D1362303

AMPHIBIANS AND THEIR WAYS

THE MACMILLAN COMPANY
NEW YORK · CHICAGO
DALLAS · ATLANTA · SAN FRANCISCO
LONDON · MANILA

IN CANADA
BRETT-MACMILLAN LTD.
GALT, ONTARIO

H. Rucker Smyth

AMPHIBIANS
AND
THEIR WAYS

The Macmillan Company
New York   1962

First Printing

The Macmillan Company, New York
Brett-Macmillan Ltd., Galt, Ontario

Printed in the United States of America

Library of Congress catalog card number: 61–10779

For Rux and Fred

Introduction

This book is primarily a natural history of amphibians. It covers the habits not only of our native frogs and salamanders but of interesting foreign species as well. Unlike many other natural-history books, it contains features found in handbooks or guides and in biology books. As in a handbook, the life cycles of a number of species are discussed in detail, and Appendix II is a chart for the identification of the families into which our native amphibians are divided. Some topics, such as respiration and cold-bloodedness, belong more to a book on biology than to a book on natural history. But a discussion of some biology in a simplified popular way is, to my mind, not only interesting but essential to the understanding of many of the habits of amphibians.

The chapters of this book fall into two categories. There are the chapters on the general habits of amphibians, and there are the life cycles of amphibians to help to give a well-rounded picture of the amphibians' ways. It is for this reason that the species treated are arranged in ecological niches rather than by families. Appendix I summarizes the differences between salamanders and frogs; Appendix II provides family identification of both orders native to this country; Appendix III is a brief discussion of common and scientific nomenclature. Although all terms likely to be unfamiliar are defined in the text, a Glossary is provided also. The annotated

Bibliography does not contain all the material consulted. It does, however, contain most of the books read, with brief comments on them. Also included in the Bibliography are herpetological magazines, records, and dealers in herpetological supplies. Prices for some of the material are given because the amateur may wish to add a few of the books to his library, and it is nice to know what they cost before walking into the bookstore or writing to the publisher to order them.

The illustrations for the book fall into two categories. All the drawings are the work of Mr. Hugh Spencer, a well-known scientific illustrator. Many were drawn from living material; photographs served as models for a few; three are adapted from drawings in other works and are duly credited. My profound thanks go to Mr. Spencer for these artistic and very accurate drawings that enrich the book immeasurably.

About a third of the illustrations are photographs taken by the author. Almost all were taken against a plain background so that they might better be used for identification purposes. All except a few of the insects were living animals, freshly captured, and released after being photographed. Those insects which were photographed dead were freshly captured and either photographed immediately after chloroforming or shortly after having been hardened in formalin.

Many people have helped me either directly or indirectly in writing this book, and it is possible to thank only a very few. Thanks must go first of all to the many herpetologists whose writings have given this author so much pleasure and inspiration and whose findinds provided most of the fascinating facts contained in this book. My daughter, Rux Smyth, has been my constant companion in all our local herpetological expeditions. She also collected all the insects and many of the amphibians for the photographs. My husband, Frederick Smyth, has tolerated sketchy meals, a perfunctory housekeeper, and even escaped amphibians hopping all over the house, with equanimity and good humor, and has encouraged me always. My friend and neighbor Mrs. James Anson has permitted us to observe and collect in her charming pond in all seasons of the year and at any time of the day or night. Mr. Charles Morgan of the Bantam Photo and Gift Shop did all the darkroom work on the photographs. In addition, he helpfully answered all my many questions, and it is largely thanks to his tutelage that any photographs illustrate this book. Mrs. Stanley Coe and Mrs. Philomen Hewitt, librarian and co-librarian respectively of the Wolcott and Litchfield Circulating Library Association went out of their way to obtain material for me. Dr. Roger Conant of the Philadelphia Zoological Garden, and Mr. Charles Bogert and Dr. Richard Zweifel of the American Museum of Natural History have been unfailingly obliging in answering fully the many questions I asked. Dr. Coleman Goin, of the University of Florida, not only answered many questions, but in addition went over the entire manuscript and made many valuable suggestions as to how it might be improved. My sincere thanks go to these and to many others who helped.

Throughout this book I have made every attempt to be accurate. Where my opinions differ from those generally accepted, I have made it clear that these were my opinions and must stand as such on their merits or otherwise. Observations made by me rather than by scientists are also clearly designated. But despite all precautions, there are bound to be some errors. I sincerely hope that these will be few and far between, and I apologize for any that occur. If the reader can find time to call any mistakes to my attention, I shall be most grateful.

Contents

Illustrations

AMPHIBIANS AND THEIR WAYS

CHAPTER 1

What Amphibians Are

You may never have heard of an amphibian watcher, for they usually go by the more formal name of herpetologists. But just as ornithologists have become known as bird watchers, so too might herpetologists be called amphibian watchers if herpetology were to become as popular as ornithology.

The amphibian watcher naturally is one who watches the amphibians—frogs, toads, and salamanders. This is a particularly fascinating hobby, and one that is especially rewarding because so many aspects of the lives of these animals may be easily observed. We can see them finding a mate and laying their eggs in the water. Because their eggs have no shell as do those of reptiles and birds, we can watch the egg change and develop into a tiny tadpole that soon hatches. We can watch the tadpole grow, and eventually see it develop arms and legs and change into an adult frog. We can see what sort of food it eats and how it manages to catch its food. In short, we can observe its entire life cycle.

There are few wild animals that can be studied as easily. Wild mammals are usually wary and secretive. You are fortunate indeed if you can catch an occasional glimpse of them. Even the more common ones, such as chipmunks, squirrels, rabbits, and mice, do not afford us very much opportunity to observe every phase of their lives. Birds can fly away from the inquisitive eye, and many will desert their nest if it is tampered with by human hands. Insects are small, and their activities are not easily watched with the naked eye. But the amphibians are large enough to be clearly seen. They cannot fly like insects and birds; they cannot run out of sight with the speed of a mammal. Most of them must come to water to breed. Many spend their early lives in a pond and some of them live their adult lives there too.

Amphibian watching also presents a challenge. Though the commoner types of frogs are easily found around ponds in warm weather, there are toads that can be found only at certain times—during a warm rainfall, for instance. Some of the salamanders may be found under rocks in streams, in the ponds, or under logs in the woods. Others you will be likely to see only at night, and a few you will be fortunate to see once a year, at breeding time.

Less is known about the amphibians than about many other groups of animals. Therefore, as you observe their habits, you may very well be the first person ever to see a certain action. Surprisingly enough, it is not necessarily the scientist who discovers a new habit; amateurs have made their mark in this respect also.

One of the most enthralling aspects of the hobby of amphibian watching is the development of the egg and tadpole. The metamorphosis from tadpole to frog is all the more startling because a tadpole looks almost as different from an adult frog as does a fish. How does a tadpole manage to change into a frog? You can gather frog eggs and watch the development from egg to tadpole to frog in the comfort of your own home, with very little trouble.

Where did the amphibian come from, and what sort of creature is it? The Class Amphibia is a very old one, dating back at least 325 million years, and possibly more. Prior to the amphibians, there were no backboned animals on land, though there were insects, spiders, and other animals that lacked an internal skeleton. There were the vertebraed fish in the oceans and fish in fresh water. But tremendous adaptations had to be made before backboned life on land was possible. A way to obtain oxygen from the air, instead of getting it from the water, had to be evolved. Furthermore, some means of progression on land had to be developed. Tails and fins were useless on land. The eye had to be provided with some protection, and with a gland to keep it clear of dust and other foreign matter. The sense organs had to be modified so that this amphibian

Eryops, a prehistoric amphibian

would have better hearing, smell, and a completely different kind of eye adapted for seeing on land. These are but a few of the many changes that had to evolve before the first backboned animals could assume a terrestrial life.

But over millions of years all this occurred. The first amphibians were undoubtedly primarily aquatic, coming on land only occasionally. Soon (geologically speaking) there evolved some species that were mostly terrestrial, while others were both aquatic and terrestrial. There were a number of these forerunners of our modern amphibians. Some were fairly large, resembling modern crocodiles. Others were small to medium in size and salamanderlike in body form. (See illustration.) Still others were similar to the modern "legless" salamander—eel-like in body shape. Some were bizarre forms such as *Diplocaulus,* with arrow-shaped heads on lizardlike bodies. It is curious to note that none of the earliest prehistoric amphibians resembled modern frogs and toads in external body form, though scientists have found many similarities in their internal skeletal structure.

Though these early amphibians bore only a vague resemblance in appearance to the modern amphibian, in habits they were very much alike. Both ancient and modern Amphibia were land and water animals, suited for life in both mediums. And when reproduction was involved, all were dependent upon water. The hard-shelled egg of the reptile to protect the egg from desiccation had not yet been evolved. The amphibian egg was and is merely surrounded with jelly, and must be laid in water unless special provision be made to prevent it from drying up.

The Age of Amphibians lasted for several million years. Gradually, reptiles were evolved, and soon the dinosaurs dominated the earth. Before the Age of the Dinosaurs had reached its peak, amphibians like those that live today had developed.

Before we describe the different types of amphibians that are extant at the present time, let us define an amphibian. An amphibian is a backboned animal with a naked skin and three-chambered heart. There are no visible scales as in fish and reptiles; no feathers as in birds; there is no hair as in mammals. The heart has two auricles

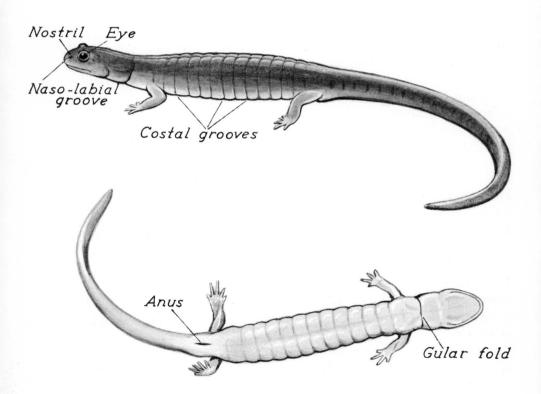

Diagram of a salamander

and one ventricle instead of being four-chambered as in mammals and birds. Amphibians, with a few exceptions, lay jelly-covered eggs, usually in water. The young amphibian is unlike the adult in both form and habits. As a larva, it usually spends its life in water, breathing by means of gills, as do fish. As an adult, it may be terrestrial or aquatic, but it usually breathes air by means of lungs and/or its skin.

The modern amphibians are divided into three groups or orders. The first of these is the order Gymnophiona or Apoda. These caecilians are found only in the tropics. They are tailless, legless, and blind. They resemble earthworms in looks and habits, for most of them lead a subterranean existence, though a few are aquatic. Since they are rare, and not so interesting as salamanders and frogs, we shall not discuss them further in this book.

The second order is the order Caudata or Urodela. These are the salamanders, many of which are lizardlike in body form; but they lack the scales and claws of a lizard and are not related to lizards. The adult salamander has a long, narrow body and a long tail. Most of them have four legs of equal size, enabling them to walk or run. In the water the tail is the sole propeller, and the legs are folded back against the body. In length and girth the salamanders vary tremendously. Some are not so big as an earthworm; then there is one, the Giant Salamander of Japan, *Megalobatrachus maximus*, which is over five feet long and as big around as a woman's thigh. This species, incidentally, is not only the largest salamander but also the largest amphibian. Most salamanders, however, are small animals.

The salamanders lay jelly-covered eggs, usually in the water, and the larvae that hatch have external gills throughout their larval life. Though they are unlike the adult salamander, they do not differ from their parents so markedly as do the young of frogs and toads. As these larvae grow, they are gradually transformed into adult salamanders.

The adult salamander has eyes that see as ours do. It depends upon its sight to warn it of an enemy's approach, as well as to help it catch its food. It lacks hearing as we know it. The salamander has no eardrums, but its front legs or lower jaw are specially modified to receive vibrations from the ground and transmit these impressions to the brain. And since it has no ears with which to hear air-borne sounds, it is not surprising that salamanders are also mute.

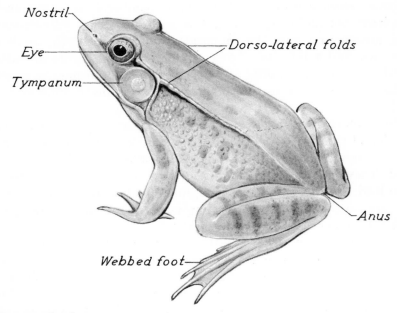

Nostril

Eye

Tympanum

Dorso-lateral folds

Anus

Webbed foot

Diagram of a frog

Those who are familiar with the aquatic salamander the Mudpuppy may insist that it has a voice. Though the Mudpuppy does make yelping sounds on occasion, scientists say that this noise is produced by rapidly inhaling or exhaling air, and that it is not true voice. To most of us, this is splitting a hair; but to be exact, any animal that lacks vocal chords, as the salamanders do, also lacks a voice. And with very few exceptions—the Mudpuppy being one of them—the salamanders are mute.

The salamander's diet, both as a larva and as an adult, is wholly carnivorous. Insects of all kinds and sizes are consumed in great numbers, and are the principal food item, though worms, smaller salamanders, and frogs are also eaten by the larger species.

Salamanders are found mostly north of the equator—Australia has no salamanders, for instance. So far as we can discover, though scientists can explain why Australia contains no native mammals except marsupials, they have never solved the riddle of why there are practically no salamanders south of the equator. Salamanders are able to live anywhere except where the soil remains permanently

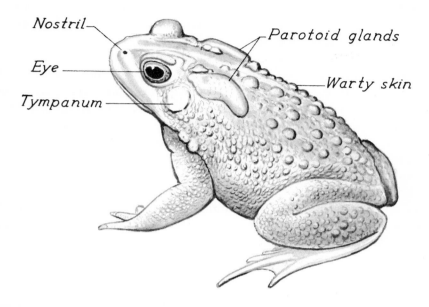

Nostril

Eye

Tympanum

Parotoid glands

Warty skin

Diagram of a toad

frozen, as in parts of the Arctic or on very high mountain peaks.

The third and largest order of modern amphibians is the order Salientia or Anura, to which belong the frogs and toads. The adult frog or toad has a short squat body and no tail. It has four legs. The front legs are short and serve to support the body when the animal is at rest. The hind legs are long—they contain one more segment than do the front legs, to be precise—and they enable the animal to hop or leap, but not to walk or run. In water, the hind legs are the propellers, and the front legs are folded back against the body. In size, frogs vary, the smallest being about a half-inch in body and head length; the largest, *Rana goliath* of Africa, attaining a head-and-body length of one foot. Usually frogs and toads are small, and even when measured with legs outstretched, most do not equal a foot in total length.

Frogs and toads also lay jelly-covered eggs, usually in water, and the tadpoles that hatch are markedly unlike the adult throughout their larval life. The tadpoles possess external gills for only a day or so after hatching. These are soon covered over by a fold of skin, making them internal for the rest of the larval life. The transformation of tadpole to adult seems sudden externally, for the gradual internal changes are not visible.

Frogs and toads depend upon their eyes to inform them of the approach of enemies or food. Their eyes are large and bulging and may be raised or lowered into the roof of the mouth. They are also undoubtedly the most beautiful eyes in the Animal Kingdom. You may think this is a ludicrous statement, but if you look at the gold-flecked eyes of a toad you will agree with Shakespeare that he "wears yet a precious jewel in his head," lovelier by far than any diamond ever could be.

Frogs and toads are able to hear as we do. In many species you can see the eardrum, or tympanum, a circular membrane located below and just in back of the eye. And since they can hear, they also have a voice. The voices of some frogs are more noise or croak than what we think of as voice, but there are others who can sing as beautifully as any bird.

An adult frog's food is similar to that of the salamanders; he too is wholly carnivorous. The tadpoles, however, with a few exceptions, are either herbivorous or omnivorous.

Frogs and toads are found throughout the world except where the ground remains frozen the year round. They are most numerous in the tropics.

We have given a bird's-eye view of the amphibian's history and a compact definition of just what they are. If you would compare a frog and a salamander feature for feature, you may refer to Appendix I, which consists of a comparison chart of the two orders. As we proceed to look at some of the interesting things about the amphibians' lives and habits, our brief definition will be expanded and you will begin to understand more clearly just what an amphibian really is and what makes him such a fascinating creature.

CHAPTER 2

Courtship and Mating

It is in spring that the average person is most conscious of the amphibian. The Spring Peeper, *Hyla crucifer,* is considered by many to be a more reliable harbinger of warm weather than is the robin. One old saying is that there will be but three more freeze-ups after the peepers are heard calling. This is akin to the superstition that if a ground hog sees his shadow on the second of February, there will be six more weeks of winter. Though the peepers are weather prophets far superior to our finest meteorologists, unfortunately they are not so expert that they can forecast just how many more frosts will occur before it is safe to set out the tomato plants.

A great many amphibians breed in the spring, but by no means all of them do. Some breed in the summer, some in the fall, some in the winter. However, in the North we are most apt to notice the breeding activity in the spring. Spring must be interpreted very loosely, for sometimes the peepers and Wood Frogs are calling before March 21st even as far north as New England. The nights are often cold and frosty, and you may wonder why these little creatures have come out of hibernation so early.

We do not begin to recognize all the conditions that cause the amphibians to emerge from hibernation and to commence courtship and mating, any more than we understand all the reasons behind bird migration. But though there is much to be learned on this subject, it is interesting and helpful to discuss a few of the factors that have an important bearing on the matter.

The prime factor governing the amphibian's emergence from hibernation is the weather. If the ground is frozen solid, the animal hibernating beneath the frost line would not be able to break through the frozen crust, even should he so desire, which he does not. For those that hibernate in the detritus of pond bottoms, ice on top prevents their escape. But the amphibian is a cold-blooded creature, whose internal temperature is nearly the same as his external surroundings, and very cold surroundings make him sluggish and incapable of the violent movement necessary to burrow out of hibernation. Therefore, until the temperature of the earth or pond water rises to a certain level, the amphibian remains in the dormant condition known as hibernation, where heartbeat and respiration are slowed to the minimum.

All amphibians are extremely sensitive to temperature changes, and notice the slightest gradations that are imperceptible to us. Furthermore, each amphibian has a temperature at which he must live for optimum comfort and activity. This varies from species to species, and helps to explain why the Spring Peeper emerges from hibernation and begins to breed earlier than the toad.

The temperature of the water is important not only because it must be warm enough to arouse those sleeping beneath it to activity but also because it must be warm enough so that any eggs laid in it will not be frozen and killed.

Humidity also plays a tremendous part in determining courtship and mating time. You will always find that the peak of breeding activities in all species occurs on evenings of high humidity—the choruses of peepers, toads, treefrogs, and frogs are at their loudest on rainy overcast days and especially nights. Naturally, the humidity of the air has more influence on those amphibians who are more terrestrial than on those who are partially or completely aquatic. But it affects them all to some extent. Perhaps there is considerable truth in the fisherman's adage that fish bite better on a rainy or dull day. Certainly it would be true if one fished for amphibians.

The weather does not, of course, completely govern courtship and mating. It is also regulated by the animal's ductless glands—especially the anterior lobe of the pituitary gland. The secretions of this gland stimulate the sexual glands, which in turn rouse the animal to mate.

We usually think of ponds and lakes as being the place where amphibians congregate to mate and lay their eggs. It is true that the great majority of all amphibians do deposit their eggs in water. The salamanders may choose a quiet pond, as do the Newt and many Mole Salamanders. They may prefer the swift-running water of a brook, as do many Lungless Salamanders. Or they may select a moist place in the woods or in the mud. Doubtless, this dry-land laying is a surprise to many. And no wonder, for it is far more difficult to find a few eggs under a stone or log in the woods than it is to see the thousands upon thousands clustered in various parts of the pond. It may be even more of a surprise to learn that some salamanders lay their eggs in trees.

Frogs and toads lay in much the same places as do the salamanders. There are pond layers, river layers, land layers, and even tree layers, though none of our native frogs lays in trees.

With the frogs and toads, courtship is always conducted very close to the place where mating and egg laying will occur. How do they court one another? Let us take a specific example, the Spring Peeper.

The peepers hibernate in the woods, beneath the earth. When the ground becomes thawed, they emerge from their winter burrows and head for ponds and swamps. On dull afternoons and in the evenings, the male sits on the bank of the pond and utters his sweet birdlike call. He takes air into his lungs and closes his mouth and nostrils. He sends the air into the vocal sacs located in the throat region. They balloon out into a glistening bubble that is almost as large as the body of the peeper. The air is sent back and forth between lungs and vocal sacs, causing the vocal chords to vibrate. An enormous sound for so small a creature emerges: *Preep, peep, peep* . . . he sings sweetly. Other males join in, and soon there is a deafening chorus of peepers all calling to the females. A female approaches one of the singing males. She is silent, for only the males sing in the breeding season. But the male senses her approach. He turns toward her, climbs on her back, and embraces her, placing his arms just behind hers in her "armpits." The couple are now ready to enter the pond and lay the eggs.

Courtship in frogs and toads consists mainly of the male's calls.

The female approaches the calling male. He may be so intent on his singing that she may even have to touch him to make him aware of her. Female toads frequently nudge males, though in other species of frogs and toads, movement in the vicinity of a calling male is sufficient to make the male cease his calling and turn to embrace the moving object.

Since the peak of the breeding activities are carried out at night, sight plays no part in the recognition of a mate. Sound and hearing and feeling are the things that count. The females are guided to the males by their calls. The males hear or feel a nearby female. "But," you may ask quite reasonably, "how do the males know they are embracing a female and not another male? And how can they be sure that they have a mate of their own species, and not a female of another species, if they cannot see her?"

First of all, the males distinguish the females by their silence. Should a male embrace another male—and this happens quite frequently—the male who is thus treated squeaks or croaks in protest, and struggles to free himself of such unwanted attentions. The female, however, is completely silent during the breeding season. Some female frogs can call at other times of the year, but when the breeding season comes they are mute.

Second, different species breed at different times. They are not all in or around the ponds at once. However, there *are* several separate species there at the same time. The males of like species tend to congregate in groups apart from others. Since each species has its own distinct song, the females naturally go toward the sound of their own kind calling.

Should the male embrace a female of a different species, however, he can tell by feel that she is not of his own kind. She must be the correct size—larger than he, and swollen with unlaid eggs, but not so large that she is of a different species. The way she moves when he embraces her may also tell him whether or not she is of his own kind.

It sometimes happens, however, that mistakes are made in the excitement of the moment. Toads, whose nuptial embrace is strong, have been known to grasp a fish and not let go until the fish was crushed to death. This is rare, but it is probably due to the fact that there weren't enough females to go around and that the urge to reproduce was so strong that the male seized the first object that nudged him.

About the only romantic part of the courtship of frogs and toads from a human standpoint are their songs. These may be as sweet as are the calls of birds, and many people mistake the trill of the American Toad and some of the treefrogs for birds. They may be plaintive, as is the lamblike bleating of the Narrow-mouth Toad. They may be insectlike, as are the calls of the Cricket Frogs. They may be squirrel-like, or like the noise of riveters; they may sound like a banjo, like a snore, or like a foghorn. It all depends upon the species, and there is but one male frog in all the world that, so far as we know, lacks a voice with which to call to his mate. This curious exception, which we shall discuss more fully later, is the Tailed Frog, *Ascapus truei*, found in parts of the northwestern United States.

When we look at courtship in the salamanders, we perceive an altogether different picture. In the first place, because the salamanders lack vocal chords they are silent. Not for them are the pleasures of serenading a lady love on a warm, humid night. Neither have they any ears; they "hear" through their front legs or, in certain aquatic species, the lower jaw, which are especially adapted to receive vibrations from the ground. So even if the males could sing, neither the singer nor the one sung to could hear the sounds. They are like the frogs and toads in that sight plays no part in the recognition of a mate. How then do the salamanders find their mates, and recognize them? So far as we know, scent is the main factor in recognition of sex and species. Females and males smell differently, and each species evidently has its own distinctive fragrance. We humans with our dull sense of smell cannot detect most of the odors that attract the salamanders to one another. The salamanders have their own built-in perfume factories. The hedonic glands, as these "factories" are aptly named, are located mainly at the base of the tail and on the underside of the head on the males. Though the females lack any readily differentiated glands, their skin secretions evidently possess the odor that enables the males readily to identify them as to species and sex.

But once a salamander finds a mate, he does not embrace her as do the frogs and toads. The salamander has more finesse, and carries

Red-spotted Newt   Diemictylus viridescens

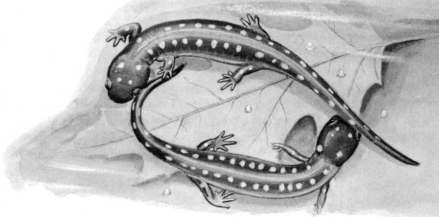

Spotted Salamander   Ambystoma maculatum

Two-lined Salamander   Eurycea bislineata

The nuptial dances of some salamanders

on a real courtship, for a very good reason. The courting varies with the species, of course. But in general he rubs his chin against her head so that she may smell his perfume. He caresses her with his tail, and he may even invite her to dance if that is the accepted thing with his particular species. The dance may consist of his transporting her on his back, or of many other "engaged" couples joining together and making various figure eights around each other. In certain species the female may straddle the male's tail, placing her head on the base of the tail, and the two will then waddle off together in this position. It is the male's object to make himself irresistible to the female, and to excite her so that mating may take place.

In most salamanders the eggs are fertilized internally, but internal fertilization is accomplished in a manner far different from that employed by mammals. When the male salamander feels that the female is sufficiently excited, he deposits, either on land or in the water, according to the habits of his species, a small jelly-covered package. This is known as the spermatophore, and each one contains the male's sperm. Next, the female comes and picks up one of these spermatophores with the lips of her cloaca, and it is placed inside her body in a special receptacle, known as the spermatheca, where the sperm remains to fertilize the eggs before they are laid.

The salamander has such an elaborate courtship because if he did not put the female in a receptive frame of mind, she might not pick up the spermatophore. There is nothing to force her to do so. In order that the eggs may be fertilized, the males must court the females.

Many species of salamanders lay their eggs a day or two after they have picked up the spermatophore. But there are others that delay. The Mudpuppy, *Necturus maculosus maculosus*, generally mates in the fall, but does not lay her eggs until the following May or June. The same is true of the Red-backed Salamander, *Plethodon cinereus cinereus*, a terrestrial species.

As we pointed out, most salamanders fertilize the eggs internally. However, there are a few exceptions. In this country there are two families of salamanders that fertilize the eggs externally. The first of these families is the Hellbenders, or Cryptobranchidae. They are completely aquatic salamanders. The male digs out a large nest in the water under a rock. The females enter, and as they lay their eggs the male sheds his sperm over them.

The other family of salamanders, the Sirens, or Sirenidae, so far as is known, fertilizes its eggs externally also. All anatomical evidence points to this conclusion. However, no one has yet observed the Siren breeding. It may seem amazing that no one has yet seen and accurately described these vital statistics of an animal found, not in darkest Africa, but in the United States. On the other hand, anyone who has ever tried to observe animals in the wild will realize how long it takes to obtain data on even the most inconsequential phase of their life cycles.

Mating in frogs and toads is a different matter altogether. Most frogs and toads fertilize their eggs externally. The male frog mounts the female, puts his arms around her, and grasps her firmly either just in back of her arms or in her groin. "Firmly" is a mild word for this nuptial embrace. If you catch a mated pair of toads, you will find it almost impossible to separate them, so tight is the male's grasp and so strong is the clasping reflex. However, it does not seem to bother the female in the least. Possibly, she enjoys this bear hug. In any case, if the pair mate on land they soon enter the water.

The female does not, however, always lay her eggs immediately. She may lay them anywhere from 3 to 26 days after pairing, the couple remaining in amplexus all during this time. What is it that governs when the eggs shall be deposited? Is it some physiological factor? Do some species require prolonged clasping in order to lay? Or does the length of time between coupling and laying depend mainly on the weather? Perhaps all of these have some bearing on the matter.

As the female lays her eggs, the male sheds his sperm on top of them. After all the eggs are laid, the female is considerably slimmer, for she may have had as many as 20,000 eggs inside her body. As soon as she no longer feels so pleasingly plump, the male releases her. Does he return to the bank and recommence his calling in the hope of attracting another female? According to one authority, frogs and toads fertilize the egg complement of but one female each year, but this may be wrong, at least for some species. It is an extremely difficult thing to prove either way.

What of the female who finds no mate? Does she lay her unfertilized eggs just the same? Evidently not. As with many unmated birds, the eggs of the female are gradually resorbed into the body. A few may emerge from the oviduct, but they are never deposited in the characteristic mass of the species as they are when the male clasps the female.

There are several outstanding and interesting exceptions to the way most frogs and toads mate. We shall discuss three of them.

The first example is the primitive aquatic Surinam Toad known as *Pipa pipa*. (See illustration, page 34.) This large flat-bodied creature lives in the ponds of South America. The mating call is a rapid clicking. This metallic sound is not produced by air vibrating the vocal chords, as in all other frogs, but by the cartilaginous disks of two bones "cracking" as the bones are moved. In much the same manner, some people can "crack" the joints of their fingers, jaws, or knees.

Clasping before laying is prolonged, and lasts at least 24 hours and sometimes longer. During this period the skin on the female's back becomes swollen and puffy. For many years it was believed that *Pipa* had a protrusile oviduct that was everted when laying began. However, it has recently been proved that this is not true. When the couple are ready to lay, the pair roll over and, while they are in an upside-down position, three to five eggs emerge and are fertilized. The pair then right themselves. The entire roll and righting take about 11 to 14 seconds, and the pair is upside-down for about one second of this entire time. When the female is ready to lay more eggs, the pair once more roll over, until, after many such turns, the entire complement of from 40 to 114 eggs are laid. The eggs are pressed into the spongy skin on the female's back by the male's ventral surfaces; the first eggs are placed near the anus, later ones successively farther forward toward the female's shoulders. One day after deposition, the eggs are half buried in the skin of the female, and by the tenth day the top membranes of the eggs are level with the skin of the back.

Our own Tailed Frog, *Ascapus truei*, is voiceless. Since he does not seem to be able to hear, and since he spends most of his time in swift-running mountain streams, a voice would be of little use to him anyway. He possesses something far more valuable, namely, a tail. (See illustration, page 206.) Actually, it is not a real tail, though it certainly looks like one. It is an organ for copulation. The male crawls along the bottom of the stream searching for a mate. When he finds a female, he embraces her and then inserts his "tail" into an extension of her cloaca, and thus her eggs are fertilized internally.

The Tailed Frog alone possesses an intromittent organ because of his habitat. External fertilization of eggs would be precarious, to say the least, in the fast-flowing water where the Tailed Frog makes his home. No sooner would the sperm be shed than the water would carry it downstream before it could possibly fertilize all the eggs of the female. So in order that the species may continue to reproduce, Nature has provided the Tailed Frog with a "tail" so that he may fertilize his eggs internally.

There are two African toads with the jawbreaking names of *Nectophrynoides vivipara* and *Nectophrynoides tornieri*. These toads also fertilize their eggs internally. But the mystifying thing in their case is how they go about it. They have no copulatory organ as has the Tailed Frog. Scientists have long been puzzled as to how the sperm is introduced into the female's body. Do they, like the female salamanders, pick up a spermatophore which the male deposits? There is no indication that they do. But scientists know that the eggs *are* fertilized internally because both species give birth to fully transformed young. The entire larval period is spent in the mother's body, and when the young are born they are miniatures of their parents. *Nectophrynoides vivipara* and *Nectophrynoides tornieri* are the only two known species of frogs and toads that are ovoviviparous, though there are several salamanders that are normally ovoviviparous and several that are occasionally so when existing conditions, such as extreme cold or high altitude, make egg laying impractical.

Let us look at some of the external differences between the sexes. With the sole exception of the Tailed Frog, these differences are secondary sex characteristics in frogs and toads. They are to a frog what a beard is to a man. With the Tailed Frog, the male is easily distinguished from the female by his longer "tail." Her "tail" is an extension of her cloaca, and is much shorter and more blunt than is his.

With the rest of the frogs and toads, we find great variety in secondary sex characteristics. About the only secondary sex characteristic that most male frogs and toads possess in common are their vocal sacs—and even here there are one or two exceptions that we shall examine in a moment. These vocal sacs are of different sizes and shapes, according to the species. They may be in the throat

American Toad
Bufo americanus

Oak Toad
Bufo quercicus

Leopard Frog
Rana pipiens

Bullfrog
Rana catesbeiana

The different types of vocal sacs in frogs

region and when in use swell out to a glistening bubble, as is true in the peepers and many toads. They may swell out in kidney-shaped masses on the side of the head, as in the Leopard Frog. Or there may be no localized swelling, but a general enlargement of the throat, as in the Bullfrog.

Vocal sacs might seem absolutely necessary to the male frog, as without them he would be unable to call to the females in the breeding season. But that is evidently not so, for some of our frogs, such as the California Toad, *Bufo boreas halophilus*, and a few others, lack vocal sacs altogether. The Tailed Frog lacks them also, but he is believed to be silent. However, the California Toad is known to have a voice—a trill, similar in character to that of our northeastern American Toad, *Bufo americanus americanus,* but lower pitched. Neither does the sound carry so well, but whether this is because of the lack of vocal sacs, as one eminent scientist believes, or because lower-pitched sounds do not seem to carry so well as those that are shrill, has not been proved.

The vocal sacs, even though they are usually present, are not very helpful to us when we pick up a frog and want to know whether or not he is a male. Unless we see his vocal sacs swelled up, we would not even know he had them. The females of some species lack vocal sacs, and in others they are greatly reduced in size. And, as we have said, the females are silent during the breeding season, though at other times of the year they may make calls similar to the males of their kind, but not so loud or so resonant.

Size is a factor in sex recognition of frogs and toads. The female is, as a general rule, larger than the male. It is just as well that she is, because she must carry him about on her back during mating and egg laying. In the water, though the additional weight does not matter so much, the female nevertheless does the swimming for both. Many males keep their hind legs drawn up on the female's back, while others allow their legs to float out behind. In a few species, if the couple is alarmed, the male may try to aid the female by using his feet in swimming motion, but their efficiency is impaired by his position on top of her. Many, however, like the American Toad, make no attempt at all to help the female in her race to escape. It seems curious to us that the male refuses to release his hold on the female and that each does not go its separate way when threatened with danger. But such is not their habit. Some species separate more easily than others, but none does it voluntarily, and often it is almost impossible to force the mated pair apart without injury, so strong is the embrace of the male.

Whereas the female is usually larger in over-all size, the male may have much larger and heavier forelegs. Perhaps he has need for powerful arms the better to grasp the female. The male toad, *Bufo boreas,* found in the Northwest and in California, has enlarged forelimbs. His are insignificant, however, compared with a South American frog, *Leptodactylus ocellatus,* whose arms are fully three times the size of those of the female!

Left: Male Green Frog, *Rana clamitans melanota.* The ear is larger than the eye.
Right: Female Green Frog. The ear is the same size as the eye.

In some species of frogs, the eardrum, or tympanum, of the male is considerably larger than the eye, whereas in the female it is the same size. A male Bullfrog can easily be distinguished from a female by this characteristic. Why the male should need a larger ear than the female has never been explained. You would think that if either of them should have a larger one, it would be the female that would have most use for it. And why, of all species, should the Bullfrog, with his tremendous foghorn cry that can be heard from a distance of half a mile or more, need a larger ear? The answer probably lies in the Bullfrog's evolution. At one time males perhaps did need larger ears, and though they are no longer useful they have not as yet been discarded.

In certain species of frogs and toads, the males have much larger thumbs. These may be swollen at the base or at the tip. This enlargement of the thumb gives the male better gripping power. Does it also help to cushion the female's skin from being overly bruised by the male amphibian's strong grasp? We have never heard this suggested as a reason—it would probably be considered rank sentimentality by most scientists—but we can see no reason why it should not be so.

There is also a difference in the shape of the toe webbing of the two sexes in certain species. A male Wood Frog can be distinguished from a female in the breeding season by his convex toe webs. The female's are concave. Of course, you have to catch the frog and spread his hind toes apart in order to see this. It can't be observed from a distance.

Some reptiles and many birds present striking color dimorphism between the sexes. This is not true of frogs and toads. Color differences, when they exist, are usually confined to the underparts, and especially the throat region. Some males have darker or more brightly colored throats than the females of the same species.

Of all the secondary sex characteristics exhibited by the frogs and toads, none is more startling than those developed by the male Hairy Frog, *Astylosternus robustus,* of Africa. All male frogs and toads need a great deal more oxygen during the breeding season than at any other time. This is due in part to their vociferous calls, and in part to the fact that their metabolic rate is heightened. Most male frogs and toads, therefore, have larger lungs to satisfy the necessary requirements of their bodies for oxygen. But the Hairy

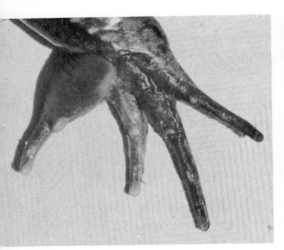 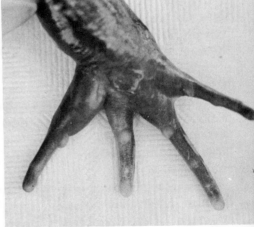

Bottom of the hand of the male Green Frog, showing the swollen thumb

Bottom of the hand of the female Green Frog, showing the thumb that is not swollen

Frog is an aquatic frog with very small lungs. Since he is a large fellow, he needs a great deal more oxygen in the breeding season than his diminutive lungs can supply. Therefore he broadens his skin area at that time, so that he will have a greater surface through which to absorb the extra oxygen needed, by growing long "hair" on his hind legs and lower sides. Of course, they are not really hairs, any more than gills are feathers, which they resemble at times. Scientists call these "hairs" vascular villosities. Be that as it may, they look like hair and they work like gills, enabling the Hairy Frog to obtain the additional oxygen necessary during the breeding season.

All in all, the secondary sex characteristics of frogs and toads are not very useful to us in helping us to tell whether our frog is male or female. It is unfortunate, but in this case there is no short cut. In order to distinguish between the sexes, you must know the secondary sex characteristics of each species.

Fortunately, the same state of affairs does not exist in the salamanders, in the breeding season. There are the larger over-all size of the females, the enlarged hind legs and/or tail of the male, differences in the colors of the two sexes, and differences in the teeth. These correspond to those secondary sex characteristics in frogs and toads. But in almost all salamanders, there are differences around

The hind foot of the male Wood Frog, showing the convex webbing

The hind foot of the female Wood Frog, showing the concave webbing

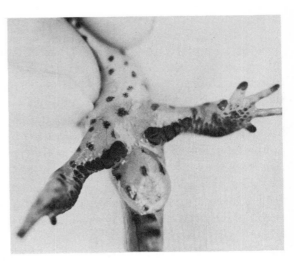

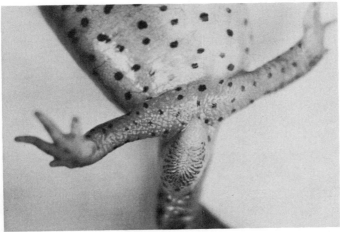

The hind legs and cloaca of the male Red-spotted Newt. Note the protuberant vent and horny excrescences on the inner surface of the legs and the tips of the toes.

The hind legs and cloaca of the female Red-spotted Newt. The cloaca is in folds, and only slightly protuberant. There are no excrescences on the legs or toes.

the vent, especially during the breeding season, though at other times these may be negligible. The male's vent is large, protuberant, and has tiny nipple-like projections. The female's vent is smooth or in folds.

Before we go on to the eggs, let me urge you to choose a warm humid overcast night in May for an outing. Wear a pair of galoshes, take a strong flashlight, and head for the nearest pond or swamp. You should have an experience that you will not soon forget. Peepers, treefrogs, toads, and frogs will be calling from all sides. You should be able to approach them easily, for they depend mainly on sight to warn them of enemies, and at night they cannot see you. Look in the water. There you will see mated pairs, salamanders and frogs, calling under the water. You will notice species you never knew existed, and species that you rarely if ever catch a glimpse of during the day. You have read how the frogs, toads, and salamanders court and mate, but there is nothing that can compare with the thrill of actually witnessing these things with your own eyes and ears. Even if you aren't a keen field naturalist, you will be amazed at all you will discover, and will be very glad that you went. Perhaps you may even be so impressed and enthusiastic that you will want to repeat the experience.

CHAPTER 3

The Eggs

The beginning of most life is hidden from us. We are unable to see the egg being fertilized; its development from a one-celled organism to an embryo of many cells is screened from our view until birth or hatching. This is true of the shelled eggs of reptiles and birds. They are fertilized within the parent's body and are then surrounded with a shell before laying. The mammalian egg is shell-less with two exceptions; but it is microscopic in size and inaccessible for observation, since it remains inside the mother's body during its development.

If we really want to find out what happens between laying and hatching, we must turn to the amphibian egg. The spermatozoa of the amphibian are microscopic in size, so that we are unable to see (with the naked eye) the egg being penetrated by the sperm. But all stages after fertilization are visible to us; furthermore, most of the changes that occur can be seen without a microscope.

To begin with, the eggs are round, though they do not remain so. They may be black or brown on top. The top part is known as the animal pole; it is the section that is alive and will grow. The vegetal pole at the bottom may be white or yellow. It consists of the food on which the egg "feeds" as it develops, for you must remember that all living things, be they animals or that most miraculous of all living entities, a fertilized egg cell, must have nourishment if they are to grow. The living protoplasm of the animal pole is lighter than the nonliving deutoplasm of the vegetal pole. Therefore, it always is uppermost. You can easily test this by turning an amphibian egg so that the animal pole faces down. You will notice that very little time elapses before it has rotated so that the protoplasm is again facing up. A few amphibian eggs are yellow or white, and are called unpigmented eggs. But though the separation of animal and vegetal poles is not readily visible in these, it exists nonetheless.

Because the eggs require a certain amount of insulation from shocks and enemies, as they descend through the female's oviduct they are coated with albuminous jelly. Depending upon the way the oviduct is constructed in different species, there may be one or more jelly envelopes, or envelopes surrounding the eggs may be lacking, and the mass of jelly may constitute the sole protection. You can get a clear picture of what an egg with its jelly envelope looks like if you make a small dot and draw a circle around it. The jelly may be clear, or it may be milky white or greenish.

Once the eggs are deposited in the pond, the jelly swells. The capacity of the jelly to absorb water is a decided benefit to both the layer and the egg. It means that the eggs and jelly, when inside the female amphibian, require little space. But once in contact with the water, the jelly swells to twice or three times its original bulk, giving far greater protection to the egg than would be the case if it did not enlarge. Of course, there are instances on record of frogs that delayed too long in laying their eggs. The water content of the body is absorbed by the jelly, which expands rapidly and beyond all bounds. The female then bursts open and dies. Fortunately, such circumstances as these occur seldom, and may be considered freaks of nature.

The eggs vary in size according to the species that lays them. But the size of the adult is no reliable indication of the size of the egg that will be laid. The Tailed Frog is only about 2 inches long, but it lays one of the largest eggs of all our native frogs. Each vitellus is approximately 5 mm., or roughly ¼ inch in diameter. Our largest frog, the Bullfrog, which may be as long as 8 inches, lays small eggs of about 1.5 mm. The smallest egg in this country is laid by the Southern Chorus Frog, *Pseudacris nigrita nigrita*, and is approximately .7 mm. in diameter. We shall allow you to figure out the equivalent measurement in fractions of an inch. Frankly, it's beyond our mathematical ability, and we are quite content to leave egg measurements in millimeters. The average salamander lays a far larger egg than do the frogs, and should you ever wish to watch the development of the amphibian egg, you would be well advised to choose those of a salamander rather than those of a Bullfrog or a toad.

The number of eggs laid also varies greatly, and, generally speaking, salamanders lay fewer eggs than do frogs and toads. The Bullfrog and the American Toad lay as many as 20,000. The Rocky Mountain Toad, *Bufo woodhousei woodhousei*, produces up to 25,000 eggs, the largest complement laid by a native salientian. The Robber Frogs of the genus *Syrrhophus* may lay as few as 5 eggs, but they are the exception. Most frogs and toads lay eggs in the hundreds or thousands, while salamanders lay in the tens or a hundred. Because of the salamander's more secretive ways, larger egg size, and internal fertilization, they do not need to lay so many eggs to ensure continuance to the species as do the frogs.

The way the eggs are laid also differs with the species. The Red-spotted Newt lays each egg separately, fastening each on the leaf of a water plant and folding the leaf around it, thus hiding it very effectively from enemies. The Spring Peeper also lays its eggs individually, but this species merely deposits each egg on the pond bottom. The Bullfrog and the Green Frog both lay theirs in a spreading mass on the surface of the water. The Wood Frog and the Spotted Salamander lay theirs in a round or oval mass attached to submerged vegetation. The American Toad and most other toads lay theirs in two long strings of jelly. The Hellbender, that large aquatic salamander, lays its eggs in rosarylike strings, as does the Tailed Frog. The Spadefoot Toads lay their eggs in bands or cylinders. It is, of course, the jelly that gives the egg mass its shape, for the eggs themselves are round, with the exception of those of the Colorado River Toad, who occasionally, though not always, lays wedge-shaped eggs. The form of the jelly is governed in part by the way the oviduct is shaped, and in part by the natural egg-laying movements, which differ in the various species.

Eggs of amphibians are identified one from another by their color, size, number of jelly envelopes, if any; shape of the egg mass, total complement of eggs, and the places in which they are laid. All of this sounds complicated, as do most things scientific at first glance.

The eggs of some amphibians: 1. The surface mass of the Bullfrog. 2. Eggs of the Red-spotted Newt laid individually among plant leaves. 3. The submerged egg mass of the Spotted Salamander. 4. The egg complement in strings laid by the American Toad. 5. Eggs in rosary-like strings deposited by the Hellbender.

However, it is not so formidable as it seems, and if you are one who enjoys finding out just exactly what species of amphibian has laid those eggs in the southeast corner of your pond, do not be overawed. Consult one of the two handbooks listed in the Bibliography, and forge ahead. You may not find that you can identify every egg that you discover with complete scientific accuracy, but you will be able to identify most, and make a well-informed guess about the others.

The eggs are laid in many places. A large majority of amphibians deposit their eggs in ponds, either spread on the surface of the water or, more often, submerged. Those species, such as the Bull-frog, that lay on the surface often lay a large number of eggs, and they also lay them later in the year. One of the reasons for this is that the surface-film eggs would freeze and decompose were they laid in cold weather. Furthermore, this type of egg has a very high mortality rate from another natural cause—hard pelting rain. The force of the rain may be hard enough to break the surface film of the water, and cause the eggs to sink to the bottom of the pond. And there they are not likely to develop because there is less oxygen on the pond bottom than at its surface, and the surface-film egg requires more oxygen than it may be able to obtain on the bottom.

More salamanders lay in the swiftly running waters of brooks and rivers than do frogs. Undoubtedly, this is primarily because most of them fertilize their eggs internally, whereas the frogs, with the exception of the mountain-stream-dwelling Tailed Frog, are unable to do so. Those salamanders that lay in rivers either scoop out a nest, with its entrance downstream, for protection from the onslaught of the cascading waters, or they attach their eggs, either singly or in a mass, to the underside of a rock.

In many parts of this country, permanent bodies of water are non-existent. Where this situation occurs, you might think that there would be no water-laying amphibians. But amphibians such as the Spadefoots, the Narrow-mouths, and some of the toads must lay in shallow water, and in dry regions they lay in mud puddles that are formed from a rain that may not recur for a year or more. Naturally, the eggs hatch rapidly, and the tadpoles are transformed in a short time into adults.

The habit of laying in the shallow water of mud puddles and swamps is not, however, confined to arid regions. None of our north-eastern toads will deposit their eggs in deep water even though it is available. If you wish to find toad's eggs, the best place to look is a swamp or a mud puddle. We have even found toad's eggs laid in a large mud puddle in the middle of a road! Lacking swamps in your vicinity, go to a small pond. Search around its shallowest edges, for it is there that you will find the toad's strings of jelly.

Very few people who do not make a study of amphibians are aware that some of them deposit their eggs on moist or dry land. This is not particularly surprising, for the chances of finding these land-laid eggs just by accident are slim, hidden as most of them are beneath rocks or logs. As a matter of fact, diligent hunting is generally required to locate them even if you know the most likely spots to search. There are quite a few native salamanders who lay on land. The Marbled Salamander, *Ambystoma opacum,* lays in a moist spot near the water, as does the Dusky Salamander, *Desmognathus fuscus.* The Red-backed Salamander, *Plethodon cinereus,* is a woodland salamander, and it lays its eggs in cavities or rotted logs. For some reason the Amphiuma, *Amphiuma means,* though it is an aquatic salamander, also lays its eggs in muddy spots on land. There are many reasons for normally terrestrial amphibians to lay on land, but why a salamander that spends its life in the water should do so is a mystery.

As to frogs, there are fewer of them, and most of them are not so common as the land-laying salamanders. The land-laying frogs in this country are confined to several species within one family, the Robber Frogs, or Leptodactylidae, of which we will say more in a subsequent chapter.

We have but one native species of amphibian that deposits its eggs in trees. This is the Oak Salamander, *Aneides lugubris lugubris,* of California. It occasionally lays on the ground, but just as frequently lays in trees.

None of our native frogs lays in trees, but there are many foreign frogs that do. All the treefrogs of the family Hylidae that live on the island of Jamaica lay in trees. Perhaps this habit arose because there are very few natural ponds and lakes in Jamaica. The type of vegetation found in Jamaica and parts of South America favored its development. The Jamaican hylas all deposit their eggs in bromeliads. Bromeliads are relatives of the pineapple, but, unlike it, they are epiphytic; that is, they attach themselves to trees and obtain their sustenance from the air through specially modified aerial roots. The bromeliad leaves form a rosette, just as do those of the pineapple. In the very center of the rosette is a hollow that generally holds a considerable amount of water. It is here that the Jamaican hylas place their eggs, and the tadpoles develop in this water. Even in the driest of seasons, the bromeliad has a store of water in the center of its leaves.

Other foreign frogs, such as the treefrogs of the family Rhacophoridae, found in Asia, deposit their eggs in trees overhanging pools, and upon hatching, the tadpoles fall into the water below and carry on their larval life there. In order to protect the eggs from drying out, the mother first deposits some albuminous jelly without any eggs. This is whipped into a frothy mass by the hind legs of one or both parents until it is as full of air as beaten egg whites. The jelly-covered eggs are then placed on top and are covered by an additional layer of jelly which is also well beaten. The outside of this nest soon hardens, while the inside liquefies, providing the eggs with a suitable medium in which to develop.

The changes in the amphibian egg from the moment it is laid and fertilized to the time it hatches are fascinating to watch. This is how most life begins and develops, from the mammal down to the lowly earthworm. If you go to the nearest pond and collect the

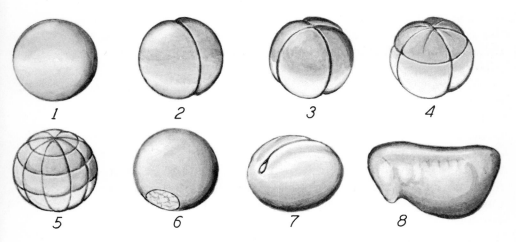

A few stages in the development of a frog's egg: 1. The unsegmented egg. 2. The two-celled stage. 3. The four-celled stage. 4. The eight-celled stage, showing the beginnings of cleavage into the sixteen-celled stage. 5. The blastula, or many-celled stage. 6. The yolk-plug stage. 7. The neural-groove stage. 8. The embryo.

largest eggs that you can find, you may watch the entire process with the naked eye or with an inexpensive magnifying glass. Suffice it to say here that the egg changes—divides from one into many cells —lengthens out, and develops, and finally the tadpole or larva wriggles its way out of the confining jelly, and hatches. The length of time between laying and hatching varies with the species and the temperature. It may be as short a time as 36 or 58 hours, as in some toads, or as long as 3 or 4 months in some salamanders. In general, salamander eggs are slower in hatching than are those of the frogs and toads.

By and large, amphibians lay their eggs and then desert them, devoting little thought as to the possible fate of the eggs. However, there are many exceptions to this rule, and some of them, especially the foreign ones, are most interesting.

Our first exception is the male Hellbender, native to this country, who, as we mentioned earlier, scoops out a nest on the river bottom, and welcomes the females as they enter to deposit their rosary-like strings. The male is a most faithful father, for he remains with the eggs, guarding the opening of the nest against all intruders, until the eggs hatch out 2½ or 3 months later, while the female goes her own way, her responsibility ended.

The female Three-toed Amphiuma, *Amphiuma means tridactylum*, who lays in the mud, remains with her eggs until they hatch. One wonders why the other subspecies, *Amphiuma means means*, who also lays in the mud, does not remain with hers.

This habit of one or both parents remaining with the eggs laid on land is quite common. We find it true of the Marbled Salamander, the Dusky Salamander, the Oak Salamander, and the Redbacked Salamander. When this habit exists, you may be sure it is necessary, not so much for the protection of the eggs from enemies as from desiccation. The damp body of the parent helps in no small measure to keep the eggs themselves moist. It has also been suggested that the skin secretions and cloacal excretions and/or secretions of the parents may serve as a deterrent to any fungus growths that might destroy the egg capsule and egg. Recent research indicates, however, that mold develops only on dead eggs or embryos. The role that skin and cloacal secretions and the brooding habit play in increasing the number of young which survive has not been fully explained to date.

When we come to the foreign species who care for their eggs,

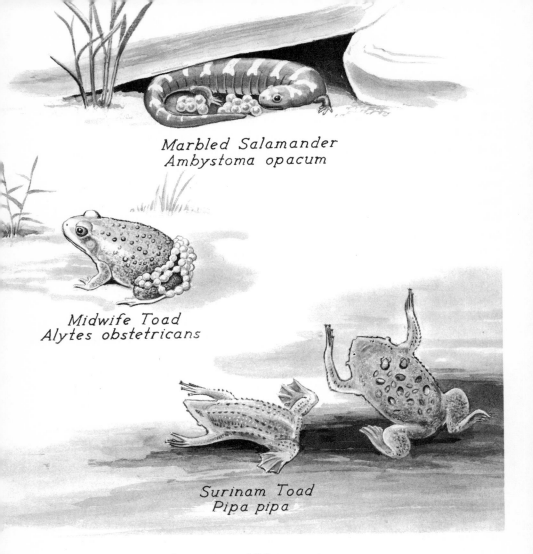

Marbled Salamander
Ambystoma opacum

Midwife Toad
Alytes obstetricans

Surinam Toad
Pipa pipa

Care of the eggs by some amphibian parents

we see all manner of strange sights. The male Midwife Toad, *Alytes obstetricans*, found in western Europe, is tied down by his parental duties. The female lays her jelly-covered eggs in long strings; the male then takes these, wraps them around his hind legs, and retires to a damp cavity. Here he remains during the day, coming out at night to bathe the eggs in dew or in a nearby pond. When the tadpoles are ready to emerge, the male goes to the water and the tadpoles hatch. One wonders how the male is able to get around at all without crushing the eggs. Perhaps a large number are destroyed, though we have never read anything to indicate it. But whether or not a large percentage of the eggs develop, Nature has amply provided for the survival of the Midwife Toad, for the female lays not once or twice annually, as do most amphibians, but three or four times each year. The male must be quite adept at carrying his burden of eggs, since he obviously gets plenty of practice.

But if you think the Midwife Toad is badly off, you have never heard of *Rhinoderma darwinii*, and others of the genus *Rhinoderma*. The males carry the eggs and tadpoles until they are transformed into fully developed frogs in their mouths—or, properly speaking, in their vocal sacs, which are necessarily quite large and elastic.

In the genera *Phyllobates* and *Dendrobates*, found in South America, the male again cares for the young. In his case, he builds a mud dam to trap water for a suitable site for egg laying. Should this artificially made pool dry up before the tadpoles are transformed, their father takes them for a pickaback ride to a nearby stream where they can complete their development. They, in turn, have special suctorial lips with which they can fasten themselves firmly to his back so that they will not be dislodged on the overland journey. Naturally, if they should fall off their life is soon ended, for though they are able to withstand short trips out of water, they are unable, while tadpoles, to live away from an aquatic medium for any extended period.

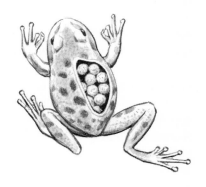

Rhinoderma darwinii   *Gastrotheca marsupiata*

X-ray views of two South American amphibians to show the position of the developing embryos and eggs

Lest you think the female amphibian has a soft life free from maternal care, observe the Marsupial Frog, *Gastrotheca marsupiata.* This animal carries her eggs about with her in a brood pouch on her back. There are other species of female frogs, of which we shall say more in Chapter 13, that also carry their eggs in pouches. The Marsupial Frog's pouch is closed except for a very small opening, and if you wish to see her eggs you must cut into her skin to do so. You may wonder how the eggs get in. Not from the inside, for the Marsupial Frog lays her eggs just as does any other frog. The answer is that after the eggs are laid and pushed up onto the back, the skin grows around them until a brood pouch is formed.

Before we leave the care of the amphibian egg, let us look at one of the most unusual of all amphibian parents in detail. The Surinam Toad, *Pipa pipa,* is a large aquatic animal. The female is dark brown or black and has a broad flat back. Her hind legs are well developed, and the feet have huge fleshy webs between the toes. The fingers on the hands are long, flat, and end in starlike tips. They are used to grasp the food and stuff it in the mouth. Pipa has no tongue. The head is flat and triangular in shape, with short tentacles and skin flaps at the corners of the mouth. These help her to find her way through the muddy pools in which she lives. The eyes are not so large as the head of a small corsage pin. Her flat back makes a good repository for her eggs. Inguinal amplexus is lengthy, and before the eggs emerge the skin on the back becomes swollen and spongy. As the eggs are expelled, they are fertilized by the male and pressed into the spongy back. They gradually sink into the skin area; by the tenth day they are level with the skin of the mother's back, where they remain. Here the eggs stay for three or four months. They change into tadpoles, and during the last month or so they eat small aquatic worms and entomostracans that enter the openings in the top egg membrane. The tadpoles grow and develop into small Surinam Toads. Then and only then do they burst forth from their cells on the mother's back and hatch. There may be 100 little Pipas hatching, and when they are all freed the mother's back is well pock-marked, and resembles a telescopic view of the craters of the moon.

CHAPTER 4

The Young

Children and adults alike are fascinated by the tadpoles and larvae of amphibians. Even very young children enjoy watching tadpoles develop. No startling changes are apparent in the growing young of most animals, which gradually become larger and less appealing. But with tadpoles we see not only rapid growth but also radical changes, and it is perhaps this above all that entertains both old and young. As with the changes in the egg, all stages of development are readily visible with the exception of those that are internal.

Before the embryo frogs and salamanders may be properly termed tadpoles and larvae respectively, they must hatch from the egg capsule and egg mass. How does "birth" take place? When the embryo amphibians have developed sufficiently inside the egg capsule, they may be seen wriggling. At first they give only an occasional twitch. As they get larger and stronger, they feel more and more cramped for space, and move frantically and almost continuously. An egg mass just about to hatch is literally seething with motion. The egg capsule that was so tough when first laid has now become weakened by the water it has absorbed. Nevertheless, the larva's struggles are not sufficient to free him. Obviously he cannot stay where he is, and survive. He needs more oxygen than he can obtain in the egg capsule. He will soon need food, for most of the yolk that nourished him has been utilized. But Nature, as always, has provided a way.

Prior to hatching, a series of glands develop on the larva's snout. These glands discharge a secretion that helps to dissolve the egg capsule. Often, the capsule is not entirely dissolved, and if you go to a pond shortly after the hatching of a group of Spotted Salamander larvae, you will find the egg mass with its broken, empty capsules. However, the capsules dissolve enough to permit the young to wriggle their way out.

But the larva still isn't free. There is a mass of jelly to traverse before he can really be considered "born." If you compare a freshly laid mass of eggs with a mass that contains larvae ready to hatch, you will immediately notice the difference between the two. In the former the jelly is firm; in the latter it is not, and often it does not even hold the egg mass together. Bits of it may break off from the original mass. The jelly is now more of the consistency of half-jellied jelly. Therefore, it is not too difficult for the young amphibian to wriggle his way through it and out into the pond.

Since frogs and salamanders constitute two separate orders, it should not surprise us that their young are quite different. Though the eggs of one may be mistaken for those of the other, no one could possibly confuse the young. Appearance and habits distinguish the frog and toad tadpoles from the salamander larvae. Incidentally, the young of salamanders are always termed larvae, while the young of frogs and toads may be called either larvae or tadpoles. Since tadpoles and larvae are so different, we shall describe them separately. And so that you may have a comparison of the two orders, the principal differences between eggs, larvae, transformation stages, and adults have been listed in Appendix I.

This country is particularly rich in salamanders both from the standpoint of numbers and of variety of species. Of the eight families of salamanders in existence today, we lack representatives of only one in this country—the Hynobiidae, found only in Asia. In general, the larvae of salamanders may be roughly divided into three types. These are the pond-type larva, the mountain-brook-type larva, and the terrestrial larva. You will notice that larval type is based primarily on the larva's habitat. Because these three types show quite distinct differences in their adaptations to their various habitats, we shall describe a representative of each type, beginning with a typical pond larva, the Jefferson Salamander, *Ambystoma jeffersonianum;* then we shall follow with a stream-dwelling larva, the North-

Pond larva

Terrestrial larva

Stream larva

Salamander larvae showing the differences in body shape, gill form, and development of tail crests. Adapted from *Handbook of Salamanders* by Sherman Bishop, with the permission of the Cornell University Press.

ern Two-lined Salamander, *Eurycea bislineata bislineata*, and complete the picture by showing a terrestrial larva, the Red-backed Salamander, *Plethodon cinereus cinereus*.

Our little Jefferson Salamander larva, a typical pond larva, after wriggling his way free of the egg capsule and jelly mass, is hatched along with the rest of its brothers and sisters, about 35 in number. It is small—no longer than ½ inch—and has a tail, a head, and a body with quite a bulge on its underside. This bulge is the yolk. It will feed on this until the mouth is open and it can obtain food from the pond. We use the pronoun "it" rather than "he" or "she" advisedly; the larva or tadpole upon hatching is neither male nor female. Its sex is not positively determined until much further along in its development—but we shall discuss this more fully later.

On either side of its head are very tiny gills, and just in front of them, at the corners of the mouth, are two claspers or balancers—one on either side. With other species, the claspers are occasionally absent, and this, among other features, aids herpetologists in identifying one species of larva from another. The claspers are tiny finger-like projections, and unless you look carefully, you may very well miss seeing them.

Upon hatching, the larval salamander lies in the water. If alarmed, it will wriggle away to a less-disturbed spot, but mostly it just rests. Sometimes you will see several larvae lying on their sides on a rock or on the bottom. Primarily they remain still because they do not need to move around to catch food. Neither the mouth nor the anus is yet open, nor is the intestine sufficiently developed to handle food.

If we return to our larva in a week or so, we wouldn't know him for the same creature. First of all, he has grown. His body is rounder, his tail longer, and it has developed tail crests—thin transparent fins extending from the tip of the tail to the head on top and from tail tip to anus below. These broaden the tail and enable the larva to swim better.

The gills have grown larger and stand out on either side of the head very distinctly. If we examine these gills closely, it can be seen that they consist of three separate stalks on either side of the head; each gill has two rows of tiny filaments on it. These gills are large and bushy in comparison to river and terrestrial types, and are quite different from both in form. Their structure ensures an adequate oxygen supply. Because pond water does not contain so much oxygen as running river water, the gills must present a greater surface to the water in order to satisfy the oxygen requirement of a pond larva.

At first we may think that the claspers are still present, but we are wrong. The claspers are gone, but upon minute observation we may see the forelegs beginning to develop. The wide mouth is now open, and is equipped with tiny spike teeth. The intestine is short, and lies in an S-shaped curve inside the body. The anus is open.

The animal is eating food of his own catching, and the larva isn't fussy as long as it is meat. Water fleas, mosquito larvae, and a host of other small animal life, tadpoles and larvae smaller that itself— all these make up its diet. Almost any living thing will do if the larva can catch it. To discover how it procures its meal, we may watch his actions with a water flea. The larva sees the flea moving, and swims nearer the better to smell the flea. Then a snap, and it is swallowed. You may watch, but you will see nothing, so rapidly does the larva act.

Our larval Jefferson Salamander already shows his salamanderlike nature. Not for him are the undignified antics of some frog tadpoles. He remains motionless for a large part of the time. But let your shadow fall on him, and he is off. Perhaps you are wary of letting your shadow fall on him, and you carefully lower your net into the water. But again, before you can scoop him up, he darts away. What has warned him, since he has no ears? His lateral line organs have notified him of danger. These show as small spots along the back and sides in regular rows. Magnification shows them to be depressed pits, each of which contains a tiny bristle. These lateral line organs are extremely sensitive to vibrations in the water. All aquatic larvae and tadpoles have them, but none are present on terrestrial larvae.

The salamander larva is almost solitary; never have I seen hundreds of salamanders seething together, as one often sees with tadpoles. He is wary and secretive, as befits his kind, and the older he becomes, the more marked are these characteristics.

This, then, is a typical pond larva. Most larvae of the families Ambystomidae, or Mole Salamanders, and Salamandridae, or Newts, as well as a few species in other families, are of this type.

As an example of a stream-dwelling larva, we shall observe the Northern Two-lined Salamander, *Eurycea bislineata bislineata*. Upon hatching, the larva resembles a tiny adult in body form. There is no great depth of body as in most pond larvae, nor is there any fin on the body. Front and hind legs are present. However, a larval Two-lined Salamander is easily distinguished from the adult not only by its smaller size but also by a tail fin and gills. The gills are different from those of a pond larva, being much smaller and less bushy.

The terrestrial larva, such as that of the Red-backed Salamander, *Plethodon cinereus cinereus*, hatches in an even more advanced state of development than either pond or stream larvae. It is much like the adults, but upon hatching, it has what are known as staghorn gills. These are flat leaflike structures, not unlike a stag's antlers in shape, with none of the tiny filaments found on aquatic gills. Filaments are useless on land. They would stick together, and so be unable to extract oxygen from the air. Within two or three days after hatching, these staghorn gills are lost, and there is little to show that this is a larva. As a matter of fact, it is not. It has already become an adult even though it is not fully grown. It must also be mentioned that terrestrial larvae never have tail or body fins; nor are lateral line organs ever present, for these can function only in an aquatic medium.

Before we go on to describe the tadpoles, let us see just how scientists manage to differentiate between different species of larvae.

In his excellent handbook on salamanders, Dr. Bishop describes all of the larvae that are known at the time of hatching. But when we catch a salamander larva, we cannot sit down and identify it then and there. We may be able to identify it if we catch it at hatching, but suppose we catch it when it is several weeks old? We may be able to identify it, but more likely, we may not. The only recourse open if we fail is to keep it until it is an adult. Nevertheless, we constantly attempt to identify what we find by size, color, type and shape of gills, shape of body, size of tail crests, claspers if present, and state of development of fore and hind limbs. Thus do the scientists identify them, and so do we also; and if we have not their success, at least it is not from the lack of trying. Do it yourself sometime. You may succeed in your identification, or you may fail; either way you will have learned a great deal about larvae in general from such close examination.

Most people have seen frog or toad tadpoles. In spring almost every pond contains thousands of tadpoles in various stages of development. But the hatchling tadpole looks nothing like what most of us think of as the typical tadpole shape. It is tiny, of course, and quite flat. When you look at this minute creature, you can find no eyes, no nostrils, no mouth, no arms. In some species, such as the Wood Frog tadpole, you can, when looking at the tadpole from above, see a head distinctly separated from the body by an indentation or neck, and a very short tail. In others, as in the Spring Peeper tadpole, the separation of head and body is not marked. Furthermore, the peeper tadpole's tail is relatively longer than that of the Wood Frog. This is not surprising, for most of the family Hylidae, or Treefrogs, have long tails with high tail crests, and are extremely graceful swimmers when they have progressed beyond the hatchling stage.

The hatchling tadpole spends most of its time resting, holding onto plants, undissolved egg capsules, rocks, or sticks by means of his oral suckers. These are two tiny suction cups that secrete a sticky substance enabling the tadpole to hold onto objects in the pond while resting.

A few days after hatching, if we look very closely, especially when the tadpole swims, we can see two tiny pairs of gills on either side of its head. Indeed, in some species, such as the Wood Frog tadpole, for instance, these external gills are visible at hatching. These grow larger for a few days, and then disappear. A fold of skin known as the opercular fold has grown from the head to the body, and within the chamber thus formed four pairs of internal gills have developed. The tadpole now has a head-body and a long tail. By this time the suckers have been lost, the mouth has formed, and the anus is open. The tadpole obtains oxygen by taking water into its mouth; the water then enters the gill chamber, where the gills extract oxygen from it; the water then passes out of the body through a hole known as the spiraculum or spiracle. The position of the spiracle is of great importance in the identification of tadpoles. In the great majority of tadpoles, the spiracle is found on the left side of the body, but there are some species in which the spiracle is located on the belly near the anus.

At this time the eyes have formed—small ones when we compare them to the eyes of fishes, or to the large bulging eyes of the adult amphibian. And just as in most salamander larvae, the tadpole possesses lateral line organs.

As the frog tadpole grows, it soon assumes the shape of an oval body and slim tail. Every species has its own characteristic body shape; but the differences between them are likely to be overlooked by the beginning observer. With practice, however, you will soon be able to distinguish some of the ones you know. The tadpole tail has both upper and lower tail crests. Depending upon the species, the tail crests may be broad or narrow; the upper crest may extend far up onto the body, or it may be confined to the tail alone. These

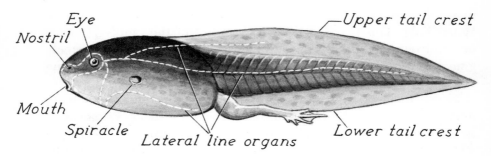

Diagram of a mature frog tadpole

differences, even more than those of body shape, seem infinitesimal.

Internally, the intestine has been formed, not in the S curve characteristic of the salamander larva, but coiled tightly as is a watch spring. In many species the intestine may be seen through the thin skin of the belly. The tadpole intestine is very long, for herbivores of all kinds require a longer intestine than carnivores. (This applies to mammals as well as to amphibians.) The frog tadpole's diet consists principally of vegetation found in the pond. That is not to say that they do not eat small invertebrates and even decaying animal matter, for they do, but the mainstay of the diet of most species is plant material. Decaying vegetation, algae, and fresh-water plants are devoured voraciously. There are a few exceptions to the rule that tadpoles are herbivorous. In this country the tadpoles of the Eastern Wood Frog, *Rana sylvatica sylvatica,* and those of the Western Spadefoot, *Scaphiopus hammondi hammondi,* are entirely carnivorous.

The difference between the tadpole mouth and salamander mouth is considered by herpetologists to be the most important difference between the two orders. The larval salamander mouth is wide and is equipped with true teeth. The tadpole mouth is small and roundish. If we look at the mouth closely with the naked eye, we can see a black horny beak with which the creature nibbles off the plant material it eats. But for the scientist the naked eye is inadequate. If you would see how a tadpole's mouth really looks, you must view it through a magnifying glass. Perhaps the clearest way to describe it is to use the human mouth as a model. Imagine, therefore, your mouth with lips open. Instead of your upper and lower teeth imagine two black horny crescents. These are the beak, or the upper and lower mandibles. This beak is lacking only in the Brevicipitidae, or Narrow-mouth Toads, in this country. Furthermore, imagine one or more rows of toothlike ridges on both your upper and lower lips. Around your lips, especially at the corners, picture a number of warts, or papillae. If you can visualize all this, you have an idea of what the average tadpole mouth looks like. (You also have an imagination of the highest order.) You may wonder why we have gone into such detail about the appearance of the tadpole mouth. There is a reason—namely, that the mouth parts are important in tadpole identification. But more of that later.

A study of the habits of different species of tadpoles could be a tremendously rewarding project. For instance, does each species have its own particular brand of behavior? Contrast, for instance, the behavior of the Green Frog tadpole with that of the American Toad tadpole. In the aquarium, you will find that the toad tadpoles swim steadily around the edge of the bowl when they are not at rest or feeding. Not so the Green Frog tadpoles. When a group of them are housed in an aquarium, you will see them "go crazy" every once in a while. They will flop every which way, much like a fish on land. They will start by swimming on their bellies, right side up, then suddenly flip over and swim on their backs, only to turn on their bellies once more. We notice that this behavior of the Green Frog tadpole is more pronounced when there are two or more tadpoles in the aquarium. Why do they act in this manner? Are they playing? What other species act in this way? Doesn't each species have its own individual behavior? To our knowledge, no

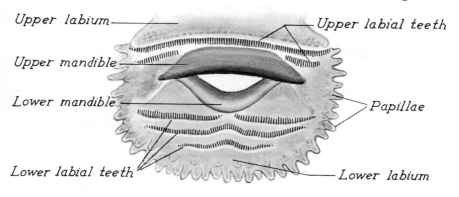

Upper labium — — Upper labial teeth
Upper mandible —
Lower mandible —
— Papillae
Lower labial teeth — — Lower labium

Mouth of the tadpole of the Green Frog, *Rana clamitans melanota*

serious study of tadpoles' ways has ever been attempted. Certainly such a project would take years—even a lifetime would not be too long—but for those whose interest in tadpoles is strong, what more rewarding and fascinating hobby could there be?

It must be admitted that there is one large hurdle to jump before such a proposition can be undertaken. One must learn to differentiate between one species of tadpole and another. Drs. Wright and Wright give a key for the identification of tadpoles in their excellent handbook. But it must be remembered that all tadpole keys are based on mature specimens just before transformation; immature tadpoles cannot be identified from a key. We shall find, too, that perhaps mature ones can't either—at least not by us. We can easily note the position of the spiracle and the position of the anus, which may open on one side of the lower tail crest or in the middle of it. But from here on, we have tough sledding. For the next step is a series of measurements in *fractions* of millimeters. We just can't measure distances between the eye and the spiracle, between the eye and the mouth, between the eye and the nostril, or between the two eyes with any accuracy on a live tadpole without injuring the animal. Nor is it much easier to take larger measurements, such as length and width of body and tail. Herpetologists who examine tadpoles naturally kill and preserve them first. This course is not prescribed for the beginning student for several reasons that will become apparent in a moment.

We may be troubled by the color. For instance, is the belly strongly pigmented, somewhat pigmented, not strongly pigmented? Do the intestines show through the belly a little, much, or not at all? These are relative values, and the inexperienced amateur is hard put to decide which alternative is the correct one.

When we observe the mouth parts, most of us will find that we are completely lost. Nor should we feel inferior because we are. Wright and Wright freely admit that no one knows how much variation is present in the mouth parts of individuals of the same species. The following example will serve as a good illustration of their remark.

One of our mature Spring Peeper tadpoles was found dead in the aquarium. Not wishing to waste the opportunity thus provided, we removed him and examined his mouth under a pen microscope with a 20× magnification. We drew a lovely picture of what we saw, and then turned to Wright and Wright to see what their picture looked like. We were nonplused to find that ours didn't look like theirs in a number of ways. The most outstanding difference—and an extremely important one—was that our peeper had four rows of labial teeth below, one row above. The key states that labial teeth on a peeper are 2 above 3 below or 2 above 2 below. Were we wrong? Our mathematical ability is of a low order, but we *can* count up to four correctly *most* of the time. We looked again at our specimen. We were relieved to find that this was one of the correct times. This peeper happened to present a variation from the norm. Dr. Liu states that the absence of one or more rows of labial teeth isn't rare, either, for the teeth often get broken.

Does all this leave us back where we started from and no wiser than before? Yes and no. If we expect to be able to identify a tadpole from a key with the same ease with which we would identify an adult, we shall find that we often fail. However, if we are truly interested in gaining more knowledge of tadpoles, we have two courses open to us. We can first of all capture a mated pair of adults, keep the eggs they lay, and examine the tadpoles from birth until transformation. This is the most reliable method. Or we can capture a tadpole and keep it until after it has transformed and can be identified as an adult. Once one is familiar with the tadpole of a certain species, one can study it and its identifying characteristics as presented in the key. We have a vicious circle here. In order to be able to identify the tadpoles, we must understand the key; in order to understand the key, we must know the tadpoles. After we have followed the key on several known species, we begin to have some understanding of the relative values referred to earlier. When we have reached this stage, we may attempt to identify unknown tadpoles either of familiar or of unfamiliar adult species.

We have, perhaps, painted a rather discouraging picture. To end on a brighter note, we must add that many tadpoles are fairly easily identified. In the chapters on the adult amphibians and their ways, we shall try to point out the outstanding identifying characteristics of some of them.

CHAPTER 5

The Big Change

We have seen how the tadpole grows larger from the time it hatches. At a certain stage in its development a radical change is made—the transformation of tadpole to adult frog or toad. When does this metamorphosis occur? The time varies enormously from species to species and also depends in part upon the temperature. Generally speaking, aquatic frogs have the longest larval period, while those frogs and toads that are terrestrial when adult have the shortest. Furthermore, species of toads found in the desert and accustomed to breeding in temporary rain pools have a shorter development than our northern toads.

To give you a better idea of the length of time, let us offer a few examples. Two Spadefoot Toads, *Scaphiopus couchi*, transforming in 15 days, and *Scaphiopus holbrooki hurteri*, transforming in 12 days, now hold the present record for the shortest period. This is not to say that these or other related species may not slightly improve upon this time in warmer, drier regions or in exceptional seasons. The record for longevity in this country is held by our largest frog, the Bullfrog, *Rana catesbeiana*, who may not transform until its third year as a tadpole in the North. In the South, transformation is normally completed in one year. Compare this to the American Toad, *Bufo americanus americanus*, in the North who completes metamorphosis in 50 to 60 days. A striking illustration as to the importance of temperature may be seen if you keep toads in an aquarium in the house. All of ours have transformed completely 38 days after hatching when kept at a room temperature of 65° to 70° F. Possibly the time would be even shorter at a higher temperature. It must be mentioned, however, that this rapidity of development may not be entirely caused by higher, more even temperatures. Light plays a part also. It has been found that many tadpoles develop faster when exposed to normal light *and* artificial light than they do when only sunlight is present.

The first sign that a frog is beginning to transform is the appearance of the hind legs on either side of the tail base. As the legs start to develop, they may at first be mistaken for the anus, for they are very tiny. Soon they are long enough to break through the skin. Gradually they lengthen out, toes are formed, and the legs thicken and look like frog's legs. When the legs are small, the tadpole drags them behind, but as the feet become well formed, the legs are used in the characteristic frog swimming motion as an aid to the tail in locomotion.

After the legs are well developed, the arms will appear. They have been forming inside the gill chamber, and when they attain a certain size they break through the skin. The left arm generally emerges through the spiracle if it is on the left side, the right arm through the opercular fold. The left arm very often appears first, but it is by no means unusual for the right one to do so.

As soon as the arms appear, the shape of the tadpole's head-body begins to change, and the tail is gradually resorbed. Day by day, it grows shorter, and as it is resorbed the tadpole utilizes it as "food," for he is unable to eat at this crucial stage of transition.

Unfortunately, we are unable to see the startling internal changes taking place at this time. But though not visible to us, they are, perhaps, even more extreme than the external changes. Lungs develop and gills degenerate. The tadpole will frequently rise to the surface of the pond to take a breath of air.

The intestine shortens and becomes the typical intestine of a carnivorous animal. The mouth with its horny beak begins to widen and change into the large frog mouth complete with tongue and (usually) true teeth. The animal's diet changes from a primarily herbivorous one to a completely carnivorous one. Insects and other invertebrates and even other amphibians, if they are small enough,

HUGH SPENC

are eaten. A few foods are rejected because of unpleasant taste, but most are consumed with relish. The main requirement is that the food be small enough to be swallowed.

The tadpole looses his lateral line organs and sheds his larval skin in one piece. Eyelids and lubricating glands form, and his eyes become large and bulging. By this time, the tail has become a mere stump, and the tiny creature is ready to assume a more or less terrestrial existence, breathing air by means of lungs, and using its hind legs for locomotion on land and in water. No longer is it a fishlike animal; now it is a diminutive frog.

When we look at a mature tadpole just beginning transformation, and compare it with the newly transformed frog a few days or weeks later, our immediate impression is that it is much smaller as a frog. But our eyes deceive us. If we measure the body of the tadpole and the body of the frog, we shall find in all but a very few cases that the measurements of the frog body equal or slightly exceed those of the body of the mature tadpole. There are a few cases in this country where the body size of the tadpole is larger by as much as 5 mm., as in the case of *Scaphiopus hammondi*. But consider the Paradoxical Frog, *Pseudis paradoxus*, found on the island of Trinidad. For years scientists had observed huge tadpoles of 14 inches in length, but had looked in vain for the adult, which, they reasoned, must really be a monstrous frog. Around the same ponds was a small green frog with a body length of 1½ inches—about the size of our Eastern Grey Treefrog. It was a long time before herpetologists discovered that this small frog was the adult of the huge tadpoles. *Pseudis paradoxus* takes several years to attain a mature tadpole size of 14 inches. After the hind legs and forelegs appear, the transforming tadpole rapidly shrinks to its mature size of 1½ inches.

We mentioned earlier that a tadpole's sex is undetermined. During transformation, the sex becomes positively established as either male or female. Each tadpole inherits his sex when born. But this inherited sex factor may be reversed by such environmental conditions as food and, above all, temperature. Though a starvation diet tends to speed transformation, such individuals are unable to reproduce when adult. Since a starvation diet must be a rare thing in the pond, perhaps this never happens in nature.

The development of a frog

But we cannot dismiss the matter of diet so summarily. We know, for instance, that the queen bee lays two kinds of eggs: unfertilized eggs, which always develop into drones or males; and fertilized eggs, which develop into either queens or female workers. And it is diet that decides whether a fertilized egg shall develop into a queen or a worker. If the larva is fed upon a specially rich diet, it develops into a large queen. If, however, the larva is fed on a less nourishing diet, it develops into a small female worker incapable of reproduction. Through some fluke of nature, it occasionally happens that a few larvae are fed on a diet intermediate between the queen and worker diets. The result is a worker of larger size than her sisters, who can lay unfertilized eggs and produce drones. When we know these facts, we wonder whether diet may not perhaps play an equally important part in the determination of sex in the tadpole. Lacking experimental proof, we can only speculate.

It has been found that high temperatures produce mostly males, while low temperatures produce mostly females. Furthermore, each species has a neutral temperature where the sex ratio is approximately equal. The neutral-temperature range is known for only a few species, but it must vary considerably. This is another reason why different species lay their eggs at different times. For if the sex ratio is too lopsided, reproduction will suffer.

A fourth factor is also known to affect the sex of the transforming tadpole. If the eggs are slow in descending from the ovaries to be laid and fertilized, the tadpoles that hatch from these eggs are likely to become male frogs. Actually, this is an extreme oversimplification of the results of blastophthoria, as this delayed fertilization of over-ripe eggs is known. Many of the tadpoles and frogs from such eggs present severe abnormalities. Some of these have improperly developed heads, swollen legs, reduction or increases in the number of limbs, and so forth. Some never develop into functional members of their sex. (There is some evidence that blastophthoria may be the cause of certain types of sexual abnormality in human beings also.)

One wonders what would happen to tadpoles hatched from eggs slow in being laid but developed at a low temperature. Would the shift be made back to female? Would the influences of slow laying, producing males, and low temperatures, producing females, cancel each other out and the sex ratio be fifty-fifty? Or does slow laying take precedence over temperature conditions?

But we are not through with complications. Tadpoles that normally would have been females but develop into males because of high temperatures or slow laying may mate with normal females. Their offspring are female. But does that mean that temperature cannot turn the tide again? Let us carry our speculation a little further.

Let m stand for a female changed into a male.

Let M stand for a normal male.

Let f stand for a male changed into a female.

Let F stand for a normal female.

It becomes immediately apparent that even apart from environmental conditions we have four possible breeding combinations. We know the results of three of them: $MF = 50\%$ M and 50% F. Fm $= 100\%$ F. And $Mf = 100\%$ M even unto the fourth generation. But what does fm produce? If we include the different environmental conditions that we know influence the final determination of sex, our calculations would give us over 100 possible combinations to choose from. We can predict with some accuracy the results of only a very few of these.

I have asked these questions to show just what a complicated process this business of sex determination in a tadpole is. And this in turn leads us to wonder if temperature and diet play any part at all in determining the sex of the mammalian embryo. There is, at present, no indication that they do, and many reasons why they may not. Nevertheless, speculations no more farfetched than these have led to discoveries in other fields.

In the salamander larva we see no such sudden transformation as the frog tadpole illustrates. In the case of the pond larva, who of the three larval types presents the most striking change, the forelegs appear soon after hatching. Granted these legs are mere buds, but they gradually grow larger and the toes form. Incidentally, it should be mentioned that the arms of the tadpole also develop before the hind legs, but since their development is internal we are not aware of this when we look at a tadpole. In the case of some pond larvae, many river larvae, and all terrestrial larvae, the arms are present at birth, though they may or may not be fully developed at that time. A few of the terrestrial salamanders have no free larval stage at all; the entire larval period is within the egg capsule, and the animal is fully transformed upon hatching.

After the arms have reached a certain size, the legs appear and develop. As with the arms, these too are present at birth in many species. Gradually, the larva grows larger. The body of the pond larva becomes more streamlined, conforming to the typical salamander outlines. The body and tail fins, where present, are resorbed into the body. The skin changes. Lateral line organs, except in a very few completely aquatic species of salamanders, are lost. The eyes become larger, and lids form.

Internally, the lungs develop except in the large family Plethodontidae, which are lungless, and the external gills gradually grow smaller until they are entirely resorbed into the body. There is no change in the shape of the intestine as with the tadpoles, for the larva is equipped at birth with the short carnivorous intestine. There is, however, a change in the teeth. Larvae, as we mentioned, have spike teeth, similar in form to our "eyeteeth." At transformation these are shed, and bicuspid teeth like our molars are formed in many species. These are found not only on the jaws but also in various spots on the roof of the mouth. They are used more for holding the food and preventing its escape than for mastication of the food, for these teeth are very tiny.

As with the tadpole, the sex of the salamander is positively determined at transformation, and, so far as is known, the same environmental factors play a part. The shedding of the larval skin in one piece, loss of gills and body and tail fin, protuberance of the eyes, formation of eyelids, and determination of sex are considered by herpetologists all part of the transformation process of the salamander. Because the fore and hind limbs and the streamlining of the body are present at birth or shortly afterward, these are not really part of the change known as metamorphosis, in the opinion of scientists.

As with the frogs, there is a tremendous difference at the age in which transformation is completed in the salamanders. Some of the terrestrial larvae hatch from the egg capsule fully transformed. Other terrestrial larvae may assume their adult form only a few days after hatching. At the other extreme are the larvae that never complete transformation. Then there are species, such as the Northern Two-lined Salamander, that do not transform for two or even three years. Most pond larvae achieve their adult form in two to four months. If we except terrestrial salamanders, in general the

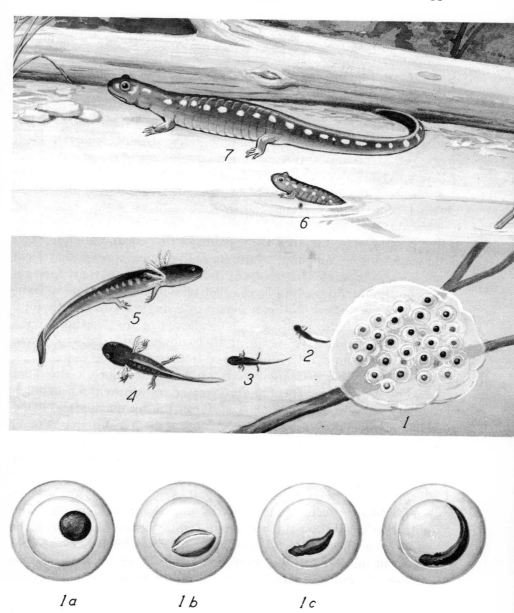

The development of a salamander

salamanders take slightly longer to transform than do frogs and toads. We rarely if ever find, for instance, a salamander laying in temporary rain pools as do some species of toads. The counterpart of rain-pool-laying frogs is found in those terrestrial salamanders that lay in moist spots.

Metamorphosis in the frog consists of a complete change of form, of diet (with a few exceptions), and often of habitat also. In the salamanders, the transformation, though less striking, is nevertheless present. Metamorphosis is governed largely by the secretions of the thyroid gland; this in turn is influenced by the secretions of the *pars anterior* of the pituitary, and also by such external conditions as temperature and diet. That the thyroid hormone is the chief agent in producing metamorphosis may be proved by anyone so inclined. Try feeding some tadpoles a few grains of thyroid and see how soon they transform, compared to others of the same species that have not been so treated. The results of thyroid feeding are most spectacular on those tadpoles and larvae that take the longest time to complete transformation. Within a month of a single feeding of thyroid, the tadpoles of the Bullfrog and the larvae of the Northern Two-lined Salamander have assumed their adult form. Both of these species have a normal larval period of from one to three years.

Though thyroid feeding speeds up transformation, it does not speed up growth, and specimens so treated transform at a size much smaller than normal. The *pars anterior* of the pituitary gland is the principal regulator of growth. Not only does it cause increase in body size, but without its secretions, the thyroid is unable to grow large enough and be sufficiently developed to secrete the hormones necessary to produce metamorphosis.

Temperature plays an important part. We find that most species of amphibians transform more rapidly in warmer surroundings. The Bullfrog, who, in the South, attains its adult form in one year, takes two or even three years to do so in the North. This is because cold acts as an inhibitor to the thyroid, slowing down its secretions so that they do not act with the same rapidity as at higher temperatures.

Diet, too, influences metamorphosis. Iodine obtained in the food stimulates the thyroid gland to greater activity. In situations where the iodine content in plants and possibly to a certain extent in the water is high, we may expect to find amphibians transforming more rapidly than in those places where the iodine content is lower. Of course, we are not likely to have the facilities to analyze the iodine content in various situations where amphibians are found. Nevertheless, it is interesting to know that this is an important factor in metamorphosis.

Apart from the iodine content in the food, an inadequate diet tends to accelerate the transformation process. When the tadpole or larva is hungry, the tail is resorbed more rapidly and utilized for food. On the other hand, low temperatures, which slow down the action of the thyroid gland, and plentiful food supply combine to lengthen the larval period.

Before we go on to describe a group of salamanders that never complete transformation and thus remain immature forever, let us examine our newly transformed amphibians.

The frog or toad that has just transformed may desert the water and assume a more or less terrestrial life with a small remnant of a tail. We commonly see this in the toads and treefrogs; doubtless it is true of certain true frogs also. However, the tail stump does not remain long; it will disappear in a day or two.

Our young amphibian varies in size. Most frogs of the family Ranidae have a transformation size larger than most treefrogs of the family Hylidae, while the toads in general transform at the smallest size of all. Some newly transformed toads are often only 7 mm.—no larger than a fly. This small transformation size is true of both the tiny Oak Toad, *Bufo quercicus,* which attains a mature size of about 1 inch, and the American Toad, which is from 2½ to 4 inches when fully grown. At the other end of the scale are the young Bullfrogs who are about 2 inches in length when they have completed metamorphosis. Transformation sizes in salamanders vary also; the larvae that hatch from eggs laid in terrestrial situations transform at an extremely small size.

Though our newly transformed amphibian has assumed his adult form and way of life, he is now really a baby amphibian, and not fully adult. Not until he is one, two, or even four or five years old will he attain sexual maturity and display those secondary sex characteristics common to his species. When he is able to reproduce, he may truly be termed an adult, but growth does not cease at that time. Indeed, though relatively little is known yet about amphibian growth, it is felt that the great majority of amphibians may continue to grow as long as they live. Naturally, when they are fully adult, they do not grow at the same rapid speed. Adult growth is not only slow, with small differences in measurement, but also sporadic, confined to periods of warmth, high humidity, and plentiful food supply.

It might be mentioned that the size of a frog is its length from snout to vent, and is measured with a caliper for accuracy; the curve of the body would lengthen the measurement, and therefore a tape measure cannot be used. If you wish to measure a frog but lack a caliper, it is simple to measure him accurately in this manner: Take a heavy sheet of paper and fold it in two, creasing it sharply. Place part of it on a table, the other part along the wall, taping the two parts in place so that a right angle is formed. Then, with a pencil in one hand, place your frog on the paper with his snout touching the paper on the wall. Put a pencil mark above his snout on the wall and a mark behind his vent on the table. Then measure with a ruler diagonally between these two marks, and you have an accurate measurement of your specimen's body length. Or you may use an ordinary compass, placing the pencil end by the snout, the pointed end by the vent, and measure the distance between these two points on a ruler.

A salamander's length may be ascertained in the same way. However, in this case it is the total length that is measured from the tip of the snout to the tip of the tail. The animal must be straight, not curled. Therefore, if possible, recruit an assistant for salamander measuring. The smaller types are particularly agile, and getting one straightened out is often a job for four hands. Lacking an assistant, pop your salamander into your icebox for an hour (not the freezing compartment). The cold will make him sluggish and more tractable.

We do not know how long a life our young amphibian can hope to enjoy. There are some figures on the life spans of certain species in captivity but none on animals in the wild. Longevity in captive specimens would probably be more striking because of lack of predators, lack of competition for food, and many other factors. From figures that we have on maximum age of amphibians in captivity, it would seem that in general larger species live longer. More species of salamanders achieve a life span of 15 to 30 years than frogs. If these were figures on animals in the wild, we might attribute this to the more secretive ways of the salamander. Since the ages are for captive animals, what reasons are there? Do the salamanders adapt themselves better to captivity? Does the fact that salamanders are mostly nocturnal have anything to do with it? Or is the salamander's way of living less active and less strenuous so that he can live longer? It may be noted that larger aquatic species of salamanders live longer than smaller terrestrial or semiaquatic varieties. Is this because they are larger or is it because they are aquatic or do both factors have a bearing on the matter?

As we know, amphibians in the North hibernate for part of the year. Amphibians in the extreme South do not, as a rule, hibernate, though they may occasionally aestivate (burrow to escape heat and aridity). The northern amphibian might be said to have an active living period of 6 to 7 months, with the peaks of activity in the spring and to a lesser extent in the fall. The southern amphibian, however, is active almost all year. Therefore, according to what Dr. Oliver calls Rubner's Hypothesis, the northern amphibian should have a longer life span as measured by years, though if life span were measured by activity periods the life spans of the northerner and southerner would be more nearly equal.

What is really needed are detailed studies of all the different species of frogs and salamanders in the wild to determine not only maximum age but also average life expectancy and growth. This can be done by anyone who is interested in making such an investigation. In order to make such a study, it is necessary to mark a large number of individuals so that they may be identified when and if recaptured. In the frogs, Mrs. Goin suggests toe clipping as the easiest way. She says that there is little blood and little pain when a toe or two is amputated with a pair of scissors. We have marked frogs and toads using this method, and we concur with Mrs. Goin's findings. The salamanders present more of a difficulty, for they are able to regenerate lost fingers and toes, and within a year or two there would be little to show that the animal had ever been marked. As we understand it, salamanders are generally marked by tattooing. But perhaps the enterprising amateur can discover a better method to be accomplished with materials at hand.

Our young amphibian, though not mature sexually, has now assumed his adult form. He may be very tiny but he is unmistakably a frog, a toad, or a salamander. We mentioned that in transformation the eyes changed, the ear developed, and the mouth changed.

Let us see just what these sense organs consist of and how they operate in the amphibian.

The eyes of the adult amphibian, especially those of most frogs and toads, are large, bulging, and unusually beautiful. The amphibian eyelids which developed at transformation consist in most species of a thickened upper lid and a lower lid, the upper part of which is transparent and folded down under the lower part. This transparent fold is known as the nictitating membrane, and can be raised up over the eye at will. Aquatic frogs frequently swim with the nictitating membrane covering the eye, lowering it as they surface for air. Both upper and lower lids proper are incapable of independent movement. However, they operate when the eye is retracted into its socket, closing over it quite as effectively as human eyelids do over their eyes. There are a few amphibians who lack eyelids altogether—among them *Pipa pipa,* who carries her eggs on her back. Pipa and others like her do have a nictitating membrane, however. Many of the neotenous salamanders also lack eyelids, but we shall tell more of them later.

The eyes themselves can be raised or lowered so that they are level with the surface of the head. This is convenient not only because of protection of the eye but also because the lowered eyes aid in swallowing food. When swallowing a very large mouthful, amphibians generally lower their eyes, which then form a bulge in the mouth cavity, thus helping the teeth in forcing the prey back toward the throat.

In Chapter 1 we mentioned that amphibian vision was similar to human vision. However, there are outstanding differences between our vision and theirs. To begin with, the amphibian eye is much more farsighted than is ours. Insects crawling under an amphibian's nose may do so with impunity, whereas those that are farther away are in danger of their lives. Humans have binocular vision; that is, they see the object viewed with both eyes at the same time. It is not possible for a human being to look at two objects in directions opposite each other simultaneously—one with each eye. Because the amphibian's eyes are placed more on the side of his head, he possesses binocular vision only at a certain distance away from him. The amount of binocular vision enjoyed varies from species to species, and depends upon the position of the eyes on the head as well as the amount of adjustment possible in the lens of the eye, which is moved forward by special eye muscles to focus. Some amphibians, such as the Hellbender, have no binocular vision at all; their vision is restricted entirely to monocular vision. All this means, of course, that amphibians do not see so well or so clearly as humans.

Since many amphibians are primarily nocturnal creatures, it surprises us to learn that scientists feel that amphibians, unlike many nocturnal mammals, are not able to see in the dark so well as the diurnal human.

Another characteristic of human sight is the ability to see color. We are not able to see all colors; ultraviolet rays are invisible to us, for instance, though they are not to certain insects. Can the amphibian see color? Or is his world like that of a dog and a cow, a world seen only in black and white and gray? It is now believed that amphibians have some color vision, but just how much has not been proved.

The pupil of the human eye is round, but we know that it is not so in all animals. The pupil of a cat's eye when partially contracted is vertical or erect. With the amphibians, we find that most of them have a horizontal pupil. But the Spadefoot Toads and the Tailed Frogs always have an erect pupil, as do treefrogs of the genus *Phyllomedusa* found in South America. Then there are a few species whose pupils present even more distinctive shapes, such as the diamond-shaped pupil of the Brazilian treefrog, *Aparasphenodon brunoi*, or the hourglass-shaped pupil of the African Sand Toad, *Bufo angusticeps*.

For ears and hearing, we find that the human being is better equipped than the amphibian in this respect also. The only amphibian who possesses an external ear opening similar to that of human beings is *Rana cavitympanum* of Siam. In all other amphibians there is no external ear opening, and the tympanum is a round membrane located behind and slightly below the eye on the surface of the skin. This tympanum is not found on all amphibians by any means. It is lacking in all salamanders and in many toads. Even when it is present, it may be indistinct.

The lack of a tympanum does not seem to prevent frogs and toads from hearing air-borne sounds, though their hearing is not so acute as is ours. We are able to hear sounds having vibrations of 15 to 20,000 cycles per second. Most frogs and toads can hear sounds having a frequency of between 50 to 10,000.

Frogs and toads also differ from us in their reactions to sound. For them, sounds seem mostly to reinforce visual awareness and body preparedness. A sudden loud noise will startle a human being into action, but the same noise merely puts the amphibian on guard and ready to flee. It seems to require vision fully to interpret the sounds it hears.

The salamanders lack hearing as we know it. They are able to feel surface vibrations through their front legs or lower jaws, depending upon the species. Many experiments have been made to prove that salamanders are able to hear air-borne sounds. In 1911 one investigator claimed that salamanders could hear. In 1927 another herpetologist was unable to substantiate those findings. The latest word that we know of is that certain salamanders can hear sounds with a frequency of up to 244 vibrations per second. Whether subsequent experiments will agree with these findings remains to be seen. In any case, it is obvious that the salamanders, if they can distinguish air-borne sounds at all, can do so only to an extremely limited extent. For them hearing consists mainly of the reception of surface vibrations through the lower jaw or the front legs.

The amphibian mouth and tongue are not at all like ours. The distribution of the teeth varies from family to family. Some toads lack teeth on both jaws; others lack teeth on the roof of the mouth. Some frogs have teeth on both upper and lower jaws and on the roof of the mouth, and this last category encompasses all the salamanders too. These teeth are very tiny and are not used for chewing. Their purpose is merely to subdue the prey and facilitate its passage to the gullet. Frogs and toads swallow their food alive and whole. If a large mouthful is taken, the eyes are lowered into the roof of the mouth to help the teeth. If the prey be exceptionally lively, the hands may also be used to cram the mouthful down. The salamanders, too, generally swallow their prey whole, but the forelegs are not used to help swallow a large mouthful. With certain of the larger aquatic salamanders, large prey is sometimes seized in the jaws and shaken vigorously by twisting the body rapidly around. This is what a dog frequently does with a woodchuck or even a meaty bone, except that the dog needs only to shake his head. The result is that the prey is torn apart either completely or partially by this treatment, and is thus rendered into a more easily swallowed piece.

The amphibian tongue is either one of two types. In most frogs and a few salamanders, it is joined to the front of the mouth and lies, when at rest, back toward the gullet. This type of tongue may rapidly be flicked out of the mouth for a considerable distance to catch an insect. Incidentally its tip is not, as a rule, rounded (though there are exceptions), but in the shape of a capital M. The other type of tongue found in many salamanders and a few frogs is mushroomlike in shape and is fastened to the floor of the mouth. It too can be projected beyond the mouth, but it cannot be extended so far as the first type. Both kinds of tongues are made sticky by the secretions of glands in the roof of the mouth. The sticky tip of the tongue is all that is needed to catch small insects. The tongue is often wrapped around larger ones. To round out our picture of tongues, we must not forget that a few aquatic frogs lack tongues altogether. Our native frogs and toads all have tongues fastened to the front of the mouth, while our salamanders have both types, according to their species.

Perhaps you may have noticed that no mention has been made of drinking. The amphibians do not drink. They do not lap water as does a dog nor suck it as does a sheep nor gulp it down as does a human. They do, however, require water, as indeed do most living things. They absorb what water they require through their skins. Some species are able to absorb water on any part of the skin. Other, thicker-skinned terrestrial species absorb it mostly through the skin of the thighs. Therefore, if you wish to give an amphibian a drink you should provide a dish of water large enough for him to get into.

The amphibian's skin is not only an organ for absorbing water but also a respiratory organ, a temperature regulator, and his main defense, as we shall see in later chapters. Therefore, it is important that it be kept in good condition. To accomplish this end, the amphibian frequently sheds his skin in one piece. He struggles out of the old one as we would out of a sweater, usually swallowing it as he goes along, though some aquatic species may allow it to float away on the water.

The number of times amphibians shed seems not only to vary from species to species but also apparently to depend on age and environmental conditions. The young amphibian is believed to shed more frequently than the adult. Green Treefrogs, *Hyla cinerea cinerea*, found in the South have been known to shed every day. Toads shed every 3 to 10 days. An adult male Bullfrog that we kept shed every other day. Little research has been done on shedding, and here again is a field where the interested amateur can score. However, one needs to be watchful; one doesn't often just happen on a shedding.

A young amphibian is like the young of other animals in many of his ways. Like them, he needs to eat more often than the adult. But more outstanding than this is his lack of secretiveness. Because he is far more diurnal than the adults, it is the young amphibian that we most often see. If we do not see him just after transformation, it is because he is very tiny and we are not looking. From the height of a human, the little dusty toad looks like a fly or perhaps a spider. But if you bend over to investigate and find a toad instead, look around you. Doubtless you will find many others nearby. Young amphibians, especially right after transformation, are gregarious, and make mass migrations away from their natal ponds. Hundreds may be seen during the early summer if you look carefully for them.

In keeping with his more active ways, the young amphibian goes into hibernation later in the fall than the mature adults of the same species, and emerges from hibernation earlier in the spring. Even year-old amphibians are less nocturnal, less wary, and more active than the older ones. Gradually, as they mature, they become more cautious, more secretive, and primarily nocturnal. You can find some of the older ones during the day if you try, but not with the ease and frequency that you find the young ones. That should not disappoint you, for the young are infinitely more engaging. The young toads are our special favorites—so quiet and tame and trusting are they.

CHAPTER 6

Forever Immature

The salamander that remains perpetually immature is a paradox. It is an adult salamander, and yet it is not. It is rare in the sense that it is difficult to observe, but common in that it exists not only in parts of America but in parts of Europe and Asia as well. There are a number of families of these salamanders that remain immature throughout their lives, but there are few species within each family. Some species of salamanders always remain immature forever; other common species, such as some Newts and the Tiger Salamander, may remain so under certain conditions; while a third, and by far the largest, group of salamanders always transform completely into adults, so far as we know.

A salamander that remains immature forever is known as a neotenous salamander. Before we attempt to describe just what such a salamander *is*, we might profitably state what it is *not*. A neotenous salamander does not remain so small as when it first hatched. Indeed, the opposite is true. Most neotenous salamanders are larger than non-neotenous species; the largest of all amphibians is the neotenous *Megalobatrachus maximus* of Japan and China. Nor are the neotenous salamanders ever immature sexually; they can and do reproduce regularly when adult.

A positive characteristic that distinguishes the neotenous salamander from those that are non-neotenous is that the neotenous salamander retains certain larval characteristics—which ones depend upon the species. Some salamanders never lose their larval teeth and/or skin. Larval teeth are spike teeth similar to our "eyeteeth," while fully transformed salamanders have bicuspid teeth, resembling our molars in the form their grinding surface presents. The larval skin is different also, just as the skin of an adult human is different from that of a baby.

Though larval skin and teeth are important characteristics of the neotenous salamander, they mean little to any but a trained herpetologist. We would be unable to distinguish the difference between the skin of a larva and that of an adult. Nor are we much more likely to pry open our salamander's mouth, get out our magnifying glass, and examine its teeth to see whether they are spike or bicuspid. However, many neotenous salamanders have a third characteristic that is a little more helpful to us in distinguishing between them and a fully transformed animal. Many neotenous salamanders never lose their external gills. They may develop lungs also, and still retain their gills. The gills may continue to grow as long as the salamander does, or they may stop growing and remain small in proportion to body size. It also happens that the gills may be resorbed into the body, while the gill slits remain open instead of closed as in fully transformed individuals.

There are several other features that may be present in neotenous salamanders, such as reduction in the size of front or back legs, lack of eyelids, and retention of tail crests and lateral line organs. Neotenous salamanders are usually aquatic; most of them are born in the water and remain there throughout their lives. But, like so many generalizations, there are exceptions, one of which we shall mention soon. Before we examine the neotenous species of salamanders in a little more detail, let us look into some of the causative factors of neoteny.

Since the neotenous salamander remains larvalike in some respects, it is only natural that we should look first at the process of transformation, and wonder why certain of their tissues failed to transform. As we know, the thyroid gland is the chief regulator of metamorphosis. Strangely enough, the neotenous salamander possesses a thyroid that functions perfectly, as has been proved in the laboratory by injecting bullfrog and non-neotenous salamander larvae with the extracts from the thyroid of neotenous salamanders.

Upon receiving the injections, these tadpoles and non-neotenous larvae immediately begin transformation. As far as we know, of all salamanders, only the Texas Blind Salamander (see Chapter 15) is lacking a thyroid. But unlike a man without a thyroid, or with an improperly functioning thyroid, where goiter and cretinism result, this amphibian suffers no ill effects, and is not very different from other salamanders who have this gland.

In normally neotenous salamanders, certain tissues are insensitive to the secretions of the thyroid, and do not change. Therefore, though the neotenous salamander begins to transform, he never completes metamorphosis because gills and/or teeth, skin tissue, and so on, do not respond to the hormones secreted by the thyroid.

There are, however, some salamanders that normally complete transformation but under certain conditions may be neotenous. Best known of these is the Axolotl of Mexico, a larval form of one of the Mole Salamanders. High altitudes or very cold water may inhibit or prevent the efficient functioning of the thyroid, as may a lack of iodine in natural food. If this type of neotenous salamander is moved to another environment where conditions conducive to transformation exist, it will complete metamorphosis. This is in marked contrast to the normally neotenous salamander, which cannot be induced to transform either by injection of thyroid or by change of climate.

There must be other reasons why some salamanders are neotenous in certain regions. The Red-spotted Newt, *Diemictylus viridescens viridescens,* that lives in the Northeast, generally transforms completely. But around Woods Hole, Massachusetts, and Long Island, New York, it occasionally remains neotenous. Neither place is at a high altitude, nor is the climate cold, and surely iodine is not lacking so near the sea.

That high altitude, cold, and lack of iodine do not always produce neotenous species is shown most strikingly by the case of the Alpine Salamander, *Salamandra atra. Salamandra atra* lives in the Alps, a region notorious for the high incidence of cretinism and goiter in humans. The Alpine Salamander lives at heights of between 2,600 and 9,800 feet, and is a terrestrial species, rarely entering the water. The young, about 20 in number, are carried inside the mother, making this species ovoviviparous. Only 2 young are born, since the others have been used as food for the survivors during development within the oviduct of the parent. These young salamanders are fully transformed at birth. Neoteny is unknown despite high altitude, cold, and lack of iodine.

You will notice that throughout this chapter there has been no mention of neotenous frogs and toads. The reason is that there is no such thing as a neotenous frog. The Salientia always complete their development and change into adults unlike their former tadpole selves. It is true that a few frogs and toads fail to develop eyelids and teeth, but this is not considered to be neoteny but merely a characteristic indicating that these species are of a more primitive type.

Why is it that among the Amphibia, the salamanders alone exhibit neoteny? We can speculate as much as we like on this question, but we still have no definite answer. All in all, neoteny and its causative factors are fields that need much more investigation and study before we can answer positively all the questions concerning it that occur to us.

The normally neotenous salamanders in this country comprise four families and a few species within a fifth. (See illustration, page 99.) The last we shall discuss in Chapter 15. The first two families are the Amphiumidae, or Amphiumas, and the Sirenidae, or Sirens. On glancing at any of the members of either of these two families, you might easily believe you were looking, not at salamanders, but at eels, which are not amphibians at all, but fish. However, the eel-like Amphiumidae have four diminutive limbs (no eel ever has legs), with but two or three toes on each (depending upon the subspecies), and are about 3 feet long. They have lost their gills—though two gill slits remain—have larval teeth, and lack eyelids.

Both subspecies are aquatic, as is normal with neotenous salamanders, but they go on land and burrow in the mud to lay their eggs. We mentioned this earlier in Chapter 3, and surely it is one of the mysteries of nature why a normally aquatic salamander should go on land to lay its eggs.

The Amphiumas, or "Congo Eels," are found along the coastal lowlands of the South from Virginia to Florida and along the Gulf Coast through Alabama, Mississippi, Louisiana, and Arkansas. They may be found in lakes, swamps, and drainage ditches throughout the area, and, once seen, cannot be mistaken for any other family.

The Sirenidae, or Sirens, the other eel-like salamanders, are different from the Amphiumas in that they possess but a single pair of front legs. They also have external gills and lungs. Their dentition is larval, and eyelids are lacking. There are two genera within this family—*Siren*, with four toes, ranging in size from 6 to 36 inches, depending upon the species, and *Pseudobranchus*, with three toes, whose specimens are considerably smaller, from 5 to a little over 8 inches in length.

The range of the sirens is about the same as that of the amphiumas, and they are completely aquatic. Siren presents an exception to the general rule that salamanders are wholly carnivorous. It is true that the greater part of its diet is made up of crustaceans, but occasionally it eats algae, and specimens have been collected whose stomach contents contained nothing but vegetable matter. Siren is an anomaly in another way; it is believed to fertilize its eggs externally.

The other two families of neotenous salamanders, the Proteidae, or Mudpuppies, and the Cryptobranchidae, or Hellbenders, are more salamanderlike in body shape. The Mudpuppies have lungs *and* bushy red external gills. They have no eyelids, but their teeth and skin are adult in form. There are seven species and subspecies of a single genus *Necturus*, and these are found in parts of the Eastern half of the country, with the area of concentration greatest throughout the Middle West. The females of *Necturus maculosus maculosus*, the Mudpuppy, the species with the widest distribution, scoops out a nest in the water, and remains with her eggs until they are hatched. Nothing is known of the breeding habits of the other six species.

The name "mudpuppy" is a curious one, and may have arisen from the fact that the animal has been heard making yelping noises. Others insist that this salamander has a doglike appearance, though my imagination has never been vivid enough to be able to see it.

The last family is the Cryptobranchidae, or Hellbenders, large flat-bodied animals with a loose skin distributed in thick wrinkled pleats on the sides. The teeth are larval and the eyelids are missing. There are no gills, but usually there are two open gill slits, one on each side of the head. Occasionally, one or both of these gill slits may be missing. The Hellbenders lay their large unpigmented eggs in rosarylike strings, and the males guard the egg complement of several females. It is found in the larger rivers in New Jersey, Pennsylvania, West Virginia, Ohio, Indiana, and Kentucky.

The Hellbender is closely related to the Giant Salamander of Japan. The latter, though much larger, and with more exaggerated folds on the sides, looks very much like the Hellbender. Both fertilize their eggs externally.

These, then, are some of the normally neotenous salamanders. Though there are four families of them, there are few species within each family. They are not very common even in the regions where they occur, and relatively little is known of the life cycles of most of them. If widespread distribution and multiplicity of species are used as the criteria of whether or not a mode of life history is successful, then it is apparent that the neotenous salamanders are not successful. It may even be that they are in the process of becoming extinct—not today or even a hundred years from now, but in a few thousand years—a relatively short period of time when viewed from an evolutionary standpoint.

CHAPTER 7

Respiration and Cold-Bloodedness

If we wish to study respiration, we can have no better subject than the amphibian. In him we find almost every kind of respiration that exists, and we cannot help but admire Nature's adaptability in carrying out one of the most important functions of life under diverse conditions. Furthermore, even if we are not especially interested in the process of respiration, questions concerning the amphibian occur to us. For instance, how does a gilled salamander larva, born on land, breathe? How do the Lungless Salamanders who lack both lungs and gills breathe? How do the tadpoles of the Robber Frogs, still encased in their egg capsules, breathe? How can a frog with lungs spend months hibernating under water and still obtain the necessary oxygen? All of these and many other questions must be answered in order properly to understand the amphibian and his ways. All may be answered if we know what respiration is and how it takes place.

Most life needs oxygen to exist. True, there are some bacteria, known as anaerobic bacteria, which can live without air—the tetanus bacillus is a prime example—but these living things are in the minority. Trees and flowers, amoebas and jellyfish, worms and slugs, insects and spiders, fish and frogs, birds and man—none can live indefinitely without oxygen. All of these take in oxygen from the air or from the water. In vertebrates, oxygen is carried to all the cells of the body by the blood. The oxygen combines with digested food and, through a process known as oxidation, produces energy. Without energy the eye cannot blink, the mouth cannot chew, the legs cannot walk, the food cannot be digested, and the heart cannot beat. Thus we see that energy is the capacity to perform work; without it, there could be none of the higher forms of life.

In order to understand how respiration can take place, we must first of all give a simple definition of diffusion. Diffusion is the spreading out of fluids or gases from the area of greatest concentration to an area of lesser concentration. It is made possible because molecules, be they molecules of oxygen, water, or gold, move. They move at different rates of speed, and the rate of diffusion depends on the weight of the various kinds of molecules. But mathematical formulas concerning diffusion need not be discussed here, for the definition just given is adequate to enable us to learn how respiration works. Diffusion is not the only process involved; a number of chemical changes also serve to speed up respiration. These are also complex, and since diffusion alone explains the respiratory process, we shall not discuss them either, though it is interesting to know that they exist. Diffusion may take place through a membrane, or there may be no membrane. In respiration, of course, a membrane is always present.

We may illustrate how diffusion in respiration works by taking the example of an aquatic salamander larva. This larva is equipped with two sets of external gills, one on either side of his head. The gills are highly vascularized; that is, they contain a great many blood vessels. The skin or membrane surrounding these blood vessels is thin. Since the water has a greater concentration of oxygen than does the blood, the oxygen diffuses through the membrane that covers the gills, and enters the bloodstream. This oxygenated blood returns to the heart to be pumped to the cells, while non-oxygenated blood enters the gills to become oxygenated. Furthermore, as the "old" blood from the body enters the gills, it contains a great deal of carbon dioxide, which is the by-product of oxidation. This carbon dioxide passes from the blood into the water, for water contains little carbon dioxide. Thus we see that respiration consists not only in the absorption of oxygen by the blood and its use by the cells, but also in the elimination of the gaseous waste products of oxidation. This removal of waste products is just as important a part of respiration as is the absorption of oxygen, for were the waste products not carried away, they would paralyze the cells and eventually kill them.

Respiration in the frog tadpoles is a little more complicated, for after the first few days its gills are internal. In this case, the tadpole takes water into its mouth. The water passes through the mouth back over the gills, where diffusion of oxygen and carbon dioxide takes place. The water then passes out of the body through a small opening, usually on the left side, known as the spiracle.

The average adult amphibian is a lung breather—some to a greater extent than others. A frog's method of respiration is slightly different from a human's because he lacks ribs (the Tailed Frog, *Ascapus truei,* excepted) and a diaphragm. This means that the air is not pushed in and out of his lungs semiautomatically as it is in man. Instead he must "swallow" his air. The air is taken in through the nostrils. Then they are closed with skin flaps, and the air is swallowed into the highly vascularized lungs, and diffusion occurs.

But no amphibian depends on his lungs solely for his supply of oxygen. The alternative methods of respiration that are used are illustrated most clearly in the case of that large family of salamanders the Plethodontidae, who have neither lungs nor gills when adult. These alternative methods of respiration are buccopharyngeal respiration and cutaneous respiration.

Buccopharyngeal respiration is mouth and throat breathing. The mouth and pharynx of all amphibians are highly vascularized. Air taken into the mouth diffuses its oxygen into the bloodstream. Nor is buccopharyngeal respiration confined only to air. Aquatic species can practice it by taking water into their mouths. The Lungless Salamanders obtain a great deal of the necessary oxygen through buccopharyngeal respiration. This is especially true of those species of plethodontids that are most terrestrial in their habits. But buccopharyngeal respiration is not confined solely to this group of amphibians. If you watch any frog or toad, you will see his throat pulsate. This is not because he is frightened, as I have heard suggested. He is practicing buccopharyngeal respiration; air is being drawn in and out of his mouth through the nostrils. Once or twice a minute, you will notice that the rhythm of these throat pulsations is interrupted. You may see a slight twitch around the waist. This is an indication that the frog has taken air into his lungs.

You may wonder why the frog does not use his lungs all the time, or why he uses them at all. He does not practice pulmonary respiration all the time probably because other, simpler methods are available to him. Furthermore, his lungs are not the efficient organs that ours are, and they do not supply him with all the oxygen his body requires. But he must use them some of the time because buccopharyngeal respiration alone does not provide sufficient oxygen either.

Cutaneous respiration is respiration through the skin. Before it can take place, two important requirements must be present. First of all, the skin must be highly vascularized; second, it must be moist. Vascularization and moist membranes are the rule if there is to be respiration of any kind, be it cutaneous, buccopharyngeal, pulmonary, or branchial.

The average amphibian's skin is constructed to make it possible for respiration to take place through it. There are exceptions: those newts and toads whose skin is dry and rough use means other than cutaneous respiration to satisfy their oxygen requirements. But the skin of most amphibians is highly vascularized; the skin is thin, or, as in thick-skinned species such as the Hellbender, the blood vessels are very close to its surface. The skin is also kept moist by virtue of its mucous glands. Curiously enough, the mucous glands function even if the amphibian happens to be an aquatic species, where presumably they are not necessary, for the water keeps the skin wet. Perhaps this is just an added safety factor provided by Nature. Should the pond dry up, an aquatic amphibian would have some chance of reaching another body of water before his skin would become too dry for cutaneous respiration to take place. The mucous glands serve another purpose for aquatic species. They act as a lubricant to make swimming more rapid.

The amphibian's ability to change color is another factor that enables him to keep his skin moist. The amphibian makes use of the principle that dark objects absorb both heat and light, while light objects reflect them. On cold dark days a frog's ground color is darker than it is on hot sunny ones. Not all amphibians can change from one color to another, as from brown to green, for instance, but all can modify the ground color from light to dark. Spots and stripes do not change very much in color, but they may appear to do so, for black spots on tan do not look the same color as black spots on dark brown. Therefore, we need not be surprised to see that the Wood Frog in the early spring seemingly has no dark mask beneath his eyes. It is there, and can be seen if the specimen is in the hand, but the animal's ground color is so dark in spring that the black mask is indistinguishable from a distance. On a hot summer day, it is a different matter. Against the Wood Frog's tan body, the mask stands out in bold relief. (See illustrations, page 135.)

Now that we have discussed the various methods of respiration, we can answer the questions we posed earlier. The Lungless Salamander practices buccopharyngeal and cutaneous respiration. The terrestrial larva of certain plethodontids uses the same methods of respiration as do the adults. He may or may not possess gills upon hatching, but if they are present they are generally lost within a day or two after emerging from the egg capsule.

With the Robber Frog tadpoles who spend their entire larval period in the egg capsule until they emerge as tiny frogs, things are a little different. Most of their necessary oxygen is obtained through the skin of their tails. Other tadpoles that have no free swimming larval stage, such as those of the Marsupial Frog, develop huge bell-shaped gills.

Before we answer the last of our questions—how a lung breathing frog can obtain the necessary oxygen when hibernating under water—let us speak a little about cold-bloodedness and what it means. Since all animals except mammals and birds are cold-blooded, or poikilothermous, it behooves us to know just what this term means. It does not mean that the blood is cold. It refers to the fact that while the internal temperature of mammals and birds remains constant regardless of outside temperature, the internal temperature of cold-blooded creatures varies with the external temperature of the air and the ground. On very cold days the internal temperature of the amphibian falls with the thermometer, for he has no way to keep himself warm inside as have we. Conversely, as the thermometer rises, so does his temperature inside rise.

This means that the amphibian's activities are curtailed, for he can only function when his internal temperature is within a certain degree range. Just as when, owing to disease, man's temperature falls below 97° F. or exceeds 101° F. he is incapacitated, so too is the frog incapacitated when his temperature rises or falls too low, though in his case this is caused, not by illness, but by external temperature.

And just as man functions best when his temperature is normal, or around 98.6° F. by mouth, so too is the frog at his most active when his internal temperature, governed by the external temperature, is at a certain point. However, unlike us, there is no given degree at which every frog functions best. Many of them find that an external temperature of between 75° F. and 85° F. suits them best; but there are others, such as the Tailed Frog and the cave salamanders, who would die at such temperatures, and who require water just a few degrees above freezing.

We all know that on hot humid days we usually feel warmer than on hot dry days. Does the amphibian feel this way also? He certainly does, and far more than we do. Here again his ability to change color comes in handy. Through it he can, to a certain extent, modify his internal temperature. But even with this useful attribute, he must carefully choose his surroundings. Now we begin to understand why the amphibians do not usually stray far from moisture or dark hiding places.

What is the result of extreme cold on the amphibian? It makes him sluggish and incapable of violent or rapid movement. If he is to survive, he must get away from it. Since it is not in his power to escape by migrating many miles as do birds, he does the next best thing. He burrows to escape it. According to the species, the hibernating burrow may be deep in the earth below the frost line, or in the muck at the bottom of a pond. There the amphibian will be safe from freezing, but he will not be warm enough to carry on a subterranean life. He is extremely sluggish, as is indicated by his slowed heartbeat and respiration. In hibernation, he is in a sleep that is so deep that all life processes are slowed to the absolute minimum.

Now we can answer the question as to how the lung-breathing amphibian can breathe while hibernating under water. It is done entirely by cutaneous respiration. But such a method is only possible when oxygen requirements are low. As the temperature of the water rises and the amphibian is aroused to greater activity, more air is needed than can be supplied by cutaneous respiration alone. Then the frog must burrow his way out of the muck and rise to the surface of the water to breathe through his lungs.

What happens if the hibernating frog doesn't burrow down far enough, and becomes frozen? The answer depends on the species and how completely the animal becomes frozen. No amphibian can be frozen solid, and live. Some can be partially frozen for a short time and still survive. Data on an amphibian's tolerance to freezing is very incomplete, and we have statistics on a few species only.

We have seen the result of extreme cold on the amphibian. In extreme heat, we find much the same reactions. In aestivation, as summer sleep is called, the animal burrows into the earth to escape high temperatures, and it goes deep enough to reach a moist spot. Though one might think that only amphibians living in the deserts of the tropics need to aestivate, such is far from the case. In the middle of a hot dry summer in the Northeast, you may find very few amphibians, especially those species that are more terrestrial. In time of drought, for instance, you may search the woods for days without finding a Red-backed Salamander. They have found surface conditions unsatisfactory, and are aestivating.

The examination of respiration and cold-bloodedness has explained many of the amphibian's ways. The phenomena of hibernation and to a lesser extent of aestivation raise a host of questions in our minds, not all of which can yet be answered. For instance: How does the amphibian know how deep to burrow to escape freezing? Why does the Leopard Frog emerge from hibernation in January and February, on days that are cold and windy, to give his woodpeckerlike call, while he is silent on days that seem warmer? Does he emerge from hibernation and then return to that state several times during the winter? Why is it that in certain years one can find many Two-lined Salamanders in January and February under logs or stones at the edge of streams, while in other, warmer winters none are to be found? Why doesn't the Two-lined Salamander hibernate in Connecticut when other species occupying the same habitat do? Or does the Two-lined Salamander sometimes hibernate? And if he does, what factors determine whether he will or will not? It is easy to ask questions, and to do so is one of the best ways we know of learning; but finding the answers is not so easy, especially when there is nothing published that you can read to satisfy your curiosity. But if you are sufficiently interested by a problem, you may be stimulated enough to be able to discover the answer for yourself through patient observations spread over the years.

CHAPTER 8

Pond Dwellers

In technical books, amphibians are listed and described by families. This is a precise and orderly way of doing things. But for many of us it is not so satisfactory as an arrangement of amphibians according to habitat. We know that skeletal, dental, and other differences are important in distinguishing one family of the Amphibia from another. But most of us are naturalists rather than scientists. We are concerned more with the animal's ways than with the type of vertebrae or teeth that he has. To us, the family and species to which a particular frog or salamander belongs is a secondary matter; we are interested in his family mainly because we should like to call him by his proper name when we find him.

In dividing amphibians into ecological or habitat groups, any number of diverse factors must come under consideration. Certain major requirements must be met before amphibians can exist and reproduce. These requirements vary from species to species, and because of them some amphibians have a very restricted distribution. Others seem to be able to tolerate a wide variety of conditions, and flourish in many different types of climate.

Perhaps the most important factors governing an amphibian's habitat are those of temperature and humidity. Amphibians cannot live in places where the subsoil is permanently frozen, for here they are unable to burrow to escape the cold, and their bodies are not equipped to withstand it as are those of certain mammals. Nor can they live in hot regions where there is low humidity and little or no rain, unless they can burrow to escape these conditions. Naturally, some species can stand hotter and drier situations better than others; the terrestrial toads are less prone to desiccation than are aquatic frogs.

Another important factor is the type and amount of water that must exist to meet the amphibian's requirements. First of all, the water must be fresh; amphibians cannot live in the sea, though a few can tolerate slightly saline water. Some species must have cold, well-oxygenated water; others need the quiet waters of a pond or the warm stagnant water of a swamp in order to raise their young or to survive themselves.

Furthermore, amphibians are extremely sensitive to the mineral content of the water and soil. Almost nothing is known about the tolerance of each species to sulfur, borax, gypsum, and so on. Certain species seem to live only in regions where there is abundant limestone; others prefer granite, shale, and so forth.

Atmospheric pressure and light also seem to play a part in the life of the amphibian, but these factors, so far as we know at present, do not govern the habitat. The scarcity of amphibians at high altitudes seems to be primarily due to low temperatures and lack of a suitable type of water rather than because of any reaction to the decreased pressure. But atmospheric pressure and light do govern the time of breeding and the rate of growth. For instance, some spadefoots cannot be induced to mate and lay without a lowering of pressure.

Ecology, or the interrelation of an animal and its environment, is a relatively new science, and though generalized concepts have been worked out, much much more needs to be learned about the amphibian's tolerance to each specific factor or group of factors.

Ponds are of many kinds. There are stream-fed ponds and spring-fed ponds, shallow ponds and deep ponds, large ponds and small ponds, woodland ponds and meadow ponds. In all of these types, you will find the Green Frog, *Rana clamitans*. The Green Frog is one of the commonest frogs in the eastern half of this country; it is not found in the states of the western half.

The Green Frog has been divided into two subspecies: the Green Frog, *Rana clamitans melanota,* and the Bronze Frog, *Rana clami-*

tans clamitans. The former is more widely distributed; the latter is found in parts of South Carolina, Georgia, Florida, and throughout the Gulf Coast states. Differences between the two subspecies are not extreme, but our color description applies to the northern variety, *Rana clamitans melanota.*

The Green Frog is a fairly large frog with a body length of two to four inches. Separating the sides from the back are two skin ridges known as dorsolateral folds. In the Green Frog these dorsolateral folds extend from just behind the eye to a point about halfway down the back, and are one of its identifying characteristics. A second feature to observe is the webbing on the hind feet. The webs extend to the very tip of all the toes except the fourth. The last two segments of the fourth toe are free of web. Incidentally, amphibian digits are counted from the inside out, the finger or toe nearest the body being the first.

As with so many amphibians, the color of the Green Frog varies. Usually the head and the forward part of the body are green; the posterior part of the back is brownish. The legs are barred and/or spotted with black, and there may be scattered black spots on the back as well. In the female the belly is white spotted with black, with the throat white. The male's belly is white, with the throat yellow. The conspicuous tympanum is larger than the eye in the male; it is smaller or the same size in the female.

What governs the color of these frogs is a problem. We have found many that appeared almost black, so dark are they, with only a small area of bright green from the nostril to below the eye and tympanum on either side of the face. Others found a few miles away were a bright green on the entire face and a bright olive on the upper back, with few if any dark spots. Does the mineral content of the water have anything to do with the coloration? We believe we can rule out temperature in these variations, for we find dark ones in warm ponds and cool springs, on cool days in spring and hot days in summer.

Age seems to be one of the factors in this matter of coloration. We notice that in any locality the younger frogs are invariably darker than the larger, older frogs. But it does not seem likely that age is the only reason for this color variation. Nor is this the only variation that exists in the Green Frog. The Wrights found that in a certain pond in the Adirondacks, the specimens had many more

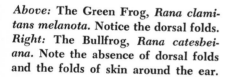

Above: The Green Frog, *Rana clami-tans melanota.* Notice the dorsal folds. *Right:* The Bullfrog, *Rana catesbei-ana.* Note the absence of dorsal folds and the folds of skin around the ear.

spots, and these were more regularly placed than on frogs found elsewhere.

All of this proves that color alone is not always a reliable characteristic on which to base identification. When someone asks us what a certain frog looks like, we usually try to describe its color first. Perhaps this is because coloration is somewhat easier to describe and creates a more vivid picture for the listener than descriptions of size, shape, and other features of the animal's appearance. But most of us note, though it may be unconsciously, the shape of the animal as well. What we all should do when observing the amphibian—or any other animal or plant, for that matter—is to picture the animal's general appearance and note how it differs from others similar to it. If we train ourselves to see these details as well as we see colors, we shall all be better naturalists.

The Green Frog is an aquatic frog and spends its life either in the pond or sitting on its edge. When it is basking, it always faces the water so that if danger threatens, it can dive into it with a splash. Incidentally, unless a frog is frightened, it generally slips into the water without a sound. Probably the splash serves as a warning to other frogs, and heightens their awareness.

The Green Frog breeds from late May to August in the North, even later in the South. The male's vocal sacs are internal, and his call sounds much like a banjo—*Plonk, plonk, plonk*. The males generally are in the water when they call; they may be floating on its surface or lying on floating water plants. Our experience has been that they are loudest in their singing in the very early morning just at dawn, though temperature plays an important part in governing the time of their calls.

The egg mass is of the surface-film type. It is less than a foot square and contains anywhere from 1,500 to 4,000 eggs. The eggs are black above, white below. Each is about 1.5 mm. in size and each is surrounded by a transparent envelope about 3 mm. in size. The tadpole has an olive-green back and a cream-colored belly. The tail is green marked with brown and has a rather pointed tip. The spiracle is found on the left side, and the anus opens on the right side of the lower tail crest.

The tadpole spends one winter as a tadpole. It seems to follow this pattern even in the South, though doubt has been expressed whether it always does so. Since the Green Frog lays much later in the South than in the North, perhaps this explains why it usually winters over as a tadpole. But why does it lay later in the South rather than earlier? We may have a case here where the amount of light plays a part in determining the breeding season and in delaying ovulation. Or it may be that midsummer in the South is too hot for proper development of the eggs, and therefore laying is delayed until the cooler weather of the fall.

Another interesting characteristic of Green Frogs found in the South is that they do not attain so large a size as those found in the North. One might perhaps expect it to be the other way around, but there is no generalization that can be made concerning the size differential of northern and southern species. Many species, such as the largest of all true toads, *Bufo marinus*, attain the maximum size only in the more southerly limits of their range. Others, as with

our Green Frog, are more common, and grow to a larger size in the
northern part of their range. This may not be entirely a matter of
inherited temperature preference, though doubtless it is an important factor.

Green Frogs are cautious animals. At first sight of danger, they
dive into the pond if they are basking, or if floating in the water
they swim away and seek cover in the bottom detritus. They seem
to have a well-developed sense of what constitutes a menace. A
Green Frog basking may allow you to approach to within a distance
of 6 feet or so. If you see him and draw nearer slowly, you may

The Green Frog floating in the water

be able to capture him—or you may not—for a jump of 2 or 2½ feet is nothing to a Green Frog, and he always aims for the water. On the other hand, if you do not see him as he sits motionless and very well camouflaged in his coat of green and brown, and blunder on toward him, you will be startled by the splash on the water. The dive is so rapid that rarely can you distinguish what species of frog has taken alarm; in such circumstances you usually have the impression of a frog smaller than is actually the case. Though we have never heard it suggested by herpetologists, it seems to me that the splash of an alarmed frog must serve a purpose other than a warning to others. Doesn't it also momentarily hide the frog as he enters the water, and thus aid in his escape? Its value in this respect is considerable, especially in shallow water, for often the frog is buried in the bottom detritus before the ripples disperse enough to permit clear sight on the part of the enemy.

In our back yard we have what we aptly call the mudhole. It is merely an excavation in the ground about 6 feet wide by 10 feet long and generally has from 4 to 6 inches of water in it. It is fed by seepage, rain, and a very small spring. It has no overflow, and the water is stagnant and covered with scum except after a heavy rain. Since we also have a river running by about 10 feet below the mudhole, it has always surprised us that the Green Frogs would bother coming to the mudhole. Perhaps it is the rich supply of invertebrate food that attracts them.

The following episode will show how wary a Green Frog can be. We spent two hours one afternoon trying to catch one in the mudhole so that we could mark him. We had boots on and had brought a good long-handled net, but we failed miserably. This particular frog jumped in the water before we could spot him. We saw him a few minutes later, only his nostrils and eyes above water, watching us intently about a foot away. At our first slow move he dived under again and hid in the muck. By this time we had got the net, and when we saw him again we managed to get it between him and open water. However, he was too quick for us, and got away. This hide-and-seek went on for some time, and with each failure on our part the time between surfacing was longer. In the end, the water was so riled up that we had to give up for the time being. Upon returning to the pond an hour or two later, we could find no sign of the frog, and it was more than a week before we saw him again. Though we tried to catch him again, we still had no success!

On the other hand, such frogs may perhaps become accustomed to people and so be less wary than usual. We have marked one, for instance, and we see him (or her) almost every afternoon. We do not see him in the mornings unless it is fairly warm—at least 70° F. On colder mornings he remains in the water, sometimes with his body half in and half out of water, sometimes submerged. We have never found him at night. I presume he buries himself in the bottom muck.

This young frog does not take any special pains to choose a concealed spot for basking. He sits in plain view, though his dark coloration makes him difficult to see when he sits still. We have found that he will dive into the water if we blunder past him. But if we approach with reasonable slowness he will remain where he is, and so long as no sudden movements are made he does not take alarm.

Of course, this young specimen—he is only 1¾ inches long, and we assume he is about a year old—is not normal. He is blind in one eye. This does not seem to be unusual, for we have found many frogs that were blind in one eye. We have no idea whether this is caused by disease or injury. We suspect the former in this case, for the eye shows no sign of any damage. It is merely milky white instead of the normal color. It is also partially contracted and partially retracted into its socket. Doubtless this blindness is a great handicap to him, and perhaps it is only this that makes One Eye seem tamer than he used to be.

However, just as one swallow doesn't make a summer, one observation, especially on an individual who has a defect, does not confirm a scientific principle. We cannot, therefore, positively assert that Green Frogs do become less wary on pleasant association with humans, for we have not sufficient proof. But it seems to be a possibility.

Mrs. Goin, in her charming book, asserts that her young Bronze Frogs, *Rana clamitans clamitans*, become very tame—some more than others. It would be interesting to know whether the degree of tameness is related to the sex of the animal involved. It would also be interesting to find out whether mature adults become tame or whether, as they get older, they become more and more wary of real or fancied danger.

The Bullfrog, *Rana catesbeiana,* is our largest North American frog and is found in every state of the Union except Alaska. It is absent from the western three-quarters of North and South Dakota, the southern tip of Florida, and the western tip of Nebraska, Oklahoma, and the middle part of Texas. Originally its territory was nearly the same as that of the Green Frog, though it extended a little farther West and not quite so far North. However, the species has been introduced in the West, and by all accounts it is thriving there to the detriment of other, smaller frogs and toads.

The Bullfrog is a thoroughly aquatic frog. It is most numerous in the larger ponds and lakes where the shores offer cover of trees, matted vegetation, and roots. The larger ponds enable him to be alone, for of all our frogs the Bullfrog is the most solitary in habit. Even in the breeding seasons when many frogs are gregarious and assemble in groups to sing, the Bullfrog remains by himself. There may be several Bullfrogs in a large pond, but each takes up his place far from his neighbor. The deep foghornlike jug-o'-rum call of the Bullfrog is familiar to most of us and is heard when the weather is warm—June or July in the North, earlier in the South. The Wrights have found that an air temperature of 80° F. and a water temperature of 70° F. are the desirable conditions that encourage the Bullfrog to begin mating. The volume of the Bullfrog's call is such that it may be heard from a distance of half a mile or more. Amazingly enough, when it is heard close up it is not so deafening as a chorus of peepers because it is deep in tone and because Bullfrogs do not sing in chorus. Never do you hear hundreds of Bullfrogs calling in the same place, as is true of peepers, toads, Wood Frogs, and many others.

The Bullfrog's egg mass is similar to that of the Green Frog. It too is of the surface-film type, laid in a spreading mass on the top of the water among branches or floating pond vegetation. It is, however, a much larger mass than that of the Green Frog. It is about 1 foot by 2 feet in area. There are from 10,000 to 20,000 eggs in this mass. The individual egg is approximately 1.5 mm. in size and is black above and white below. There is no envelope surrounding the egg. The egg masses of the Green Frog and the Bullfrog look very much alike. However, the much larger size of the mass, the larger egg complement, and the absence of jelly envelopes make it simple to distinguish the eggs of the Bullfrog from those of its smaller cousin.

Unfortunately for the amateur, it is extremely difficult to tell the difference between the tadpoles. The Bullfrog tadpole is, of course, much larger—5½ inches total length just before transformation as compared to the Green Frog's 3½ inches. The tip of the tail is blunt rather than pointed. In the North, the Bullfrog tadpole generally spends 2 or even 3 winters in its larval form. This extended larval period is, as we mentioned before, very much shortened in the South.

As an adult the Bullfrog resembles the Green Frog, but it is not difficult to tell them apart. The Bullfrog has no dorsal folds, though he does have a fold of skin that is very noticeable, beginning at the back of the eyes and going above and around the tympanum and down to the forelegs. The toes of the hind feet are always fully webbed. When a Green Frog and a Bullfrog are placed side by side, one is immediately impressed by the difference of their postures. The Green Frog sits much straighter; that is, his forelegs raise the forepart of his body higher off the ground than do those of the Bullfrog. The Bullfrog's natural posture seems to be a more crouching one, with the body almost parallel with the ground. (See illustrations, page 81.)

In coloring, the Bullfrog and the Green Frog are similar. However, though the Bullfrog usually has green on his head, this does not usually extend onto the back. Furthermore, both Bullfrog males and females have a white throat, and the underparts of both sexes are usually white, though I have found individuals whose undersides were marked with black. The outstanding difference between the sexes is the tympanum larger than the eye on the male. Bullfrogs —or at least those that we have seen—do not show any spotting on the back, nor are the legs barred with black, though there may be a few black spots. We don't notice any marked differences in coloring between individuals in one locality and another or between young and mature specimens. However, along the Gulf of Mexico many of the Bullfrogs appear almost black and have a belly mottled extensively with black.

The Bullfrog is, as we said, a very large frog. He is not only long; he is also broad of body, and is quite heavy with long, well-muscled legs and tremendous fully webbed feet. A couple of years ago, we caught two Bullfrogs—both males—shortly after they emerged from hibernation. One weighed ½ pound and had a body length of 6 inches. The extended hind leg measured 7½ inches. Incidentally, this frog was blind in one eye and was missing a thumb on one hand. The other frog was smaller—¼ of a pound in weight with a body length of 5½ inches and a leg length of 7 inches. Females are even larger, and specimens of 8 inches in body length weighing ¾ of a pound to a pound are not uncommon.

Since the Bullfrog is so large, it need not surprise us to learn that his diet is more varied than that of most frogs and toads. As with most frogs, the bulk of the diet is made up of insects. But small birds, smaller frogs, and young turtles also play a part in filling up the capacious stomach of our largest frog. Because the Bullfrog can and does consume other frogs and toads, herpetologists lament his introduction into the West.

The introduction of new wildlife into areas outside its natural range seems generally to create problems and undesirable results not foreseen by the introducer. Many examples can be cited. The mongoose introduced into the West Indies to help control rats has all but wiped out several species of native birds. The rabbit, introduced into Australia, multiplied so rapidly and caused such damage that measures were taken to eliminate it.

To see how the elimination of a species native to an area can cause harm, we may take the example of the French doctor who objected to the wild rabbits destroying his garden. He inoculated several rabbits with the deadly myxomatosis. It had the desirable effect on the rabbits around his garden, but it also had international repercussions which he probably did not anticipate. Myxomatosis spread to all the rabbit population, both wild and domesticated, of Europe, and despite desperate attempts to prevent its spread into England it jumped the Channel and decimated the rabbit population there also. The result to man has been disastrous, for not only do many people depend on the rabbit for food but so also do many predators. Many natural predators, such as foxes, for instance, have become scarce, and rodents far more destructive than the rabbit are multiplying.

At present, the result of the Bullfrog introduction into the West concerns only those people who hate to see indigenous species become extinct. *Rana fisheri,* a small spotted frog, similar to our Leopard Frog, has almost disappeared from its restricted locality around Las Vegas, Nevada, and the Bullfrog has taken its place. There are several other frogs, found only in certain small areas, which may well be doomed to extinction if the Bullfrog gets into their territory. But this may not be the sole repercussion of the introduction of the Bullfrog. What other more far-reaching effects may occur we can only imagine.

Why was the Bullfrog introduced? So far as we know, it was to cater to the frogs'-legs trade. Originally, perhaps, the Bullfrogs were confined by frog farmers, but a few escaped and they soon multiplied and spread.

To see a Bullfrog swim is to witness frog swimming at its best. The forelegs are folded back against the body and the muscular hind legs with their huge webs propel the animal swiftly through the water, seemingly without effort on his part. It is not always easy to see a Bullfrog swimming in a pond or lake, for they are so alert that they swim beyond your view or bury themselves in the muck almost before you catch a glimpse of them. They are much less wary at night, and you will probably get your best view of them then. We have noticed too that Bullfrogs are less alert upon first emerging from hibernation. For several days after they make their appearance in late spring or early summer, they may be caught or observed with a facility that might lead the uninitiated to believe that they were a docile and inactive species.

For some reason the Bullfrog is quite frequently the star performer in frog-jumping contests. Actually, the Leopard Frog of the fields, the Green Frog, and even the tiny Cricket Frog are able to jump farther, and of course their jumping ability, when related to body length, far exceeds that of the Bullfrog. The distance of the average Bullfrog's jump is about 26 inches as compared to the Leopard Frog's 36 inches, the Green Frog's 32 inches, and the Cricket Frog's 33 inches.

The Bullfrog and the Green Frog are not the only frogs that are strictly aquatic. Throughout Florida and along the coast of Georgia, Alabama, Mississippi, and Louisiana, the Pig Frog, *Rana grylio,* is common in habitats similar to those preferred by the Bullfrog. It may be distinguished from the Bullfrog by its slightly smaller size and longer first, second, third, and fifth toes on the hind feet. During the breeding season, its grunting calls have earned for it its unflattering common name.

The most aquatic of all frogs are not found in this country. They are the aglossal (meaning without a tongue) toads of the family Pipidae found only in Africa and South America. We described one of these primitive toads, *Pipa pipa*, earlier. The African genera *Xenopus* and *Hymenochirus* are similar to *Pipa* in habitat and general appearance, though they are not quite so broad and flat, nor do they possess the starlike fingertips or mouth tentacles so characteristic of *Pipa pipa*. Their life cycles do not present a striking divergence from the norm, for they lay their eggs among water plants, and the tadpoles hatch and develop in the usual way.

Of the pond-dwelling salamanders, most, with the exception of certain neotenous species, belong to the family of the newts, the Salamandridae. This is not to say that all salamandrids are aquatic, for some of them are not, but many of them have a life cycle similar to that of the Red-spotted Newt, *Diemictylus viridescens viridescens*, and the two other subspecies, *Diemictylus viridescens dorsalis* and *Diemictylus viridescens louisianensis*. These three subspecies of *Diemictylus viridescens* are found in the eastern half of the country as well as in the southeastern part of Canada.

The courtship of the newt is considered to be more elaborate than that of the ambystomids, or Mole Salamanders. The breeding activities are carried on in the middle or late spring. The male seizes the female around the neck or forearms with his hind legs. He is facing in the same direction as she. He frequently twists the fore part of his body around so that he may press his neck, equipped with hedonic glands, to her snout. The tip of the tail is also lashed back and forth in order to direct the odors emitted from his cloacal glands toward her nose. When the female is sufficiently aroused, the male deposits his spermatophore in front of the female's snout. She moves forward and picks it up with her cloacal lips.

The female deposits her fertilized eggs singly, fastening each to water plants. They are extremely difficult to find both because they are quite small and because the water plants act as an excellent camouflage. The female will very often place her egg on a leaf and then, with her hind legs, fold the leaf over the egg, so that it is hidden completely. The spherical egg is brown above, yellowish beneath. There are 3 oval envelopes, and the egg and its envelopes measures only about 2.4 mm. by 3.6 mm. The eggs hatch in about a month.

The larva is greenish yellow with a grayish line on either side of the center of the back. The tail and body crests extend almost to the head. The larva has balancers upon hatching, buds of forelegs, no hind legs, and the gills of a pond-dwelling larva. These gills, though small at hatching, rapidly grow large and bushy, soon exhibiting their characteristic form. The newt larva soon develops the deep body and dorsal keel found also on many aquatic Mole Salamander larvae.

After an aquatic larval period of two or three months, the little newt has developed arms and legs and a granular skin. It has lost its gills and body and tail crests. It becomes a brilliant light red above, with a row of black-bordered round spots on either side of the backbone. It is yellow beneath. With this coloration, it leaves its natal pond and takes to the woods. It is no longer a larva, but neither is it an adult newt. It is, at this stage, known as an eft. The eft spends its terrestrial life in moist situations, usually in the woods, hiding under stones and other suitable cover. However, efts do not seem to be so secretive as many other types of salamanders, and on damp days it is not unusual to catch sight of one abroad.

The eft stage of the Red-spotted Newt may extend for 1, 2, or even 3 years. During the winter the eft hibernates underground in the woods. In certain localities the eft stage never occurs. We also sometimes find neotenic newts. At the end of the eft stage, the eft migrates back to the pond. He enters the water to take up his aquatic adult life. Within a week he has developed the tail crests and smooth skin of the adult newt. His orange-red coloring has been transformed into a drab olive, but he retains the row of black-ringed red spots on either side. The belly is yellow marked with black spots.

The newt is about three inches long when adult, and has a body build midway between the stout-bodied ambystomids and the slim-bodied plethodontids. The adult male newt may be distinguished from the female in the breeding season by his protuberant vent, larger tail crests, and the horny black excrescences present on the tips of the hind toes and the undersurfaces of the hind legs. (See illustrations, page 24.)

Newts seem to enjoy certain kinds of ponds, but just what distinguishes these from others not densely populated with newts still remains to be discovered. We find very few newts and efts in the ponds and woods near our house. But the other day, on stopping at a roadside pond a few miles away, we were amazed to find hundreds of newts swimming in its waters. This particular pond is spring fed, about ten feet deep, with very steep banks. It was filled with aquatic grasses, and its waters were brown, making it impossible to see clearly beyond a depth of two or three feet at the most. Obviously, the shallower ponds with their gravelly bottoms and lack of aquatic grasses do not appeal to the newt so much as do the deeper grass-filled ponds. Perhaps the mineral content of the water is also an important factor in governing the habitat they prefer.

For some obscure reason there are relatively few representatives of the Salamandridae in the western half of the country. But along the northwestern coast we find the Northern Rough-skinned Newt, *Taricha granulosa granulosa*, with a life cycle similar to that of our Red-spotted Newt. Other species found in restricted localities may also have terrestrial efts and aquatic adults. Some newts have only an aquatic larval period, the adults being terrestrial except during the breeding season.

Europe seems to have far more representatives of the Salamandridae than do we. The males of a number of European newts of the genus *Triturus* develop high dorsal crests during the breeding season. On several species these crests on the back have wavy, sawtoothed edges. The life cycles of the pond-dwelling newts of Europe do not differ very much from those of our native *Diemictylus viridescens viridescens*.

Before going on to the stream dwellers, we must emphasize that the ponds attract many amphibians that are not permanent residents. Almost all of our frogs and many different kinds of salamanders congregate around the ponds during the breeding season. Many of the frogs and toads also return to the pond on occasion for moisture. So when you visit a pond even outside the breeding season, do not be surprised to see other amphibians that are visitors rather than inhabitants.

CHAPTER 9

River and Stream Dwellers

There are many different kinds of streams. Some are small, with muddy bottoms, and flow very slowly through woods or fields. The inhabitants of this type of stream are likely to be much the same ones as those found in ponds or ditches. There are brooks with a gravelly bottom that are roaring torrents of white water during periods of maximum rain or snow, but they slow up to become trickling brooks in the summer. There are mountain streams that start high in the mountains and consist of very cold cascading water year round. Then there are the rivers, large and small; but we shall use the term to designate those bodies of running water usually of sufficient depth to permit boating of some sort even in periods of drought.

Rivers and streams, whatever their type, have one important feature common to them all. All have running water, constantly changing. This water is better oxygenated than the still water of ponds and lakes. Therefore, it should not surprise us to find that many neotenous and Lungless Salamanders live in rivers and streams. They have become admirably adapted to swift-water dwelling; you will not usually find them or their larvae in the ponds of forest or field.

What adaptations have been made to enable these amphibians successfully to make their homes in the rivers and streams? Differences between pond dwellers and stream dwellers are marked in egg, larva, and adult.

The eggs of stream-dwelling salamanders are large and unpigmented. An unpigmented egg is not, as the term implies, transparent, nor are all of them white. Many unpigmented eggs *are* white; some are yellow; all are very light in color. The vegetal pole is not visible in these unpigmented eggs. Unpigmented eggs are usually larger than pigmented eggs, and in general they are deposited singly or in a number of small clusters and are hidden rather than exposed. Most stream dwellers either deposit their eggs under stones or else select spots where quiet pools are formed; a few scoop out a nest so that the eggs will have a better protected place in which to develop. It can easily be seen that the unprotected clump of eggs laid by many ambystomids would be easily washed away and dashed against rocks by swiftly running water. Therefore, it was necessary for the stream dwellers to modify the primitive form of the egg mass before laying could take place in swiftly running water.

In this country we have, properly speaking, only one true mountain-brook-type frog. Because the Tailed Frog is a unique animal in more ways than one, we shall devote Chapter 16 to a full discussion of him, his eggs, and his larvae. Africa and especially Asia have several true mountain-stream frogs.

Frogs of the African genus *Heleophryne* produce large unpigmented eggs, few in number. This much has been ascertained by dissection. Whether they are laid on land, as Dr. Rose suggests, or laid in the brook is not known, as the eggs have never been found in nature.

We know a little more about the Asian mountain-brook forms largely owing to the work of Dr. Liu. *Staurois chunganensis* attaches its unpigmented large eggs to the underside of rocks in the mountain streams where it lives. The eggs of other mountain-brook dwellers are not known.

We see that the true mountain-stream frogs, whose eggs are known, produce unpigmented large eggs, and these are concealed under rocks so that they are protected from the onslaught of rushing water. What advantages a large unpigmented egg has over a small unpigmented one is hard to imagine.

Stream-dwelling salamander larvae have short gills, and these, as a general rule, are not very bushy, though there are exceptions. Their bodies are more elongated, and the tail crests are reduced in size. Body crests so characteristic of the pond-dwelling larva are absent altogether.

The stream-dwelling tadpole also has similar modifications in body shape, tail crests, and in the form of the mouth. The typical cascade tadpole body is shaped like a canoe paddle and is much flattened. The tail muscles are thick and powerful, the tail tip rounded and blunt, the tail crests low and thick. All of these adaptations make the stream-dwelling tadpoles very powerful swimmers. Because the flattened body and low tail crests offer the least resistance to the current, the animal is unlikely to be caught by the rush of water and dashed to his death on a nearby rock. A useful adjunct to these is the mouth shape of the true stream tadpole. Those species found in the fastest waters have large suctorial lips with which they adhere to the rocks while resting. In addition, many tadpoles of the Asian genus *Staurois* have a large adhesive disk on the belly, formed by the lower lip and a semicircular ridge of skin on the belly.

Mention should also be made of another curious mouth-part adaptation found on the tadpoles of *Megophrys minor* of western China and *Phyllomedusa guttata* of Brazil. These tadpoles are surface feeders and have what are known as funnel or umbrella mouths. The umbrella mouth is located on the tip of the snout, not, as with other tadpoles, on the underside. The lips are large, and the lower one may be folded up so that it completely covers the mouth opening. When these tadpoles are feeding, they face upstream and extend the lower lip. The oncoming water pushes food particles into the funnel thus formed. Then the mouth parts (there is no horny beak) either accept the food into the mouth or reject it.

The umbrella-mouth tadpoles have the true stream-dweller's body and tail. However, they do not live in as swiftly running water as those tadpoles with suctorial mouths. Nor are the adults aquatic, as are the adults of the true cascade-type tadpoles.

Stream-dwelling adult amphibians often have lungs that are much reduced in size. In water, the lungs act as hydrostatic organs providing buoyancy, which is undesirable from the standpoint of a stream-dwelling amphibian. And since the water of streams is well oxygenated, the animal usually has no trouble in satisfying its oxygen requirements with reduced lungs.

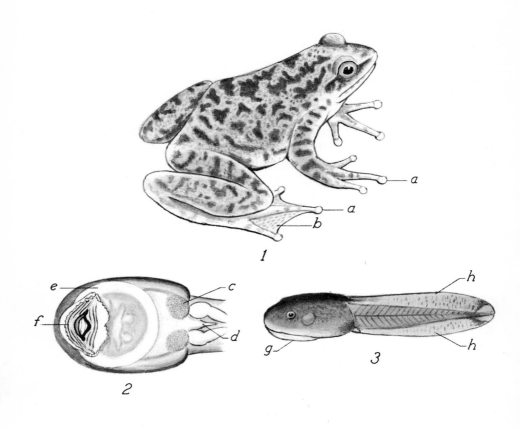

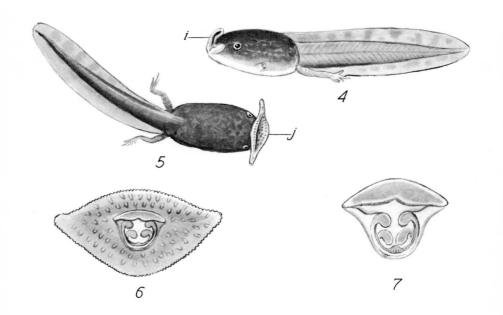

Among the salamanders, we find many plethodontids, or Lungless Salamanders, living in rivers or streams. The Plethodontidae, our largest family of salamanders, are either terrestrial or stream dwelling. Those that are terrestrial often lay on land, but those that return to the water to lay their eggs always return to streams. The outstanding exception is the Four-toed Salamander, *Hemidactylium scutatum*, a terrestrial plethodontid who lays in wet spots on the edge of ponds or swamps and whose larvae possess the long bushy gills and body crests of the pond-type larva.

Astylosternus robustus, the Hairy Frog of Africa, whom we mentioned earlier, is believed to be a mountain-brook dweller. His reduced lungs are adequate for his needs except during the breeding season, when the metabolic rate of the males is much increased. To accommodate the greater oxygen requirement at that time, the males develop "hairs" that act, as we pointed out, much as the skin and external gills do.

But the Hairy Frog does not look very much like other true stream-dwelling frogs as typified by *Staurois* and *Rana margaretae* of Asia. These adults have a rather flat slender body with long legs. The toes are fully webbed, and all digits are equipped with large, well-developed toe disks. In addition, there is generally a sexual dimorphism in size—the males being much smaller than the females. This feature is of considerable advantage to a couple in amplexus in running water, for the water thus passes over and around them rather than sweeping them with it.

These then are some of the adaptations made by the amphibians to enable them to live in running water. Let us now look at the detailed lives of a few of these stream dwellers.

Adaptations for swift-water dwelling: 1. The mountain-brook-dwelling frog, *Staurois lifanensis*, showing (*a*) the enlarged digital disks and (*b*) the fully webbed foot. 2. The tadpole of *Staurois kangtingensis* showing (*c*) the ventral poison glands; (*d*) the ventral spiracular tube; (*e*) the ventral adhesive disk; and (*f*) the large suctorial lips. 3. The tadpole of *Staurois lifanensis* showing (*g*) the ventral adhesive disk; and (*h*) the low tail crests. 4. The tadpole of *Megophrys minor* with (*i*) the umbrella mouth parts closed. 5. The tadpole of *Megophrys minor* with (*j*) the mouth parts open as when feeding. 6 and 7. Two magnified views of the mouth of the *Megophrys minor* tadpole. Adapted from drawings of I. S. Wang in *Amphibians of Western China* by C. C. Liu, with the permission of the Chicago Natural History Museum.

The Greater Siren, *Siren lacertina,* is a large eel-like neotenous salamander found throughout Florida and along the coasts of Virginia, North Carolina, South Carolina, Georgia, and Alabama. It does not confine itself to swiftly running streams, though it is found there frequently. It may also be found in ditches, ponds, swamps, and lakes.

The Greater Siren attains a maximum size of 3 feet, and may be as big around as a woman's wrist. It has small gills and front legs only. Although the animal with its long streamlined shape appears to be all tail, close examination shows that it is really all body, the head and tail combined consisting of only about ⅕ of the total length. Its coloring is inconspicuous. The back and sides are gray, very faintly marked with yellow; the belly is blue, marked with muddy yellow.

Little is known about the breeding habits of the Greater Siren. Anatomical evidence indicates that the eggs are fertilized externally, but no one has ever seen Siren breeding. The eggs and larvae are rarely found in nature. Siren has laid eggs in captivity. These were brown above, white below, surrounded by 3 jelly envelopes. They were laid singly and, including all envelopes, were about 9 mm. in size. But herpetologists do not jump to the conclusion that the eggs need necessarily be laid singly in nature just because they were so deposited in the laboratory. Captive specimens do not always lay in their characteristic manner.

Although the adults of the Greater Siren have long been known to science, the eggs and larvae are seldom found in nature even by herpetologists who are looking for them. They are probably well hidden in water weeds or in mud. Much much more needs to be learned about this species before we have a reasonably complete story of its life.

The family Sirenidae consists of nine subspecies within two genera: *Siren,* with four fingers, and *Pseudobranchus,* with but three. The eggs and larvae of the Dwarf Siren, *Siren intermedia nettingi,* have been found in nature and described. These eggs were found in April, deposited in an aquatic nest, and were in a mass. Eggs and larvae are also known for a few other species.

The eel-like salamander *Amphiuma means tridactylum* is another neotenous stream dweller. In contrast to the Sirenidae, the Amphiumidae lack gills as adults and possess both forelegs and hind legs.

Greater Siren
Siren lacertina

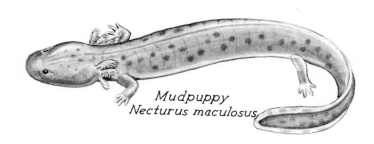

Mudpuppy
Necturus maculosus

Congo Eel
Amphiuma means

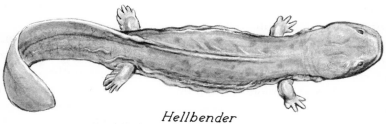

Hellbender
Cryptobranchus alleganiensis

Representatives of the four families of neotenous salamanders found in this country

The legs are so small that they may easily be overlooked. Therefore, the Amphiumidae are frequently mistaken for eels. These diminutive limbs have but three toes, instead of the more usual four in front and five behind. Furthermore, the toes are greatly reduced in size, the first and third being, as a general rule, mere buds. Unlike most salamander toes, there are no bones in Amphiuma's toes. They are merely supported by cartilage. This, incidentally, is true of the toes of the Sirenidae also.

The Three-toed Amphiuma is a very long-bodied animal, and specimens measuring 40 inches are not unusual. It is found in parts of Alabama, Mississippi, Louisiana, and Arkansas. The other subspecies, *Amphiuma means means*, the Two-toed Amphiuma, has a slightly broader distribution, being found along the coasts of Virginia, North Carolina, South Carolina, Georgia, Alabama, Mississippi, and throughout Florida.

In color the Three-toed Amphiuma is inconspicuous, and is brown on the back and upper sides. The lower sides and belly are gray.

It is surprising to find that such a thoroughly aquatic salamander leaves the water and excavates a shallow nest beneath a log in which she lays her eggs. Evidently, the eggs are generally laid in the fall, though specimens have been found brooding eggs in winter. The female does not always burrow in mud, but quite frequently chooses soil that is fairly dry and that may be some distance from water. The eggs are deposited in rosary-like strings and are large—about 9 mm. The female coils around them during an incubation period of from 1 to 2 months.

How long do the hatchling larvae remain in the nest before going to the water? No one knows, but if one lived in the same part of the country as the Three-toed Amphiuma, one could have a great deal of fun in trying to find out.

The Proteidae, or Mudpuppies, have the broadest distribution of any of the neotenic salamanders found in this country. Because a list of states in which they are found would be lengthy, we shall merely say that Mudpuppies are found in parts of every state in the eastern half of the country, New Hampshire and Maine excepted, but the area of greatest concentration is in the Middle West. Mudpuppies seem to prefer larger swift-running rivers, and most prefer clear water.

The Mudpuppy, *Necturus maculosus maculosus,* has the widest distribution of all the species, and may be found not only in the clear running waters of large rivers but also in the more sluggish and muddy water of canals and drainage ditches. It is the largest of our native mudpuppies, and may attain a maximum length of 1½ feet. The average specimen falls far short of this, however, and is about 1 foot. Its legs are short and strongly made, with four toes on each of the four digits. The Mudpuppy has gills that are large and bushy and red in color. It also has lungs when adult.

The Mudpuppy has a reddish brown back with black spots scattered over it. The underparts are light gray and may or may not be marked with darker spots.

The mating season of the Mudpuppy is in the fall months of September, October, and November. There has been but a single recorded instance of its courtship activities. The male swam around the female and crawled over her tail and between her legs. The female remained quite passive during this display. After the female has seized the spermatophore, she does not immediately lay her eggs. Implantation is delayed, and the eggs are not deposited until the following May.

The female excavates a nest under a log or stone with its entrance facing downstream. We almost always find stream nests with entrances so oriented, for if the entrance faced upstream the eggs might be damaged by the force of the oncoming waters. In this nest the female Mudpuppy deposits from 20 to 150 eggs, attaching each egg to the roof of the nest. These eggs are nonpigmented, yellow in color, about 5 mm. in diameter, and surrounded by 3 jelly envelopes. The female remains with the eggs until they hatch 1 month to 2 months after laying. She may even remain with the larvae until they leave the nest.

The larvae possess both fore and hind limbs upon hatching; however, the toes are not developed until later. The larval Mudpuppy does not attain sexual maturity until it is about 5 years old at a length of 8 inches.

The Mudpuppy's food consists principally, not of insects, as with most amphibians, but of crayfish. Water weeds are also consumed, with insects and fish coming as third and fourth in preference.

The most unusual neotenic salamander in appearance is undoubtedly the Hellbender, *Cryptobranchus alleganiensis*, and its very close relative, *Megalobatrachus maximus*, the Giant Salamander of

Japan and western China. The Hellbender is very large, averaging about 1½ feet, but females have been found that were nearly 2½ feet long. The body is broad and flat; the legs are short and stout with four toes on the forelegs, five on the hind. The skin is thick but highly vascularized; it is also loose, and on either side it falls into deep wrinkles. In color, the Hellbender varies from light brown or rusty red to almost black with scattered darker spots. Underneath, it is of a similar but lighter color.

The Hellbender is found in the swifter waters of large rivers in parts of New Jersey, Pennsylvania, West Virginia, Indiana, Ohio, Kentucky, and North Carolina. It is rarely seen, for it is not only completely aquatic but also thoroughly nocturnal, hiding by day under rocks in the water and coming out only at night to forage for its food.

The breeding season is in the late summer and early fall—the end of August through September. The male excavates a nest under a large rock and lies there awaiting the arrival of the females. When one appears, he pays little or no attention to her until her eggs start to emerge from her cloaca. The sight of the eggs stimulates the male to activity, and he seizes them and fertilizes them externally as they are laid.

The egg is unpigmented, yellow in color, and about 6 mm. in size. However, the 2 envelopes with which it is surrounded make the whole much larger—about ¾ of an inch in diameter. After the female has finished laying, she departs, leaving the male to guard the eggs. The egg complement of several females, each laying from 300 to 400 eggs, may be entrusted to his care. The larvae hatch in 2 or 3 months and have both fore and hind legs. The gills, which are small are retained for a year and a half.

The Giant Salamander of Japan and western China is very similar to our Hellbender. Surprisingly enough, though, it seems to prefer smaller streams, despite its immense size of 4 feet and girth roughly the same size as a woman's thigh, and its weight of 60 pounds.

All of these neotenous salamanders have established records for longevity in captivity. The prize must go to *Megalobatrachus maximus,* a specimen of which lived in the Amsterdam Zoo for 52 years. The Hellbender is second with 29 years. Third is the Amphiuma, or Congo Eel, with 27 years, and fourth is the Greater Siren with 25 years. We might expect the Mudpuppy to come next on the list, but unfortunately I have been unable to find any record of its life span in captivity. However, it does not really matter, for life spans in captivity cannot be taken as reliable indicators of life spans in the wild.

These, then, are some of the stream dwellers. All are neotenous and most are difficult to observe. Let us now turn to the more typical and common salamanders—the plethodontid stream dwellers.

One of the commonest species of stream-dwelling salamanders is the Northern Two-lined Salamander, *Eurycea bislineata bislineata*. Its range extends from Virginia north to Maine, from the Atlantic Coast on the east to Indiana on the west. It is a slender-bodied salamander of about 3 inches when adult. But this average measurement may be shorter in the more southern portions of its range or longer in the more northern parts.

The upper parts are yellowish tan in color with small black spots scattered over the back; on many individuals the spots form a line down the middle of the back. The tan back is separated from the sides by two black lines—one on each side—that commence behind the eyes and extend back to the tip of the tail. The underside is yellow. (See illustration, page 229.)

As with all plethodontids, nasolabial grooves are present. These are very tiny grooves running from the base of the nostril to the upper lip. They serve to free the nostril from water and are equipped with glands that flush dirt from the nostrils and grooves. In order to see these nasolabial grooves on a salamander as small as the Northern Two-lined Salamander, a magnifying glass is required.

The difference between the males and females is not, as in so many salamanders, in the character of the vent, but in the character of the snout. During the breeding season the male's snout is apt to be somewhat swollen around the nasolabial grooves—and in some individuals small cirri may be formed. These cirri are blunt finger-like appendages on the edge of the upper lip, and when they are present the nasolabial groove extends over them.

The Southern Two-lined Salamander, *Eurycea bislineata cirrigera*, carries this development of cirri further. The males always have well-developed cirri. Another difference between the sexes in this species is that in the males the teeth on the edge of the upper jaw—called premaxillary teeth—are frequently elongated and extend forward so that they are exposed. The Southern Two-lined Sala-mander is similar to the northern variety in looks and habits, but it spends more of its time on land in swampy places, returning to the stream for breeding and egg laying. It is found in the states of North Carolina, South Carolina, Georgia, Alabama, the northern end of Florida, and the southern tip of Mississippi.

We cannot call the Northern Two-lined Salamander completely aquatic, for though it does live in brooks it is found on their banks or even some distance away quite frequently. I should very much like to know just what conditions or factors prompt them to leave the water. In the winter, especially in the more northern portions of its range, it is said to hibernate on stream bottoms. We have been amazed, therefore, to find Two-lined Salamanders in January and February under rocks on the shore during periods of thaw. On other February days, when the weather seems to be much warmer, not a salamander is to be found. The governing factor in this case may be the water temperature. The Two-lined Salamander is one of those species of amphibians that depend almost entirely on low-ering temperatures to warn them that it is time to go into hiber-nation (or emerge from it). They are not like many amphibians (the toads, for instance), who dig their hibernation burrows long before the real cold weather comes.

We suspect that the Northern Two-lined Salamander is not a true hibernator when it makes its home in the swiftly running brook water which, even in subzero weather, forms only a thin coating of ice, not secure enough to support a man's weight. It unquestionably remains on the bottom, but perhaps, though sluggish and inactive during these periods of extreme cold, it is not truly hibernating. Another argument in support of this theory of mine is that the Two-lined Salamander evidently breeds quite early—in middle or late winter with us. During the spring and summer months, it is not difficult to find this salamander by overturning rocks in shallow waters or in wet spots on the bank. In some years these salamanders are very common in such locations; in other years, in July and August, we find the adults more frequently away from the stream, burrowed under well-decayed logs in the nearby woods. The North-ern Two-lined Salamander seems to prefer gravelly streams and rivers. In Connecticut, at any rate, we have never found one in a slow-running muddy-bottomed brook. This may be, of course, because with a swift-running stream at our back door we go to muddy slower-running brooks infrequently.

The courtship of the Two-lined Salamander is a fairly elaborate affair and is carried on in the water. The breeding season is in winter, from January to March or April. The male noses the female and rubs his snout and chin against her face. The secretions from the glands found there arouse her to straddle his tail, facing in the same direction as he. She then places her chin on the base of his tail where another scent gland is located. In this position the two walk off along the stream bottom until the male deposits his spermatophore, which the female retrieves.

The female glues her eggs singly to the underside of rocks on the stream bottom. These eggs are unpigmented—as indeed are all plethodontid eggs—white or yellowish in color and about 3 mm. in size. They are surrounded by 2 jelly envelopes. Each female lays about 30 eggs, though several females may utilize the same rock.

These eggs are not easy to find. We have been actively interested in amphibians for about seven years. Each year, almost daily from June through August, we have searched for the eggs, looking in shallow water and deep water, still water and swiftly running water and all the gradations between. We have looked under small stones and rocks so large that had they not been under water we could never have budged them. Nor have we been alone. Our daughter, an ardent herpetologist of eight, has for four years been searching for these eggs, both with us and on her own. We had begun to suspect that we were late in looking for them, for we frequently found what we believed to be Two-lined larvae of hatchling size— about ½ inch—in May and June. This year we began egg hunting as soon as the height of the stream waters permitted. On May 27th our daughter came rushing in with the news that she had found them. Sure enough, under a small flat rock no larger than my hand were 20 eggs with pale yellow embryos ready to hatch at any moment. The rock was in shallow quiet water near shore—though when the salamander laid, the rock must have been under water at least a foot deep and perhaps more. After this momentous find we continued searching for an hour longer, but we saw no more eggs. Doubtless most of the others had already hatched.

So if you have trouble finding the eggs of the Two-lined Salamander, don't give up in disgust, for you are not alone. Keep looking, and one day you (or your inquisitive child) will be lucky enough to discover them.

The larvae of the Two-lined Salamander are not difficult to find, and you will, if you look sharp as you overturn rocks in shallow water, see them in all stages of development, during the spring, summer, and fall. This is because this salamander has a larval period of from 2 to 3 years. The larvae are easier to find in the summer months when the brook waters are lower and shallower, for it is difficult to spot one of these tiny creatures in deep running water.

The Northern Two-lined Salamander is a very agile species, and can elude your grasping hand with the greatest of ease just when you are sure you have captured it. Quite frequently, if the animal's body squirms away, but you have a firm grip on the tail, you will find that you have *only* the tail, wriggling violently in your hand. The salamander has broken off his tail and departed with little or no inconvenience to himself. The best way, therefore, to catch a Two-lined Salamander is to grab with both hands.

Another common Lungless Salamander is the Northern Dusky Salamander, *Desmognathus fuscus fuscus*, whose range is similar to that of the Northern Two-lined Salamander, but extends slightly farther South into the northern half of South Carolina, Georgia, and Alabama. Another subspecies, *Desmognathus fuscus ariculatus*, extends along the coasts of the southern states of North Carolina, South Carolina, Georgia, Alabama, Mississippi, Louisiana, and the northern half of Florida.

The Northern Dusky Salamander, *Desmognathus fuscus fuscus*, is not really a stream dweller. It lives on the edges of streams, never straying far from moist soil. It is often found in the water during the summer, but it exhibits its terrestrial habits in its choice of egg-laying site. It hibernates, however, under water in the streams and seems to be more of a true hibernator than does the Two-lined Salamander. We find the Dusky Salamander out of water in midwinter infrequently.

The Dusky Salamander is a larger, stouter-bodied species than the Two-lined Salamander. It is between 3½ and 4½ inches in length, the males being somewhat longer than the females, and sometimes attaining a length of 4¾ inches. Our local Dusky Salamanders are brownish black above. The underparts are pink, heavily speckled with blue-gray. But *Desmognathus fuscus fuscus* is one of those amphibian species that show considerable variation in color and pattern. Many individuals are light brown or brown above, with two darker, irregularly marginated lines dividing the back from the sides.

Unlike the tongue of the Two-lined Salamander, which is of the mushroom type, fastened to the floor of the mouth, the Dusky Salamander's tongue is fastened in the front of the mouth like those of most frogs and toads.

The life cycle of the Northern Dusky Salamander is a rather curious one and might be compared to the newt's life cycle in reverse. After a courtship on land, the female makes a nest under stones or logs in a damp spot near a stream. Here she lays her eggs, about 20 in number. She remains with them, brooding them faithfully until they hatch. The young larva remains on land for about 2 weeks. At the end of that time, it moves down into the water, develops a tail fin and the typical gills of a stream dweller, and remains aquatic for the rest of its larval period. After 8 or 9 months, it transforms, and leaves the water to spend its adult life along the stream margins.

The Northern Dusky Salamander, *Desmognathus fuscus fuscus*. This specimen has lost a part of his tail, but it has healed, and regeneration has begun.

You might think that the stouter-bodied Dusky Salamander was less agile than the Two-lined Salamander. And as you lower your hand to capture a specimen, the animal never appears to move. The Two-lined Salamander squirms out from under your descending hand. The Dusky Salamander eludes your grasp altogether by jumping. We shall discuss salamander jumping more fully in Chapter 18, and here merely suggest that you use both hands when capturing a Dusky Salamander.

These are not the only stream-dwelling salamanders of the United States, but they are among the most common. There are several plethodontids found along the northwestern coast, and also a stream-dwelling ambystomid, but these are limited in their range, and one, at least, is rather rare.

But though the West has been neglected by stream-dwelling salamanders, more stream-dwelling Salientia are found there. These frogs do not, however, show the adaptations of a typical mountain stream or cascade frog mentioned earlier. They are not found in waterfalls or rapids, and evidently no adaptations are needed to enable them to survive in the streams they inhabit.

The California Yellow-legged Frog, *Rana boylei boylei,* is one of these brook dwellers. It is found along the coasts of southern Oregon and northern and central California. It occasionally inhabits lakes, but above all, this frog prefers streams with a rocky bottom, though it is not unknown in those having a mud bottom. It seems to prefer slower-running brooks, but it never inhabits those that dry up completely in summer.

The underparts of many western frogs are red in color. The Yellow-legged Frog may be distinguished from all of these by the fact that the underparts of the legs and around the vent are yellow, never red. The rest of the belly is white, and the throat is generally marked with black. Above, it may be black, grayish-brown or greenish, with indistinct spots or blotches. The upper surfaces of the legs and arms are barred with black. There is generally a lighter area on the snout between the two eyes.

Unlike many frogs of the family Ranidae whose skin is quite smooth, the skin of the Yellow-legged Frog is warty or tuberculous, and resembles a toad's skin. There are one or two other western frogs whose skin is rough, but not to such an extreme degree as is the skin of the Yellow-legged Frog. The body shape of *Rana boylei*

California Yellow-legged Frog
Rana boylei

Canyon Tree Frog
Hyla arenicolor

Two frogs found living in or near streams

boylei is also rather toadlike, for it is small—about 1½ to 3 inches in length—and very broad. Unlike a toad, its legs are long, and extensively webbed.

This stream dweller is very shy and difficult to catch. It is completely aquatic and is rarely found more than a foot or two away from the banks of streams. If alarmed when basking, it immediately dives into the water, taking refuge under rocks or in the mud.

No one has recorded or described the calls of the males, but the breeding season is in April and May. The males may be distinguished from the females by the thumb, which is greatly swollen at the base.

The eggs are laid in a submerged mass, with a total complement of about 1,000. The egg, black above, white below, is small—about 2 mm.—and is surrounded by 3 distinct envelopes, the largest being 4.5 mm. in size. The egg mass is not always found in quiet pools as one might suppose, but frequently in shallow water that flows steadily. Eggs have even been found in swiftly running water. In this connection it would be helpful if herpetologists would measure the speed of the water so that every one would know just what "swiftly running" means. They might, for instance, drop a chip of wood on the water and time the number of seconds it takes to cover a prescribed distance. Then we amateurs could perform the same experiment and thus determine whether our water was running at a speed greater than, less than, or equal to the herpetologist's water at the time of his observation.

The incubation period for the eggs of *Rana boylei boylei* is not known, but one might expect to find it slightly longer than that required for frog eggs laid in the pond. The tadpole is olive green, and transforms after a larval life of about 3½ months.

Another stream dweller is the Canyon Treefrog, *Hyla arenicolor*, found throughout Arizona and New Mexico and in parts of southern and Lower California, western Texas and Mexico. The Canyon Treefrog belongs to the family Hylidae, or Treefrogs. Actually, this is a misnomer, for many treefrogs almost never climb trees. The Canyon Treefrog is one of these, and is semiaquatic or aquatic in habit, rarely being found very far from the gravel-bottomed clear streams it seems to prefer.

In appearance, the Canyon Treefrog is similar to the Eastern Grey Treefrog of the Northeast. It is of moderate size for a hylid, being from 1¼ to 2¼ inches long. It has a granular skin and conspicuous toe disks on all its digits. There is no webbing between the toes. It is brownish or grayish above, with small scattered black spots. The upper parts of the legs and arms are barred with black. The belly and throat are white or light tan; the undersides of the arms, legs, and around the vent are orange or yellow.

The authorities seem to be somewhat at odds about the voice of the male Canyon Treefrog. Some say that it is a short trill similar to the one made by the Eastern Grey Treefrog, *Hyla versicolor versicolor*. Others describe it variously as goatlike, sheeplike, ducklike. We have not heard this frog calling, so our opinion does not add to (or detract from) the confusion. Admittedly, it is difficult to describe sounds verbally. One might suppose, though, that the accounts would be more similar. A duck quacking most certainly does not sound like a sheep bleating or like the trill of a bird. However, the voices of many Salientia sound differently at different times. The trill of the Eastern Grey Treefrog sounds very different when the weather is cool than it does when he is singing alone or in chorus at the height of the breeding season. Furthermore, the calls of many frogs are ventriloquial, and the same call may sound unalike to two observers, each occupying a separate vantage point.

Then too, the location of the frog itself makes a difference. Some species call from under water as well as from above. The underwater call sounds slightly different from the one voiced in air. All of these factors help to explain why we sometimes find a great disparity in the descriptions of voice by herpetologists.

However, the calls of frogs and toads are being recorded. This is a great help to the amateur, who can thus hear the voice of various species separately and in chorus, in different mediums and at different times of year. There are two such records that we know of on the market today. They are listed in the Bibliography.

The Canyon Treefrog has a breeding season extending from March to July. The eggs are laid singly, and may be found either floating on the water's surface or attached to leaves at the bottom. The tadpole has an olive-colored body and tail. Its tail crests are often mottled with orange or red, and the center of the belly is pink. The tadpoles transform in 1½ to 2½ months.

These, then, are a few of the stream dwellers. You will find many others if you look for them. You will also find stream visitors, or species that live mostly by its banks rather than in the water.

CHAPTER 10

Swamp and
Ditch Dwellers

Swamps provide a bridge between permanent lakes and ponds and dry land. A swamp is land that is saturated with water but not covered by it. During certain seasons of the year, the entire swamp area may be flooded; in other, drier times, the peripheral areas of the swamp may be quite dry, while in its center the ground may be saturated and riddled with scattered small pools. The water of swamp pools is not usually running water but is stagnant, with relatively low oxygen content. These swamp pools may nevertheless be clear, or they may be so dirty from decaying vegetation and animal matter that they can sustain very few kinds of animal life.

Similarly, ditches are a bridge between rivers and streams and land. Ditches may be large drainage ditches, which are more like canals, with a huge volume of water, or they may be merely roadside ditches no more than a foot or two wide. In ditches, the oxygen content of the water is lower than in rivers, and the water is more or less stagnant.

Of course, it is difficult to generalize about ditches and marshes and the amphibians who live in or around them. Depending upon the season and the rainfall, a swamp or a ditch may become a lake or a stream; in seasons of extreme aridity they may become dry land. Habitat conditions are constantly fluctuating, and as they change, so do the animals who inhabit them.

112

The largest of our native toads is the Colorado River Toad, *Bufo alvarius*. Though the Giant Toad, *Bufo marinus*, attains a larger size in the more southerly portions of its range, the length of the Giant Toads found in the United States does not quite equal the large size of 7 inches often attained by *Bufo alvarius*. In fact, next to the Bullfrog, the Colorado River Toad is our largest salientian.

Most true toads are dry-land dwellers coming to temporary pools only for breeding, but the Colorado River Toad is more aquatic, and lives around cattle-watering troughs, swampy land, ditches, and irrigated fields. It is found in Arizona around the Colorado and Gila rivers to the borders of Nevada and New Mexico respectively, and down into the Mexican state of Sonora.

We usually think of swampy areas as being humid, but when we do we are thinking of southern swamps, not the wet areas of ground found in this part of Arizona. For this is a desert region where the air is dry, and though few amphibians can tolerate such low humidity the Colorado River Toad is well equipped to withstand it. He has a smooth but very thick skin with a few small round warts scattered over his back. The parotoid glands so characteristic of toads are large and slope down sharply toward the arm. In addition, there are several large warts on the legs—one on the femur, or first segment of the leg, one or more on the tibia, or second segment of the leg. In color, this toad is greenish with brown or orange warts. The underparts are white. The eyes are large and very beautiful, with the dark pupil and yellow iris veined with red.

The males may be distinguished from the females by their heavier arms and by the horny excrescences on top of the fingers. The voice of the male when held in the hand has been variously described as a chirp similar to the note of the American Toad, a cluck like contented chickens, and, when in chorus, loud calls. They breed at night in shallow ponds, during or after rains, from March through August. The eggs, about 8,000 in number, are laid in strings of jelly. They are black or very dark brown above, light below. The vitellus is sometimes round, but just as often it is wedge-shaped, and triangular in outline.

It is interesting to speculate as to how the eggs become wedge-shaped. Do some females always lay round eggs and others wedge-shaped ones? Or does a female lay wedge-shaped eggs one year and round eggs another? If the latter be true, what governs the shape of the eggs? Has age any bearing on the matter? Going a little further, does one find a preponderance of one egg shape during drier or wetter periods or earlier or later in the year? Does the shape of the egg influence in any way the length of the incubation period? If so, how? We don't know the answers to these questions, but discovery of the facts is well within the range of the amateur.

The tadpoles of the Colorado River Toad have never been precisely described for science. They have been seen, but evidently a large-enough series have not been collected and studied.

Colorado River Toads are not especially numerous. One is fortunate to find them when they are breeding, for evidently they are rather scarce at other times. They are quite secretive, and seek cover during the day in moist spots under watering troughs. By night they are seen more frequently, but they are never common.

In sharp contrast to our largest toad is the smallest of all our native Salientia, the Little Grass Frog, *Hyla ocularis,* found along the coasts of North Carolina, South Carolina, Georgia, and throughout Florida. One needs sharp eyes to see this tiny little fellow, for he is slender of body, and only about ½ inch long when adult. This frog is usually some shade of brown or tan on top, but sometimes specimens that are grayish-green or brownish-red are found. The most constant identification mark is a dark line running from the snout through the eye back to the arm or beyond it, though in some specimens this line may be missing. Sometimes one finds a dark triangle between the eyes and a central dark back stripe and two dark side stripes, but quite often these markings too are absent. The vent is whitish or very light tan with dark speckles that are sometimes scant, sometimes profuse.

For so small a creature, the Little Grass Frog has amazingly long but very slender legs. And though it lives in swampy areas around pine woods and cypress ponds, its toes are nearly webless. The round digital disks characteristic of all the Hylidae are distinct but so tiny as to be of little practical use in climbing. However, this frog does not climb very much or very high, confining its climbing to low bushes. It is more often found on the ground around the swampy edges of ponds and in marshes.

The Little Grass Frog is able to turn its head up, down, or to either side without turning its body. Most frogs are unable to do so. A few, such as the Eastern Grey Treefrog are able to cock their

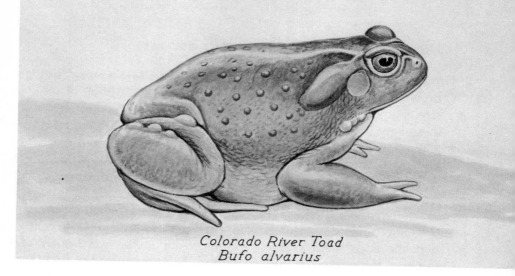

Colorado River Toad
Bufo alvarius

Little Grass Frog
Hyla ocularis

Southern Cricket Frog
Acris gryllus

Some swamp- and ditch-dwelling frogs

heads slightly, but have not the freedom of head movement of the Little Grass Frog.

The males may be distinguished from the females by their "pleated" throats; that is, the skin on the throat is not smooth but falls into wrinkles or folds. The vocal sacs when expanded form a large round throat bubble. The call is loud for so small a creature. It is very high-pitched and quite cricketlike in quality—or it may sound like the peeping of newly hatched chicks. The breeding season is an extended one from January to September, though Dr. Conant states that they may breed the year round in Florida.

About 100 eggs are deposited singly in shallow water. They are brown above, cream below, and are very tiny—about .7 mm. in size. The envelope measurement does not exceed 2 mm.; obviously, these eggs are hard to find. The tadpole is greenish in color on top, with scattered black spots. The tail is long, and the tail crests are high and extending far up on the body.' After a larval life of 1½ months to 2½ months, the tadpole transforms into a tiny frog ¼ to ⅜ of an inch long.

Though the Little Grass Frog seems to prefer swampy ground, they may sometimes be found in quite dry areas. Mrs. Goin tells us that she finds them around her place, not in the wet winter and summer, but in the dry spring and fall. Why does she not find them in wetter weather? It is known that amphibians make long (never exceeding two miles and usually less than half a mile) migrations to and from suitable breeding sites. Dr. Oliver says that these distances are in marked contrast (especially in some species) to their normal everyday travels, which in many species do not exceed a circle with a radius of a few hundred feet. Possibly these facts may help to explain why Mrs. Goin found *Hyla ocularis* during dry weather. They may have been merely journeying to or from the breeding sites.

It is believed that most amphibians do not breed more than once a year. But when we realize that the Little Grass Frog breeds during any month of the year in Florida, and that Mrs. Goin's captures were in the spring and fall, we wonder whether this species may possibly breed twice a year. A widespread marking of breeding individuals over several years would be necessary to prove or disprove this theory. It would be a good project for some ambitious amateur herpetologist residing in Florida.

Another small frog belonging to the family Hylidae is known as the Cricket Frog, genus *Acris*. Some species of Cricket Frog are found throughout the eastern half of the United States, New England, New York, North Dakota, most of Pennsylvania, West Virginia, and South Dakota excluded. All of them are swamp dwellers with similar appearances and life histories.

The Southern Cricket Frog, *Acris gryllus gryllus,* is found in the coastal lowlands of North Carolina and South Carolina and most of Georgia, Alabama, Mississippi, and the western arm of Florida. Elsewhere in Florida, it is superseded by the Florida Cricket Frog,

Acris gryllus dorsalis, which differs from it principally in thigh pattern. The color variation of the Southern Cricket Frog is extreme; individuals of black, brown, red, green, or gray may be found. The markings are variable also, and may be dark or red. Often there is a triangle between the eyes, with the apex on the snout, and another triangle just behind this, with the apex turned toward the rear. There may be, in addition, a central back stripe and a side stripe. The legs are barred with dark. There is also a light line running from the eye to the arm.

Probably the most reliable identification mark is the thigh pattern, which is, unfortunately, not visible when the frog is at rest. In order to see it, you must catch your frog and straighten out one hind leg. On the rear of the femur, you will find a dark evenly edged stripe on the Southern Cricket Frog. In addition, the upper part of the thigh and around the anus is sprinkled with small tubercles. In the Florida Cricket Frog there are no anal turbercles, and there are *two* stripes. In the Northern Cricket Frog, *Acris gryllus crepitans,* anal warts are present, together with one irregular edged dark stripe. The Northern Cricket Frog also has more extensive webbing on its toes.

The Southern Cricket Frog is a small frog from ¾ to 1¼ inches in length. It has a slender body, long legs, and feet that are more completely webbed than those of the Little Grass Frog. Its finger and toe disks are small and are not used for climbing. It is more like the true frogs in appearance than are other hylids. The Southern Cricket Frog spends most of its life in swamps and bogs in fairly open situations. When alarmed, this little frog shows its aquatic affinities by heading straight for water, and with a leap dives down into the muck to hide.

While the female's throat is a light tan, that of the male is a much darker brownish yellow, sprinkled with black dots. This marked throat discoloration is a reliable indicator of sex. The vocal sacs expand into a round throat bubble when the male is calling. Miss Dickerson tells us that the voice may be imitated by hitting two marbles or pebbles together several times with increasing rapidity. I have tried this. Neither the marbles nor the pebbles sound very much like the recording of the Southern Cricket Frog's voice, but of the two the pebbles make the better approximation. The breeding season is from February to October in periods of maximum rainfall.

The eggs number about 250 and are laid singly, either attached to water weeds or on the bottom in the shallow water of temporary pools. The eggs are a little larger than those of the Little Grass Frog but not enough larger to make them readily visible. The tadpole is olive in color with a black tail tip. As with so many of the hylids, the tail crest is high and the body deep. The spiracle is found on the left side. It is not just an opening in the body in this species, but is equipped with a tube that stands out at an angle from the body, with the opening at its end. The larval period is an extended one of 2 to 3 months or even longer.

The Southern Cricket Frog is the commonest frog within its range. It may be found in every month of the year, though naturally it is less frequently collected during the colder months of December, January, and February. Does this frog hibernate or not? Some say that it does hibernate on land. Others say that it does not but that during the colder months of the year it goes to the larger bodies of water so that it may take refuge there in the advent of freezing weather. Which of these opposite schools of thought is right? We don't know, but perhaps they both are for their own locality.

The Southern Cricket Frogs are active creatures; moreover, they are found both during the day and at night. Owing to the small size, however, they are easily overlooked or mistaken for grasshoppers. Their long legs make them wonderful jumpers. They vie with the Leopard Frog for the maximum distance jumped by our native frogs. But if the distance jumped be related to body length, they are far and away the best jumpers we have, for they can jump between 35 and 40 times the length of their own bodies. Imagine, for comparison, how far a six-foot man should be able to jump in order to compete—240 feet! The world record for the standing jump is only a little over 12 feet. The world record for the running broad jump, made by Jesse Owens in 1935, is 26'8¼". Let us assume that Owens is 6 feet tall. You may work out his relative jumping ability accurately if you like. I am content to say merely that it is a little over four times his height. However, frogs make standing broad jumps, and here we find that an exceptional man can jump only about twice his height. Of course, frogs and men are built quite differently, but, this comparison demonstrates the disparity in their relative jumping abilities clearly.

Familiar to most people living in the eastern half of the United

States, southern Florida excepted, is the Spring Peeper, *Hyla cruci-fer crucifer*. But is is principally by voice that he is known, for though it is a common species, most people have never seen this small creature. He is an inhabitant of woodland swamps, though during the breeding season most ponds have a chorus of peepers on their banks. These small treefrogs are brown or tan in color with a dark X mark on the back. Very often the marking is not a perfect X but is incomplete or modified so that it appears like an inverted Y. There is a V mark between the eyes and an inverted V joining the dark barred hind legs. The underparts are cream-colored. This creature is about ¾ of an inch long and has the typical toe disks of a hylid, though it does not climb very much. Actually, its toe disks are very efficient, for it can and does cling to the upright sides of an aquarium for days.

The males are considerably smaller than the females, and during the breeding season are much darker in over-all color. In fact, sometimes they are so dark that the characteristic markings are all but indistinguishable. The male also has a dark throat, which is lacking in the female. The breeding season is early. The Wrights say April marks the height of the breeding activities, but we hear calls as early as the middle of March in our vicinity. Farther south, the breeding season is much earlier—even as early as November.

The vocal sacs of the male swell into a glistening round flesh-

The Northern Spring Peeper, *Hyla crucifer crucifer*

colored throat bubble as he utters his sweet *Preep, peep, peep.* Generally, unless the day is warm and overcast or rainy, the peepers do not begin calling much before four o'clock in the afternoon. But finding them in daylight, even though the chorus be deafening before your approach, is difficult. For as you draw near, the singers in your immediate vicinity cease their calling. Being small, and choosing stations that are partially concealed, they are most inconspicuous. We find the same caution at night during the colder weather of early spring. Though herpetologists insist that hearing plays no part in stilling the calls of amphibians, the Spring Peeper has made us skeptical of this dictum.

We regularly go to two ponds for our amphibian watching. One, on the edge of the woods, was once a gravel pit, long since abandoned. It is an ideal peeper breeding place, for the pools are surrounded by low shrubs. The footing at night, however, is not very good, for the banks are steep and gravelly. We have gone there on dark moonless nights with dark clothes. Though the peepers were singing when we arrived, they soon stopped as we approached—as quietly as possible, but not very quietly because of the gravel. If the peepers didn't hear us, how did they know we were there? We switched off our lights. We were unable to see each other five feet away. Can we nevertheless assume that the peepers could see us?

Our other observation place is a spring-fed pond in an open situation surrounded by lawn on one side and a mowed field on the other. On bright moonlit nights, further brightened by a street light and our flashlights, we clomp loudly over and see hundreds of peepers in no way disturbed by our presence. The peepers start breeding in this pond two or three weeks later than in the gravel bank.

It is our theory that when the nights are warmer and the peepers are in chorus stage, they are oblivious to noise and even sight of danger in the evening. But at the start of the breeding season, and when the temperatures are down in the 40's, they are much more aware of danger. We feel that hearing plays a part in stilling their calls on cold dark nights. Though experienced herpetologists do not think so, no other explanation occurs to us.

You might think that frogs in amplexus would be easy to distinguish from unmated ones. Such is sometimes the case. But it is almost uncanny how much two peepers in amplexus resemble a single peeper. The female is larger than the male and markedly lighter in color. The male clings tightly to her, flattening his back and keeping his legs well drawn up. From a slight distance, in poor light, they appear as one peeper. Any single peeper in the pond is suspect, however, for they usually call from land, though they generally choose the damper spots on the bank. You will be surprised, especially when you first go collecting, to find out how many single peepers turn out to be a pair.

When a mated pair of frogs is captured, the male will very often croak in protest, especially if he is touched. We do not find this true of the male peeper. Though peepers in amplexus are more easily separated than the American Toad, for instance, we have never heard a male utter a peep in protest when handled. Their behavior when accosted by another male when they are unmated is different. Then they peep loudly in protest, and give a sort of body shrug, which in most cases is sufficient to induce the embracing peeper to cease his unwelcome attentions.

The eggs, about 1,000 in number, are laid singly. They are black on top, white underneath, and are about 1 mm. in size. We well remember the first time we captured a mated pair and confined them in an aquarium to obtain the eggs. On the bottom of a white refrigerator dish was a little dirt from the rock that we had put in with our specimens. The next morning, at first glance, we thought that the peepers had not laid! A closer look showed we were mistaken, but the few grains of dirt and sand made the eggs difficult to distinguish. This brought home, more clearly than previous fruitless searching in the pond had, the extremely small size of a peeper egg.

The incubation period of the peeper egg in the field has never been accurately determined. In an aquarium, we find it to be between 4 and 5 days, when kept at a room temperature of between 65°F. and 70° F. Since the water in which the peepers lay is much colder—sometimes only a few degrees above freezing—we may expect to find that the field-incubation period is considerably longer.

The tadpole is sandy in color on its back. The belly is white or cream. In certain positions the characteristic V-shaped indentation of the tail crest by the anus is clearly visible. Hatching evidently exhausts these small mites, for afterward most of them lie inert on the aquarium bottom or pond bottom. In the pond they show up quite clearly against the dark bottom if one knows what to look for. About a week later, the peeper tadpoles have assumed their characteristic shape. When viewed from above, the body is oval in outline. The tail crests are transparent. The belly has become a beautiful iridescent shade of reddish gold with a very metallic sheen. By this time they are eating. When at rest, they no longer lie on their sides on the aquarium bottom, but cling to its sides in an upright position, heads up, tails down.

The field-incubation period is 3 months or longer. In our aquarium we find it is about 46 days. As soon as the legs appear and are well developed, the dark markings of the adult peeper appear on the back of the tadpole. The gorgeous iridescent belly is lost. The arms then emerge, and the small creature immediately starts to go toward land. They do not wait for the tail to absorb before assuming a more or less terrestrial existence. Possibly these tailed peepers stay fairly close to the water until their tails are resorbed, though we have not observed them closely enough to be absolutely sure of this. It seems that they do not remain near the pond as long as young toads, but this is a purely subjective impression and may not be correct, because there are so many more little toads around a pool that one is bound to see more of them as successive batches transform.

Outside the breeding season, Spring Peepers are scarce and hard to find. They evidently leave the more open situations where they have bred, and retreat to more secluded ones. Finding them becomes more a matter of good luck than anything else. They seem to prefer woodland swamps, and are more numerous in wet situations where much low brush and shrubbery abounds. Occasionally, one may find them in marshy fields also, but they are not nearly so numerous there.

We know that the peeper is among the first frogs to leave hibernation and start breeding. When does he return to the hibernation site in the fall? We do not have any precise time, and it would, of course, vary with the locality. We do not believe that the peepers have an innate sense of when to hibernate, as does the American Toad. With the peeper, we believe temperature is the sole governing factor, for this year—a rather warm fall—we heard scattered calls in a woodland swamp as late as November 1st. When the Spring Peeper does hibernate, it is on land, under the earth. But even in the North he does not remain there for long—2 or 3 months at most. Then he is out again to tell us that spring will soon arrive.

Our next two swamp dwellers are salamanders. Although they are not closely related, they have several characteristics in common. Both are plethodontids; both are small; and both have but four toes on all four feet, instead of five behind and four in front as do most salamanders.

The first of these is the Eastern Four-toed Salamander, *Hemidactylium scutatum*. It is found throughout the northeastern states and the Middle West as far south as northern Georgia. It is absent from most of Maine and the more northerly portions of New York, New Hampshire, and Vermont. This salamander is from 2 to 3 inches long, the males being smaller. The back is reddish brown in color; the belly is white distinctly marked with black spots. There are, as we said, but four toes on all the feet, and at the base of the tail there is a constriction. This constriction is an indentation around the tail. It marks the place where the tail will break off if grasped by an enemy.

The Eastern Four-toed Salamander is found in areas of sphagnum bogs, either in the woods or, less frequently, in the open. The breeding season is in the late summer and early fall. The courtship is much like that of the Two-lined Salamander. The pair walks along, the female behind the male, with her chin on his wagging tail. The eggs are not deposited until the following spring. The female selects a cavity under moss or among grasses very close to a pool of water. She lies on her back and lays about 30 eggs. These are deposited singly, but close together. The jelly surrounding each egg is sticky, and it may appear that several eggs have been deposited together, so closely do they adhere to one another. Such is not the case, however, for they are not united by a common jelly envelope. The vitellus is large—up to 3 mm. in size—and is surrounded by 2 jelly envelopes making egg and jelly a little over 5 mm. in total diameter.

The female remains with the eggs for at least part of the incubation period of a month to two months. Dr. Oliver tells us that in the more southerly regions of their range—specifically Virginia—the female broods the eggs for about half of the total incubation period. In New York and Michigan she remains with them until they hatch. This difference in the length of the brooding period is very interesting, and prompts us to wonder whether the eggs laid in Virginia might be smaller than those laid in the North, or whether the salamander may be larger in the South. This question is not such a nonsequitur as it might seem to be. Scientists seem to feel that the exhaustion of the female after laying plays a part in determining the length of the brooding period. *Hemidactylium* is a small salamander, but it lays a very large egg. If we put only the vitelli of the total egg complement together in a line, we find that this small creature has laid eggs that are equal to or exceed her own body length. It is small wonder that she is exhausted after this feat. It may be found that in the South, *Hemidactylium* is larger, the eggs are smaller, the total complement is less, or a combination of these factors is true. If so, the shorter brooding period in the South may be partially explained.

We say "partially" advisedly, for female exhaustion after laying does not completely explain why *Hemidactylium* broods. It is not at all uncommon to find a communal nest where a number of salamanders have deposited their eggs in close proximity to one another. In this case, not all the layers remain with the eggs. A few only remain on the nursery detail while the others depart. What determines which females shall stay? Is it those that laid their eggs first that remain? Or do the first layers depart as later arrivals deposit their eggs? Does age or size play any part in determining which shall remain with the nest? Someday we may know the answers.

When the eggs hatch, the larvae wriggle down into the water. Unlike all other plethodontids, these larvae are pond larvae similar to those of the Mole Salamanders in body form. The tail fin extends up onto the back, and the gills are large and bushy. The larval period is about 1½ months. The transformed salamander, only about ¾ of an inch in length, leaves the water and takes up its adult life on land in the moist mosses where it was born.

The Dwarf Salamander, *Manculus quadridigitatus*, found along the coasts of the southern states from North Carolina to Texas, is about the same length as the Eastern Four-toed Salamander, but it is more slender and has a very long tail. In color and shape of head, it looks very much like the Two-lined Salamander. Its back is bronzy tan occasionally marked with darker spots and dashes. On each side there is a dark line that runs the entire length of the body. The belly is yellow. Despite the similarity of color and markings, the Dwarf

Salamander may be distinguished from the Two-lined Salamander by the fact that the former has but four toes on its back feet, whereas the latter has five toes.

The male Dwarf Salamander has cirri extending from its nasolabial grooves, as well as elongated premaxillary teeth that are slanted forward and are therefore exposed during the breeding season. These teeth are found on the triangular-shaped bone (the premaxillary) that forms the tip of the upper snout. The male Dwarf Salamander is not unique in this respect. Many of the plethodontids—the genus *Eurycea* especially—have these monocuspid elongated teeth. Their function has not been fully explained. It is true that during the breeding season the males rub the females with their snouts, and it is felt that the exposed teeth provide extra friction.

For many years herpetologists insisted that amphibian males did not bite or grasp a female in the fashion of many breeding mammals. This statement is now open to question, for quite recently the male Slimy Salamander, *Plethodon glutinosus glutinosus,* was seen holding the female's body or tail gently in his mouth during courtship. In addition, when a male Slimy Salamander attempted to court other males, quite frequently the courted male bit the courting one severely, though sometimes it was the courting male that attacked the one he was courting when he discovered the latter was not a female.

So far as we know, no one has ever seen any such behavior as this on the part of the Dwarf Salamander. But since the males of many species of salamanders develop specialized premaxillary teeth, perhaps more thorough investigation of their habits may disclose that they use these teeth during courtship.

The Dwarf Salamander breeds and lays its eggs in winter from December through February in the larger pools of swamps or slow-flowing permanent ditches. The eggs are deposited singly or in small groups on the undersides of logs or vegetable debris in water. The total complement may be as high as 50, though smaller numbers are more common. The eggs are about 2 mm. in size, white in color, and surrounded by 2 envelopes. The larvae are found in March, and after a larval period of 2 or 3 months they complete their transformation and assume a more terrestrial existence.

These are but a few of the swamp and ditch dwellers you may find. Most notable of the omissions are the Chorus Frogs, genus

Pseudacris. These belong to the family Hylidae. They are small—most do not exceed 1½ inches in length—brightly colored little animals. They are generally marked with five rows of spots or five stripes on the dorsum. Representative species may be found throughout most of the United States, New England excepted.

Forest and Field Dwellers

Just as there are many types of ponds, streams, ditches and swamps, so are there many types of forests and fields. There are forests that consist of deciduous trees, and there are those whose stand is principally coniferous. There are the immense rain forests of the Northwest and the tropics and the drier jungles. There are the forests made up of large trees of tremendous antiquity, and thickets made up of new trees and saplings. The same variety is present in fields. There are plowed fields and fields under cultivation. There are hayfields and land which is used for pasturage. We could go on almost infinitely, describing the type of soil, the moisture content, and so on, and we should not be straying from our subject in doing so either. Mineral content, moisture content, amount and type of vegetation—all these are pertinent factors in the make-up of an ecological niche or habitat.

Forests and fields have one broad characteristic common to them both. They are both more or less dry land. The forest dwellers, as a general rule, prefer the darker, damper atmosphere, where cover such as rocks, leaves, leaf mold, and logs is always readily available. The field dwellers can tolerate the more open situations found in most fields. Those who are least susceptible to desiccation are often found in plowed fields. Let us examine a few of these dry-land dwellers; first, the more moisture-loving woods dwellers, then the

The Spotted Salamander, *Ambystoma maculatum*

grass-field dwellers, and last the dwellers of plowed field and areas sparsely vegetated.

Of all the dry-land amphibians, none is more moisture-loving than the Spotted Salamander, *Ambystoma maculatum,* found throughout most of the northeastern half of the United States, Florida and southern Georgia excepted. Herpetologists tell us that these salamanders live in the woods, hiding by day under logs and rocks during rainy weather. We are told that during drier weather, they make shallow burrows underneath the surface. It is fortunate for us that the scientists give us this information, for few of us would be able to find it out for ourselves. Though we have looked long and persistently in wet weather and dry, making lengthy excavations to explore tunnels with openings under logs and rocks, we have never been fortunate enough to find a Spotted Salamander outside the breeding season. This might not be so extraordinary if this creature were small and slim-bodied, or inconspicuously marked. But it is not. It is a large, stout-bodied animal, almost 7 inches long, black in color with a row of yellow or orange spots on either side. It is a very striking animal, and one couldn't possibly overlook it, especially when one is searching for it.

Neither is the Spotted Salamander rare; indeed, it is among our most common salamanders, as anyone can prove for himself by going to the ponds at night in the early spring. Though the Spotted

Salamander may be seen in ponds found in the open, it is the woodland ponds that they prefer and where they are most numerous. Here they may be counted by the hundreds during the evening; and a little later their egg masses serve as proof that one has not counted all that were present.

The males are a little larger than the females, and have a protuberant vent. So swollen is it that one can sometimes distinguish the sexes while they are swimming. The nuptial dance consists of both sexes swimming over and around one another, the males nudging each other and the females. "Dance" is a good description for these courtship activities, but one must not interpret the dance too literally. There is nothing organized or stylized about it. Occasionally the dance is carried on in a very limited area; there are many participants and the water fairly boils with their activities. More often, there are scattered groups of fifteen or twenty salamanders seemingly swimming in haphazard fashion. But as you watch, you will see that they do indeed twine in among one another, over and below, then swim off only to return in ones and twos to nudge one another again. Usually this is done in a leisurely manner—unhurried caresses in passing one another by. Every so often a salamander will surface, gulp a breath of air, and return to his courtship activities. We might mention that Spotted Salamanders appear to be a different color at night than when seen in daylight. As you look at them by flashlight, they have slate-gray bodies with light gray spots.

The following morning one finds the pond bottom littered with the white gelatinous bases of the male spermatophores; they show up clearly against the dark leaves of the bottom. Not a salamander is to be seen. It is as if they had vanished into air. Where have they gone? We do not know. We do not find them under logs or stones by the ponds. Nor have we found them under logs and stones on the pond bottom, though it is possible that they may be there. Do they leave the pond and burrow in during the day? This seems a not unlikely possibility.

The breeding season extends over a week or two in any given locality. The Spotted Salamanders are not like some of the burrowers that we shall describe later, whose breeding activities are completed in one or two nights. The breeding season is in March or April.

The eggs are laid several days after impregnation in a roundish mass attached to submerged vegetation. They may be deposited in several small masses or one large one. The total complement ranges from 25 to 250 eggs, with larger, older females laying the larger number. Generally, we find that most large egg masses contain approximately 100 to 125 eggs. The egg itself is dark brown above, whitish below. The envelopes that surround the egg may be clear or they may be light green. The green coloring is caused by algae that penetrate the capsule and grow there. Surprisingly enough, the alga does the egg no harm; indeed, algae and eggs are mutually beneficial. The algae give off oxygen as a by-product of photosynthesis. This additional oxygen in the egg capsule makes larger embryos, a lower mortality rate, and a shorter incubation period. The algae benefit from the carbon dioxide given off by the embryo as a waste product of respiration. When does the alga enter the egg capsule? At any particular stage in the egg's development? Why does one find some eggs with algae, while others in close proximity have none? These are interesting questions that may someday be answered by herpetologists.

The mass of jelly may be clear or it may be milky white. We find both kinds in any given pond. What governs the color? Does it depend on the female who lays the mass, or are environmental conditions responsible?

The incubation period is between 1 month and 2 months, depending on the temperature. The larva is a light sandy or greenish yellow color with darker spots scattered over the back. Balancers are present at hatching, as are the buds of the forelegs. The dorsal fin is high and extends up as far as the forelegs. Transformation occurs after a larval period of 2 to 4 months. The adult coloration complete with spots is usually assumed within a week of metamorphosis.

Of all our local salamanders, the Spotted Salamanders are our favorites. The plump body, the head with its large dark eyes and bluntly rounded snout, and the docile, gentle manner make this animal very engaging. How aggravating it is not to be able to find him outside the breeding season! What we should do is to keep them in a terrarium. They evidently live to a considerable age when properly cared for. Dr. Oliver tells us that the maximum age recorded for a captive is 25 years.

The Slimy Salamander, *Plethodon glutinosus glutinosus*, is another stout-bodied woodland salamander. It averages slightly smaller than the Spotted Salamander, being about 6 inches long, though larger individuals have been found. It belongs to the Plethodontidae, as is evidenced by its nasolabial grooves. Its head is different from that of the Blunt-mouthed, or Mole, Salamanders, the snout being more pointed. Its range is about the same as the Spotted Salamander's, but extends a little farther south, down into half of Florida, and not so far north. It is entirely absent from the New England states.

The Slimy Salamander has a black back with numerous scattered white flecks. The belly is slate-gray. This salamander gets its popular name from the copious sticky secretions produced by its mucous glands. Do these exudates help keep this salamander's skin moist under adverse conditions? Probably. All Lungless Salamanders are easily killed by desiccation, but this is more marked in the Slimy Salamander than in some of the other woodland salamanders, such as the Red-backed Salamander, for instance. The Slimy Salamander is found under surface materials in the woods, occasionally in caves or in rock crevices, and very often, especially during dry periods, it burrows into the soil.

Very little is known about the breeding habits of the Slimy Salamander. By piecing together scattered accounts and evidence gathered through dissection, it seems probable that the mating season is in the fall, in the North, while the laying season is in the early spring. However, this may not hold true in the South, for eggs attended by a female were found in a cave in Arkansas in August. Eggs and mother have been found in West Virginia in June. The eggs, about 15 to 18 in number, are laid in a small mass. Dr. Bishop feels that in the North the eggs may be found in the hiberation sites deep in rock crevices. It will be no simple matter to find them, but their discovery and precise observations on the larvae that hatch would indeed be a nice feather in an amateur herpetologist's cap.

Far more common and less secretive is the Red-backed Salamander, *Plethodon cinereus cinereus,* found in the Northeast as far south as North Carolina and west to Indiana and Wisconsin. This salamander prefers coniferous woods, and we find them more frequently in the vicinity of evergreen trees.

The Red-backed Salamander has two color phases. All of them have a bluish-black or charcoal-gray belly liberally speckled with bluish-white flecks. Perhaps we should say almost all of them have mottled bellies. Once we found a Red-back whose belly was dark gray with only a few widely scattered white specks. The red-backed phase has a broad band of red or orange extending from the head back to the tail. The sides are black. The lead-backed phase is a uniform dark gray or black on its back. Some individuals are intermediate between these two phases, with the dorsal stripe of a faded gray interrupted in places by the darker gray of the sides. In some localities Red-backed Salamanders may predominate; in others, Lead-backed Salamanders are more frequently found; in still a third place, they may be found in approximately even numbers. Dr. Conant tells us that at high elevation Lead-backs may be scarce or absent altogether. But whether it is a Red-backed Salamander or a Lead-backed Salamander, they are the same subspecies, *Plethodon cinereus cinereus.*

A few days ago we listened to a discussion of industrial melanism in the Pepper-and-Salt Moth in England. In areas near large industrial cities, tree trunks and vegetation are blackened from soot. In these regions the black, or melanistic, variety of the Pepper-and-Salt Moth predominates in a 3 to 1 ratio. In regions not polluted with industrial smog, the normal coloration predominates—also in a 3 to 1 ratio. Both the melanistic and the normal coloration are valuable to the animal in the preferred environment. We are not suggesting that industrial melanism is responsible for the two-color phases of the Red-backed Salamander, but we wonder whether, in situations where one or the other color phase predominates, there is not some good reason why it does. In other words, in some way not known at

The Red-backed Salamander, *Plethodon cinereus cinereus*

present, either phase may perhaps have a definite survival value for its possessor.

The Red-backed Salamander varies in size from 2½ to 3½ inches, and though the Lead-backs appear a little smaller, it is probably their dark color that gives us this impression. The males are shorter than the females, with a more swollen snout. The premaxillary teeth are enlarged in the male—but you will need a magnifying glass to see this feature. The breeding season is in the fall on land, from late September to late November.

The eggs are not deposited until the summer following impregnation; June or July are the usual months. These eggs are laid in cavities in or under rotting logs. They are fastened in small groups by a common stalk to the roof of the cavity and are usually attended by the female. The total complement is small—from 3 to 13 eggs—but the vitellus is large and may measure up to 5 mm. in diameter. This egg is surrounded by 2 jelly envelopes. The eggs are unpigmented, as is usual with the plethodontids, and take from 1 to 2 months to hatch. If the larva is to have a red back, his dorsal band will be present at hatching. The gills are of the "staghorn" terrestrial type, and are at their largest in the embryo, though they are present on the hatchling. By the time the larva is a few days old, however, they have been completely absorbed. Within a week or two after hatching, our little Red-backed Salamander looks just like his parents, but he is only about ¾ of an inch long—a tiny mite of a thing. Not until he is 2 or even 3 years old will he attain sexual maturity, and begin to reproduce.

For a Lungless Salamander, *Plethodon cinereus cinereus* can tolerate amazingly dry conditions. This is all the more surprising since it is a fairly small salamander, for the skin area is proportionately larger in a small animal than in a larger one when the surface is related to weight. We might expect to find that the larger plethodontids are less prone to desiccation, but such is not always the case, as a comparison of the large Slimy Salamander and the small Red-backed Salamander proves.

During the winter months the Red-backed Salamander hibernates underground. The depth to which it burrows varies considerably, and may be as shallow as 3 inches or as deep as 15 inches. Possibly in the more northerly portions of the range they may hibernate even below this maximum recorded depth. In this species hibernation is governed principally by lowering temperatures, and is not dependent on any inherent rhythm. Dr. Oliver gives us some very interesting facts concerning the Red-backed Salamander's hibernation. He reports that one investigator found that the mortality due to hibernation was as high as 57 per cent. How such an exact figure could be determined, we cannot imagine. Is it really true that over half the Red-backed Salamanders die from cold every year? We do not feel that we are being disrespectful if we view this figure with skepticism. Perhaps the mortality rate *is* this high in certain years or in certain unfavorable localities. But perhaps this high percentage does not hold good for all years in all localities. How was this figure arrived at? Was it done by finding a hibernation site and counting the animals that were dead and those that were alive? Or was it done by marking off a collecting area and making a fall count and a spring count? Either of these methods has its flaws. In the first case, hibernation sites are difficult to find, and one cannot feel sure that one has not found the ones that are less suitable. The second method also has its disadvantages. Though one does not see hundreds of terrestrial salamanders gathered together in a common breeding site, there still exists a certain gathering together of the clan. We find more Red-backed Salamanders clustered together in scattered groups in the fall than at any other time of year. The fall count is therefore apt to be large. However, we don't think that the smaller spring count necessarily indicates a high hibernation mortality rate. Whereas in the fall there are two urges that prompt these salamanders to collect—the breeding season and then hibernation—in the spring neither of these conditions is present. Probably the salamanders emerge in small groups at different times, and scatter. Though scientists can predict to the exact hour when the vernal equinox will occur, they cannot predict with equal accuracy just when each salamander will emerge from hibernation.

Be all this as it may, it seems certain that whatever the percentage, the hibernation mortality rate of the Red-backed Salamander is high. Though Nature has not provided the Red-backed Salamander with an innate knowledge of when to hibernate, she has partially compensated him in another respect. It has been found that in the winter, the water content in the body is greatly lowered. It is believed that this enables the animal better to withstand low temperatures without freezing.

Above: The Eastern Wood Frog, *Rana sylvatica sylvatica*, in light summer colors
Right: Wood Frogs in amplexus. Note the darker color of the male and his convex toe webbing. The female is larger, lighter in color, and has concave toe webbing.

The prize for the earliest spring breeding frog in the North goes, not to the Spring Peeper, but to the Eastern Wood Frog, *Rana sylvatica sylvatica*. Herpetologists are not in agreement as to whether the Wood Frog should be divided into subspecies or not. Some authorities divide the Wood Frog into three subspecies: *Rana sylvatica sylvatica*, found in the northeastern United States; *Rana sylvatica cantabrigensis*, found in eastern Canada; and *Rana sylvatica latiremis*, found in western Canada and Alaska. Others feel that only two subspecies are called for: *Rana sylvatica sylvatica* and *Rana sylvatica cantabrigensis*. Still a third group feels that the color differences and leg length as related to body length are not sufficiently constant and distinct to warrant subspecific division. The latter group feels that the relatively longer legs of our United States Wood Frog change gradually to the shorter leg of the Northern Wood Frog and that this, therefore, is not an innate characteristic but merely one produced by physical differences in their range. We amateurs are not qualified to judge who is right in this controversy. Let us therefore take the middle course and assume, as a great many herpetologists do, that this species is divided into two subspecies. Perhaps industrious amateurs in northern Minnesota and Wisconsin, where *Rana sylvatica cantabrigensis* occurs, will, through leg and body measurements of many individuals, be able to shed some light on the confusion.

Our Eastern Wood Frog, *Rana sylvatica sylvatica*, is a small brown frog of from 2 to 3 inches long. In the cool spring water of the ponds where it breeds, the male appears to be dark or reddish-brown, unmarked except for the light line along the upper jaw and the light-colored dorsolateral folds. But after the breeding season, in the warmer weather, its color lightens considerably and the dark mask in back of the eye and dark lines from eye to snout stand out like dark brown velvet against the light tan of the rest of the body. You will notice, if you look closely at the photograph of the Wood Frog in his summer dress (page 135), that the lower part of the iris is considerably darker than the upper part and blends into the mask. This indicates the purpose of the mask. It breaks up the conspicuous eye on an animal which is otherwise inconspicuous against the leaves of the forest floor. The mask, therefore, is an excellent camouflaging mark. Sometimes the Eastern Wood Frog has barred legs and a few dark spots scattered over the back. The belly is white except where the hind legs join the body, where it is a light greenish color.

The Eastern Wood Frog is, as we said, a very early breeder. As a general rule, they do not breed in the North before the middle of March or early April, but farther south they may start their breeding activities in February. Water temperature has been found to be a reliable indicator of when a number of frogs will lay their eggs. The average water temperature is 50° F. when the Eastern Wood Frog lays its eggs.

The males may be distinguished from the females by their toe webs, which are convex, while those of the female are concave. The vocal sacs of the males are internal, and show only as a generalized throat swelling when expanded. The males lie on the surface of the water or may call under water. The voice usually resembles the quacking of ducks, and many hundreds all call at the same time. The call does not carry well, and is inaudible a very short distance away. Sex recognition is almost entirely by trial embrace. All nearby moving objects are seized; those which croak or whose bodies have not sufficient girth are released promptly.

The breeding period in any given pond is short; the peak of the breeding activities is over in 2 or 3 days. When you hear hundreds of "ducks" quacking in a pond where there are no ducks to be seen, you may be sure you have come upon Wood Frogs breeding. But though your ears assure you the frogs are there, your eyes may not convince you. We have found that during the height of breeding activities in woodland ponds, the frogs are almost oblivious of our presence, even in the daytime. But where large breeding groups have chosen a pond in a more open situation, they seem to be more alert to danger and the greater number of them choose to call under water rather than while floating on its surface. However, though the Wood Frog is hard to see in his dark spring dress, once you have spotted him on the pond bottom he is quite easy to scoop up with net or hand. He flattens himself out on the bottom and depends on protective coloration and absolute immobility to save him. As your hand slowly descends, he is not so apt to dart away to another spot as are many other frogs.

The eggs are laid in a roundish mass attached to submerged vegetation. There are from 2,000 to 3,000 black eggs in a mass. Each eggs is surrounded by 2 jelly envelopes; only the outer one is distinct. The vitellus is small and averages under 2 mm. in size. Because these frogs are early breeders, they choose the warmest parts of the pond in which to lay their eggs. This often means that they lay close to shore in shallow water. Twenty-five or more bunches of eggs are often found laid so near to one another that soon after the jelly has swelled, it is impossible to tell exactly how many masses have been deposited, for each merges into the others around it.

Laid in such shallow water, the eggs are very vulnerable to desiccation and freezing. The shallow water of ponds often evaporates rapidly in the warmer days of spring. Many of the uppermost eggs are left high and dry, and these, naturally, do not hatch. However, the same high temperatures that cause rapid evaporation of the pond water also hasten the development of the egg. Dr. Oliver gives us the precise hatching time at different temperatures. At a water temperature of 50° F., eggs hatch in 275 hours, or a little over 11 days, whereas the eggs hatch in 3 to 4 days at a temperature of 68° F. Eggs that are near the surface may be killed by freezing temperatures. But even though the top of an egg mass may be frozen, the eggs of the lower part will develop normally. The eggs and embryos of the Eastern Wood Frog can tolerate a considerable temperature variation—a 38° F. variation, to be precise—and as long as water temperatures do not fall below 37° F. or rise above 75° F., these eggs will hatch satisfactorily. Moreover, for some reason, eggs develop faster when temperature variations occur; the shortest incubation period is found in those eggs which are initially subjected to a low temperature and which finish their development at a higher temperature.

The tadpole of the Eastern Wood Frog is greenish olive in color, with a high tail crest. It is wholly carnivorous in diet. We often see groups of these tadpoles all nibbling on the freshly killed body of some unfortunate casualty of the breeding season. We see them nibbling at other tadpoles' tails. Is this because food is scarce, or have they, as do so many animals, some way of knowing that the one they attack is unhealthy and not long for this world? Or is it plain cannibalism? Of course, their diet also consists of the minute insects and entomostracans found in the pond.

The Wood Frog tadpoles have a larval period of 1½ to 2½ months. As they transform, they leave their natal ponds wearing the light summer dress that makes them so inconspicuous in the forest.

Outside the breeding season, our best collecting results have been in wooded spots near our river. We have found Wood Frogs in the forest near small trickling springs, but not so often as we do near the river. Perhaps it is the younger ones, always more gregarious and less elusive than any older adult amphibian, that prefer the damper, more open areas around the river. Though the Wood Frog is common, he is hard to find outside the breeding season. His alertness and shyness are all the more noticeable because this behavior is so unlike his behavior in the spring.

True land frog that he is, the Eastern Wood Frog hibernates under the soil of the forest floor. But as one might expect from a frog that can breed in such cold weather, the Wood Frog is also able to tolerate colder weather in the fall than many other species can. The latest date that we have found a Wood Frog was September 29th. However, since we do not know the home range of any particular individuals, we have no way of knowing the precise hibernation date. It seems quite likely that these frogs may be found abroad in October also, and even later in the more southerly portions of their range.

The Oak Toad, *Bufo quercicus*, is our smallest native toad. Its maximum size does not exceed 1¼ inches, and it is for this reason that it is frequently mistaken for a young Southern Toad. The Oak Toad is found along the coasts of our southern states from North Carolina south to Florida and west to Mississippi.

The Oak Toad varies in color from almost black to a light gray. There is always a light-colored stripe extending from the tip of the snout to the vent along the middle of the back. In addition, there are, in the lighter-colored individuals, four or five pairs of black spots on either side of the vertebral streak. Many of the tubercles are red, and those on the black-barred arms and legs are frequently spiny. The palms of the hands and soles of the feet are orange.

When one looks closely at the Oak Toad, the first thing that becomes apparent is the extreme shortness of the head in relation to the rest of the body. The parotoid glands are oval and elongate, as a general rule, though an occasional specimen may have parotoids that are roughly triangular in outline. If we take a specimen in hand, and look at his foot, we find that the outer-sole tubercle is small, the inner one large and equipped with a cutting edge.

The breeding season is an extended one from April to September. However, these small toads do not go to the breeding ponds until warm rains occur. Unlike many toads, the vocal sac of the male Oak Toad is kidney-shaped when expanded. This characteristic indicates that this toad is closely related to the large Great Plains Toad, *Bufo cognatus*, and the Texas Toad, *Bufo compactilis*, whose males also possess kidney-shaped vocal sacs. The voice of the calling Oak Toad is most unfroglike, and resembles very closely the peeping of baby chicks. Only the lower part of the male's throat is discolored, while the rest of the throat and underparts are grayish white. Like most male toads, the Oak Toad male has dark excrescences on the first, second, and third fingers of the hands.

Though almost all true toads lay their eggs in strings of jelly, the Oak Toad, perhaps because of its minute size, proves an ex-

Giant Toad
Bufo marinus

Oak Toad
Bufo quercicus

Slimy Salamander
Plethodon glutinosus

Some of the inhabitants of forests and fields

ception to this generality. We find female Oak Toads laying their black eggs in short bands of ⅜ of an inch or less in length with 4 to 8 eggs in each bar. The vitellus does not exceed 1 mm. in size. These bars may be scattered haphazardly close together, fastened to water vegetation, or they may be deposited so that they resemble the spokes of a bicycle without the wheel rim. In more precise scientific language, these bars may radiate out from a common focus. The total egg complement of 600 to 750 eggs is small for a toad.

The incubation period for these eggs is not known. Although the Wrights describe the tadpole as being small, grayish in color, with an upper tail crest marked with black, and a purplish-colored belly, they include no specific measurements of tadpole sizes just before transformation, nor do they include this species in their tadpole identification key. From this, we conclude that less is known about the Oak Toad tadpole than about many other species of tadpoles.

This small toad is a resident of the sandy pine barrens of the South. Its breeding habits and the cutting edge on the inner-sole tubercle of its foot might lead one to guess that this was a fossorial toad. Actually, this is far from the case. Most toads are primarily crepuscular or nocturnal animals when fully adult. Though the Oak Toad is no real exception, curiously enough these little fellows are found abroad during the day more frequently than most toads. When they do hide during the day, they may be found under logs or in very shallow burrows whose opening is shielded by vegetation. This type of burrow is quite different from those dug by the true burrowing amphibians, as we shall see in the next chapter.

Doubtless, more scientific arguments have been fought over the Leopard Frog, *Rana pipiens,* than over any other species found in this country. The battle has been going on for years, and still continues. The question is over the subspecific division. Wright and Wright devote about forty pages of absorbing discussion to *Rana pipiens,* its various color forms and mutations, and give their viewpoint on each of the subspecific divisions proposed. From their summary of the species and the controversy over it we can see most clearly the enormous pains the conscientious herpetologist takes to ensure that a given subspecies be a valid one. He must collect hundreds of specimens in the field throughout the animal's range. He must observe many individuals in nature, as well as preserved specimens. He must examine eggs and tadpoles. In the case of *Rana pipiens burnsi,* once advocated as a subspecies, it is now fairly well established that *burnsi* is merely a color phase of *Rana pipiens pipiens,* and not a valid subspecies at all. This was finally settled by embryological and genetic study. *Burnsi's* eggs were structurally indistinguishable from those of *pipiens pipiens.* It was found that these eggs differed by one color gene only. So when one finds a brown unspotted frog in Minnesota or the borders of states surrounding it, one must correctly call it *Rana pipiens pipiens* (*burnsi* mutant). Such is the exactitude of science.

We are in no position to enter into this fascinating argument. Let us therefore stay clear of it as much as possible and consider the Leopard Frog as one species, bearing in mind, of course, that color variations and slight differences in body measurements do exist. Some variety of *Rana pipiens* is found throughout the United States and Canada. The western states of California, Oregon, and Washington have this species only on their eastern borders, however.

The Leopard Frog is a slender, smooth-skinned frog with long legs. The dorsal ground color is brown, green, or tan. The prominent dorsolateral folds are light in color. Between these ridges are two or three rows of *irregularly placed white-bordered round* spots. The sides are also spotted with white-bordered black spots. The legs are barred with *light-bordered* black bars. The underparts are glistening white with *no orange* on the underside of legs or groin. Occasionally the underparts of the legs may be a light yellow, and, *in Arizona only,* they may be orange. The italicized words are most important, for we have another frog, the Pickerel Frog, which we shall discuss in a moment, that resembles the Leopard Frog and is distinguished from it by the differences in the italicized details only.

The Leopard Frog is a beautiful frog. Fortunately, it is among our most common frogs, so we can enjoy its beauty as often as we like. Though it hibernates in the water, it emerges from hibernation early and may begin breeding as early as March 15th. One may generally hear scattered calls of solitary males as much as three weeks before the breeding season really begins. Not until the water attains a minimum temperature of 41° F. does the Leopard Frog start laying its eggs.

Unlike many Salientia, both the male and female have a voice, though during the breeding season we presume that the females are normally silent. The vocal sacs of the male swell out on either side between the angle of the mouth and the shoulder. The call is difficult to describe so that one who has never heard it can imagine it. The start of the call sounds somewhat like a woodpecker tapping on a dead tree, and this sound is followed by several throaty croaks. The frogs call while in the water, either when floating on its surface or when submerged. Sex recognition is by voice; when other males are clasped, they croak in protest and are usually released immediately.

The egg complement of between 3,500 and 4,500 is laid in a mass attached to aquatic vegetation. The vitellus is black above, white below, and is about 1.6 mm. in diameter. It is surrounded by 2 envelopes. The incubation period varies with the temperature of the water. Dr. Oliver tells us that at a constant temperature of 68° F., the eggs will hatch in 4 days. But in nature we are more apt to find that the eggs have a longer incubation period, especially in the North. It usually ranges from 2 weeks to a month.

The mature tadpole has a brownish body with translucent tail crests finely speckled with black. The belly is an iridescent cream color, with the intestine showing through the skin. The tadpole attains a mature size of about 3¼ inches before transforming, after a larval stage of 2 to 2½ months.

Thousands of Leopard froglets may be found basking on the shores of their natal ponds in July and August. In all probability you will not even notice them until you approach closely and hear the splashes as they jump into the water. By all means catch one so that you can look at it closely. Note the long slender body and legs with very narrow waist. See the pointed snout. The feet are only partially webbed. These features indicate that it is a land frog of extreme agility. The ground color of the upper parts is light tan, or greenish, depending on the individual. The white-outlined dark-brown spots stand out clearly against the lighter background on a warm day early in July. It is hard to believe that this frog is so difficult to see in his natural surroundings.

We do not know how long he stays near the banks of the pond where he was born. Unfortunately, we do not live near enough to a pond where Leopard Frogs breed in great profusion to be able to make the daily observations necessary to establish this. It is not too long, but whether "too long" means several days or several weeks we cannot say. Be that as it may, during the latter part of July and throughout August and most of September we begin to find the current year's crop of Leopard Frogs hopping around the field and the untrimmed edges of the lawn.

We rarely if ever spot this small creature before it spots us and jumps to elude us. Its hop is long and low, and generally it jumps three or four times, each jump being in a slightly different direction. Of all our frogs, the Leopard Frog is the longest jumper in terms of distance jumped. Its prodigious leaps exceed even those of the Green Frog, and Dr. Oliver tells us that a leap of a little over 44 inches has been recorded for this frog.

The Leopard Frog is a frog of grasslands, preferring the damper parts. You are not likely to find him jumping around in a cornfield or wheatfield. He prefers pasture lands, and the moister parts of them at that. You may find him among your untrimmed lawn borders, or, in the early morning, when the grass is dew-drenched, even out on the lawn itself.

As the Leopard Frogs grow to the adult size of from 2 to 4 inches, they are more wary and stick to the longer grass. We do not find adults with anything like the frequency that we find the young.

As the temperatures begin getting colder in the fall, the Leopard Frogs head for the ponds to hibernate. In the warm days of fall, they may be seen swimming about, but as the water grows colder they remain on the bottom and finally dig into the detritus to spend the winter. They must dig deep enough so that the body temperature does not fall below 31° F. Below this, the Leopard Frog will die, for the coordinating centers of the nervous system cannot function.

How does the Leopard Frog fare in hot weather? Can he, being a dry-land frog, withstand great heat? Surprisingly enough, we find that he cannot. The maximum temperature he can survive internally is only a fraction over 64° F. This helps to explain why we occasionally find desiccated Leopard Frogs on the roads or on a plowed field in summer. They got too hot while crossing it, and died. This also explains why the Leopard Frog prefers long grass and moist spots.

Twin brother to the Leopard Frog is the Pickerel Frog, *Rana palustris,* found in the eastern half of this country as far west as Texas. It is absent from Florida and the southern portions of South Carolina, Georgia, Alabama, Mississippi, and Louisiana.

Like the Leopard Frog, the Pickerel Frog is a spotted frog. However, its spots are squarish with dark borders, arranged regularly in two rows between the dorsolateral folds with an occasional third spot in between. The sides are also regularly spotted. The underparts are white except for the undersurfaces of the hind legs and groin, which are orange or dark yellow. Probably the most outstanding characteristic of this frog is its odor, which once smelled is unmistakable. Unfortunately, the young are more difficult to separate from young Leopard Frogs. The undersides of the young Pickerel Frog's legs are not orange, but yellow or flesh-colored, and the acrid Pickerel Frog odor is not present. To add to the confusion, the spots of young Leopard Frogs are not always light-bordered. But with a little practice, one can usually tell the difference by the way in which the spots are arranged. These, regularly arranged in rows in the Pickerel Frog, cover a larger area than do the spots of the Leopard Frog, in which there is a greater proportion of ground color. The Pickerel Frog nearly always has a ground color of tan or brown, and rarely if ever exhibits the green color sometimes found in Leopard Frogs.

The skin secretions of the Pickerel Frog produce the animal's characteristic odor. They are extremely toxic to other animals—even to amphibians of a different species. But we shall discuss the protective properties of this frog's skin secretions in the chapter on defense. What we should like to ask here is why the young do not have the adult odor. Is it because their skin secretions are not toxic? No, it is not. We have seen a very hungry Garter Snake mouth a

The Pickerel Frog,
Rana palustris

young Pickerel Frog but refuse to eat it. However, from the snake's behavior, we believe that the skin secretions of the young are not so potent as those of the fully matured adult. Though the snake refused to eat this frog, it did repeatedly bite it, and showed no sign of discomfort after doing so. This is not the case when a snake makes a mistake and seizes an adult Pickerel Frog.

The Pickerel Frog is a slightly smaller frog than the Leopard Frog, being between 2 and 3 inches long at maturity. It emerges from its hibernating retreat in the pond a little later than the preceeding species, and begins breeding when the water temperature is 57° F. or above. Unlike the Leopard Frog, it has no large external vocal sacs and its snoring call produces only a small swelling between the ear and arm on the sides of the head. The males are equipped with the enlarged thumb pads of most ranids.

The eggs are brown above, yellow below, and are a fraction of a millimeter smaller than those of the Leopard Frog. The total complement of 2,000 to 3,000 is laid in a mass of jelly, attached to submerged vegetation in shallow water. After an incubation period a little longer than that of the Leopard Frog, the Pickerel Frog eggs hatch.

The mature tadpole is about 3 inches in length, with a cream-colored iridescent belly. The intestines are visible through the skin. The tail crests are not transparent and are heavily washed or blotched with purple or black. After a larval period of between 2½ and 3 months, the tadpoles transform into small Pickerel Frogs about an inch long. These little fellows are even more beautiful than the Leopard Frogs. You will find, if you examine them closely, that all of them have a very metallic luster, making their ground color appear bronze, gold, or copper, depending on the light. These frogs are living gems; few people who have ever seen one closely would dispute it.

Just as the Leopard Frog is hard to see against a natural background of grass, so too is the Pickerel Frog. The photograph showing this camouflage (page 231) was taken on the lawn. If the subject had been posed in meadow grass, you would have seen nothing but grass in the picture.

The Pickerel Frog seems to head for its hibernation pond fairly late in the fall, and not before the first frost. We have found them on land as late as October 6th, though at this time of year they are easier to find in the river, where many of them probably hibernate, even though it is too swift a stream in which to breed in the spring. However, the ones we find there are immature adults, never full-grown frogs. Is this because the adults prefer the quieter ponds, or is it merely that we do not see them because they are more secretive than the young?

The North American continent is not the only continent where spotted meadow frogs are found. In Africa there is the Spotted Grass Frog, *Rana grayi,* who resembles our Leopard Frog in markings and our Green Frog in body build. This frog has a very unusual habit that makes it worthy of brief mention. Though it often lays in water in the manner of most Ranidae (all except one other), it also sometimes lays its large eggs in depressions in the earth near a pond. The outer egg capsule is clear, hard, and glassy so that no dirt adheres to it. The eggs may be washed into the water by rains and may hatch there, or they may hatch on land. In the latter case, the tadpoles wriggle the short distance necessary to reach the water. Dr. Rose, who gives us these interesting facts about *Rana grayi,* wonders whether there may not be two subspecies of this frog— one that lays on land and one that does not. Or is *Rana grayi* one species with individuals laying on land or in the water, depending on weather conditions or other external factors? As yet, no taxonomist has gathered enough specimens of this frog to determine whether or not it should be split into two subspecies.

The Marbled Salamander, *Ambystoma opacum,* belongs to the Mole Salamander family. Its breeding habits, however, are quite different from those of all the other members of the family. This salamander is found in the eastern part of the country as far west as Texas and as far north as Connecticut. It is absent from the southern part of Florida.

Its habitat is much drier than that preferred by most ambystomids. It is found on sandy or gravelly hillsides. There is one spot near our home that should be ideal for the Marbled Salamander, but we have never succeeded in finding one. Since we live in the northerly portions of its range, they are, we feel sure, not at all common here. Although herpetologists tell us that they are less moisture-loving than many others of the family, it seems probable that they are quite secretive, as are so many other Mole Salamanders.

The Marbled Salamander is stout-bodied with a blunt snout. It is among the smaller members of the family, being only about 3 to 4 inches in length. The ground color is black, dark brown, or dark gray, with the belly of a little lighter hue. This dark ground color is interrupted by bands of white or light gray. In some individuals the bands are narrow. In others, they are so extensive that the creature appears to be white with a series of large black blotches down the center of the back. (See illustration, page 34.)

The males may be distinguished from the females by their smaller size, protuberant vent, and by their coloring. The male's bands are white, while those of the female are gray. Dr. Bishop's handbook gives us, among others, three photographs of adult Marbled Salamanders. Two of these are females with narrow gray bands. The remaining photograph is that of a male who appears white with black blotches. Naturally, one cannot draw any conclusions at all from only three photographs. But it did occur to us to wonder whether perhaps all males may not be more extensively marked with white than the females. To prove this, however, would require extensive collecting of both sexes throughout the range area. Possibly there is nothing at all that would warrant such investigation.

Unlike other ambystomids, the Marbled Salamander breeds in the fall, from September to December, depending on the temperature. Naturally, it breeds earlier in the North, later in the South. The courtship is on land. The eggs, between 50 and 225 in number, are pigmented. The 2.7 mm. vitellus is surrounded by 2 envelopes. These eggs are deposited singly in a depression on the ground, under leaves, bark, stones, and so on. The spot chosen is one that is likely to be flooded by fall rains, and therefore it must be very close to the pond. The female remains with the eggs, but for just how long has not been determined. If the rains come soon after laying, and flood the eggs, she leaves them. But suppose a month or two elapses before the rains come? Will she stay with her eggs all that time? What *is* the maximum length of time that this species will brood? The eggs themselves have a very variable incubation period of from 13 to 207 days, according to Dr. Oliver. This is necessary, of course, for eggs whose hatching is dependent on rain to wash them into the water or flood them. They are evidently unable to hatch on land.

After an aquatic larval period of 5 to 6 months, they transform, and leave the water. At this stage they are from 2½ to 3 inches in size, dark brown or black with light specks liberally sprinkled over the ground color. We do not know how soon they develop their adult marbling. As a matter of fact, the precise number of days or weeks necessary for any species of newly transformed amphibian to attain mature adult coloration is known for very few species.

The Giant Toad, *Bufo marinus,* was for some years considered to be the largest toad in the world. It still ranks among the biggest, for specimens of 9 inches have been found in British Guiana. This very large animal never attains such an immense size in this country —7 inches is its maximum growth here. It is found in a very small section of southwestern Texas in Zapata, Starr, and Hidalgo counties along the Rio Grande. Recently, it has become established in southern Florida also. It becomes more common and larger in Mexico and South America.

The Giant Toad is found around houses, gardens, fields, and water tanks. During the day they generally hide under logs and rocks or in shallow burrows. In color, this toad is brown, reddish, green, or black on the dorsum, with enormous triangular pitted parotoid glands. Underneath, it is a pale yellow or dirty white. Its voice is described as a low trill; when they are singing in chorus in the tropics the noise is evidently deafening.

Depending upon where it lives, the Giant Toad breeds at different seasons. The Wrights tell us that they breed from February to July in Bermuda, in Trinidad from August to October, and in British Guiana possibly the year round except for February and October. In certain areas this toad may lay twice a year, though this has never been proved as a definite fact, nor do we know in what regions it may breed biannually. In the United States the breeding season depends upon rains, and the Giant Toad may breed any time between March and September.

Like most toads, *Bufo marinus* lays its eggs in strings of jelly, but I have never been able to find a description of the size of the vitellus, number of envelopes, or the total complement. The eggs may hatch in less than 3 days. The tadpoles resemble those of the American Toad, and transform after a larval period of about 1½ months. Most amphibians cannot tolerate salt water. The eggs and tadpoles of the Giant Toad, however, actually develop faster, with a lower mortality rate, in slightly saline water (15 per cent salt water). We shall have much more to tell about the Giant Toad in later chapters

Above: The American Toad, *Bufo americanus americanus*
Right: The American Toad from the rear

when we examine the subjects of defense and economic importance.

Another dweller of plowed fields and gardens is the American Toad, *Bufo americanus americanus,* found throughout most of the eastern half of the United States. In Florida and parts of North Carolina, South Carolina, Georgia, Alabama, and Mississippi, it is replaced by the Southern Toad, *Bufo terrestris,* of similar appearance and habits. Within its range, the American Toad is likely to be confused only with Fowler's Toad, *Bufo woodhousei fowleri.* Differentiation between the American Toad and Fowler's Toad is not always easy because the two sometimes hybridize, and the offspring thus show some of the characteristics of both species.

Typically, the American Toad has a short, very broad body, and measures from 2 to 4 inches in length. Fowler's Toad is shorter—

The sole of the foot of the American Toad. Notice the large black outer-sole tubercle and the smaller inner-sole tubercle.

from 2 to 3 inches—and is more slender in body build, with longer legs. Both are some shade of brown, reddish, drab olive, or gray above. This ground color is punctuated by dark spots. In the American Toad, there are only one or two *large* warts in each of the dark spots. In Fowler's Toad three or more warts are enclosed by the dark spots. The belly of the American Toad is dirty white with scattered dark spots. That of Fowler's Toad is of the same color with but one black spot on the chest.

The two species of toads are also differentiated by structural differences. The most outstanding are in the shape of the parotoid glands and in the cranial crests or ridges on the head. These crests are not folds of skin but are made by bony ridges of the head underneath the skin. If you look at the diagram of the toad (page 7) and the photograph of the toad's back (page 150), you will notice that in both, the parotoid glands are kidney-shaped. This is a characteristic of the American Toad. The parotoids of Fowler's Toad are oval. Look at the photograph and diagram again. Notice the two ridges between the eyes, known as the supraorbital or interorbital crests; the ridges in back of each eye, known as the postorbital crests; and (in the photograph only) the short ridges that join the postorbital crests to the parotoid glands. These last are known as the preparotoid longitudinal crests. In the American Toad the postorbital crest is either separated from the parotoid gland, as in the diagram, or connected to it by a preparotoid longitudinal crest, as in the photograph. In Fowler's Toad, however, there is no preparotoid longitudinal crest, and the postorbital crest touches the parotoid gland horizontally.

And while we are talking about identification by crests, we might add that the supraorbital crests of the Southern Toad are thickened and clublike where they end at the back of the head.

The cranial crests of toads provide a valuable means of identification of many species of toads, which is the reason we discussed these rather technical details here. They are of value, however, mostly in adult identification, for immature toads do not always show the clear crest development manifested in the adults.

The American Toad emerges from hibernation in March, April, or May, depending on the temperature. It breeds later than the Wood, Leopard, and Pickerel Frogs, for, unlike them, it breeds in temporary rain puddles or in very shallow water. Sometimes, the eggs are ruined by freezing, but generally the toad does not start breeding until the danger of freezing water is past.

The song of the toad is a high musical trill. It is of almost unbelievable sweetness, whether heard close at hand or from a distance, in chorus or solo. The breeding male seems slim and alert—quite unlike his fat, dusty midsummer self. As he sits in or on the edge of his puddle, he takes air into his mouth and forces it into his vocal sacs. Pushing himself very erect with his forelegs, his throat expands so that it forms a grayish white bubble, flecked with charcoal-gray. The sweet trill emerges. At the end of the call, as the bubble reduces, the male toad looks amazingly like a child drawing a large bubble of bubble gum into his mouth. I have never heard toads trilling in the morning. But they are often heard from noon far into the night in humid or rainy warm weather.

Male toads, at the height of the breeding season, are very eager. They quite frequently grab rocks or other males in their anxiety to find a mate. When a male is grasped by another male, he struggles and gives a series of soft rapid chirps. This is generally sufficient to inform the other male that he has made a mistake. The more alert the male, the better his chances of securing a mate are, for Dr. Oliver tells us that it has been found that males far outnumber the females at the breeding ponds. We wonder whether there is a reasonably constant ratio of this imbalance between the sexes. In our mudhole we found the ratio of males to females to be about 5 to 1. But since the mudhole is artificial and not an ideal breeding habitat anyway, we cannot assume that this ratio would hold true in other, more natural breeding ponds.

Male American Toad singing

Sooner or later a large female, swollen with unlaid eggs, will approach and nudge a singing male. Instantly he embraces her, and the pair are ready to begin to lay the eggs. The female finds a spot to her liking. The male lowers his legs so that they are between the female's and places his feet on or near her anus. Not until his feet are in this position will the female express any eggs. If you watch the breeding pair closely, you can see one side of the female's body expand, contract, and return to normal position, followed by the same movements on the opposite side. As these contractions occur, the eggs are expelled in two strings of jelly. The male contracts his stomach, and you can see him jerk slightly as he forces out his sperm to fertilize the emerging eggs. After a few eggs are expelled, the couple surface to breathe (the two strings of jelly trailing from the female's cloaca), and one can see their nostrils rapidly "blick" open and shut. Then they submerge and more of the

American Toads in amplexus laying. Note the paired dark strings of eggs. At this stage the jelly is almost colorless, and has not yet swelled.

eggs are laid. As the eggs emerge, they look like black-and-gray beads.

If one returns to look at the eggs an hour or so after the pair has finished laying and separated, one will find that the eggs in their inner compartments have turned and are now so oriented that the black part is facing up, the grayish-white side down. The jelly has swelled and shows clearly. The strings lie partially coiled, twined over and through vegetation and on the pond bottom. The eggs themselves are very small, with a vitellus measuring between 1 and 1.4 mm. The total complement may be as high as 20,000 or as low as 4,000. In a day or two the coils have straightened, and the egg mass is difficult to see, so discolored is it by the mud of the pond.

In 3 to 12 days, the eggs are all hatched, and the tiny black tadpole begins his life in the puddle. But whether in the puddle or in the home aquarium, the toad tadpole is a cute little morsel. His upper parts are a velvety black—though close examination in a strong light may show that some tadpoles are not quite so black as they first seemed, but are a very dark brown instead, with tiny flecks of greenish bronze. The tail crests are a translucent milky white, and the tail itself is rather short with a rounded tip. When viewed from above, the body is vaguely triangular in outline—the tip of the triangle being the snout, with the base just above the tail insertion.

The behavior of toad tadpoles is quite different from that of most frog tadpoles. They are extremely gregarious, and group together in bunches. We do not notice this in the aquarium, but in the puddle it is a quite frequent occurrence. Why do they swarm in this manner? Do toad tadpoles do so naturally? I don't think the latter is true, for we have never seen this swarming together in the aquarium. In captivity, the little fellows rise to the surface and swim round and round the bowl with rapid lashings of their small tails. We do not see swarming so frequently in larger ponds where ample room for development exists and where the tadpoles need not fear desiccation because of water evaporation. It has been suggested by herpetologists that this swarming of toad tadpoles may in some way hasten transformation. It is an interesting theory, but there is no proof that it is true (and none that it isn't).

The larval period in nature is a little less than 2 months. In the home aquarium, at an average room temperature of from 68° F. to 70° F., we find the larval period to be 34 to 40 days. This short tadpole stage makes these tadpoles ideal specimens for children to observe. In those species of amphibians that have a larval period of 2 to 3 months, the changes are slower and the children's interest is apt to fade away before the final transformation occurs. But with toad tadpoles changes occur rapidly, and thus the imagination and enthusiasm remain to the end.

The newly hatched toadlet is tiny—often less than ¼ inch long. He is no larger than a fly, and far more engaging. Now that he has assumed his adult form, he is a dusty dark-brown color, with fine stipplings of bronze still remaining. For a while this tiny fellow will stay near the water, but as the days pass he will become increasingly a dry-land creature. A week or two after transformation, the toadlets may be found hopping all over the lawn and fields. But you need watchful eyes to see them, so well do they blend in with their surroundings and so small are they. Unlike the adults, the toadlets are markedly diurnal. If a warm rain occurs soon after transformation, you may be fortunate enough to see a mass migration away from the natal ponds and puddles. Thousands of little toadlets may be seen at this time, and this is undoubtedly where the ancients got the idea that toads were rained down from the sky.

We see more adult toads during the months of July and August than at any other time of the year. They have taken up their summer residence in and around our lawns and gardens. Though they hide by day under rocks and logs or in the earth, we can see them in the evenings or at night. According to Dr. Oliver, their nonbreeding home range rarely exceeds an area 100 feet square. Where ideal conditions exist, it may be much less. The adult toad in the photographs (pages 150, 151) is a dear friend of ours. She lives in one of our puppy yards, where she is not annoyed by our cats and the dogs —even the puppies pay little attention to her. By day she sleeps under the puppies' bench, and is always at home when a photographic model is needed. By night she can be found abroad in the puppies' yard—an area 20 by 15 feet. We saw her nearly every evening last summer, and have never found her in any of the adjacent yards. Will she be there next summer, or will she change her residence? We can hardly wait to find out if she will return to us and her home range after breeding next spring.

Toads, unlike many amphibians, do not depend solely on lowered temperatures to start hibernating. Our toad disappeared on September 8th, exactly ten days before the first frost occurred. This was not unusual, for toads usually do burrow in before the first frost. How much before it? Is our observation of ten days an average figure? How can a toad "know" that frost is soon coming? Do the shortening days and lengthening nights inform it that it is time to dig in for the winter? We do not know much about the factors that may influence hibernation time, but undoubtedly it will be found that in many species hibernation is caused by a number of complex, interrelated phenomena.

We like all amphibians for their own unique qualities, but we must admit that of them all we are fondest of the toad. How it is that this gentle, placid creature with a jewel of an eye is regarded by many as the personification of ugliness we shall never be able to understand. Of all our amphibians, the toad is the easiest for most people to observe, for he is of moderate size and spends much of his active life in and around gardens. Perhaps you too will come to love this quiet, useful animal if you get to know the individuals around your home.

CHAPTER 12

The Burrowers

As we have seen, many amphibians spend a good part of their lives hiding, either in the water under the detritus, or on land under leaves, rocks, or logs. Others, such as many of the toads, dig shallow burrows in the earth, hiding there by day or in periods of extreme heat and aridity. But there are some amphibians who spend almost their entire lives underneath the ground, emerging only for breeding or at night during a rainstorm. As one might expect, some fossorial species are more secretive and subterranean in habit than others. And since we find burrowers in many different families, the adaptations that enable these species to lead a subterranean existence vary considerably.

Before we discuss these adaptations, we must first examine the methods employed by the fossorial amphibians to dig their burrows. One might suppose that they would dig in headfirst, but such is not always the case. The salamanders invariably tunnel in the earth headfirst, but so far as we know now, only two of the Salientia do so. The first exception is, curiously enough, not a burrower at all but an aquatic frog, *Xenopus laevis*, closely related to *Pipa pipa*. We shall discuss Xenopus more fully in Chapter 20. The second headfirst burrower is *Hemisus marmoratum* and others of the genus found in Africa. Other subterranean Salientia dig their burrows with their hind feet, tunneling in backward. Though this seems like

158

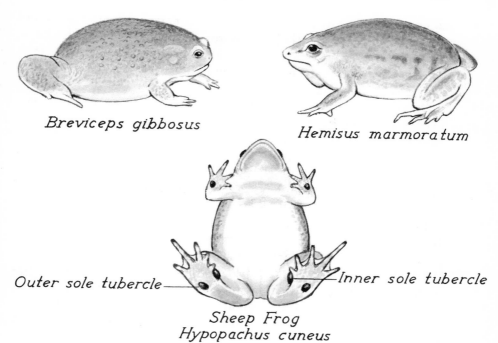

Breviceps gibbosus

Hemisus marmoratum

Outer sole tubercle

Inner sole tubercle

Sheep Frog
Hypopachus cuneus

**Adaptations for burrowing, showing differences in head shape and body form
and development of sole tubercles**

an awkward and inefficient method to a human, actually it is the
sensible way for a frog. We must remember that the hind legs of all
Salientia are powerful, while the forelegs are weak and serve mostly
as a support for the front part of the body. But though most Salientia
burrow in backward, it may be that further study of fossorial species
will reveal that there are a few others with pointed snouts, like
Hemisus, who burrow in headfirst.

Adaptations for a subterranean life are many, and we find them in
the body form, the eyes, and other sensory organs, the mouth, the
skin, and even in breeding habits. The body form of burrowing
amphibians seems to be either one of two types. Most of the fossorial salamanders belong to the family Ambystomidae. These salamanders have a stout body with a blunt head. Many of the burrowing toads also have a stout body, almost as broad as it is long, with
a blunt snout and a flat head. At the opposite extreme, we find that

some of the Narrow-mouth Toads have a narrow pointed head and a wide waist, giving their possessors a rather wedgelike shape. Hemisus is of this type, as are our native Narrow-mouths. It is among this group that we may expect to find others, such as Hemisus, who may be headfirst burrowers.

One of the more curious habits of many burrowers is their practice of inflating their bodies when in their tunnels. Many of the Salientia, such as the Spadefoots, the Asian Kaloula, and the African Breviceps, commonly inflate their bodies with air while in their burrows, and even out of them when threatened. The latter practice is surely a good defense, for an inflated round toad body is difficult to grasp and hard for reptilian enemies to swallow.

But does body inflation inside the burrow also serve as defense? It may make the animal more difficult to withdraw and may also prevent visitors to the burrow. But is this its primary function? Or is the body inflation merely a type of innate behavior known as thigmotropism? Thigmotropism means that an animal tends to place its body in situations where as great a surface as possible will be in contact with some solid object. Perhaps defense is only an adjunct to this inborn reaction.

There is an Australian burrower, known as *Chiroleptes*, which inflates its body not with air but with water. This amphibian has the ability to absorb water with extreme rapidity and to such a degree that it becomes as round as a ball. This amphibian camel can utilize this stored water in periods of drought.

As with body form, we find two types of eyes in the burrowers. The Spadefoot Toads have large bulging eyes with vertical pupils, while many of the Narrow-mouth Toads have small beadlike eyes. The African genus *Breviceps* has large bulging eyes, but we find that the eye placement diverges from the norm. Whereas the eyes of most frogs and toads are so placed that they gaze sideways and/or upward, the eyes of Breviceps gaze forward, and in one species, *Breviceps rosei*, the gaze is directed down. The forward placement of the eyes is of definite value, since side vision is useless within the narrow confines of the burrow.

At least one amphibian is equipped with sensory papillae. This is *Rhombophryne testudo*, found only on the island of Madagascar. These papillae, which are found on the face, are analogous to the mammalian shrew's long whiskers and the curious proboscis of the

Star-nosed Mole. They serve as sensory receptors in the darkness of the burrow.

The mouth too has become modified in many Narrow-mouths. Because the diet of many of these fossorial amphibians consists mainly of ants, termites, and other small burrowing insects, they have no use for the very wide typical frog mouth, any more than an anteater needs the wide mouth of a hyena. Therefore, the mouth of many Brevicipitidae is markedly smaller than the mouth of most other amphibians.

Modifications for a fossorial life have also been made in the skin. Most burrowers have relatively smooth skins—not usually quite so smooth as those of aquatic frogs, but much less warty and granular than most toads. Furthermore, the skin on the head and back of many burrowing toads is permeated with a secondary deposit of bone, and this skin adheres to the bones of the skull. This is true of all the Spadefoot Toads, as well as others.

Bufo empusus, a Cuban toad, has this modification to an extreme degree. What possible use is this bony head to him, since he tunnels in feet first? It serves as a door to his home, blocking it effectively from all comers. Our native Spadefoots do the same thing, and we shall examine the curious posture that these animals assume in their burrows a little later. This bony deposit in the skin is not confined to burrowing amphibians alone. Why other amphibians should possess a bony head is hard to imagine, for so far as is known they have no possible use for it.

But of all the modifications for a fossorial existence the most useful is the development of the spades. If you look at the bottom of the hind foot of a toad (see the photograph, page 151), you will notice two tubercles on the sole of the foot. In most of the burrowers, one or both of these tubercles are greatly enlarged, depending on the species, and the skin has become hardened or cornified. The outer margins of these tubercles are formed into sharp cutting edges.

The Mexican burrowing toad, *Rhinophrynus dorsalis,* not only has these spades but the first toe has only one segment, and this is shovel-like in shape. This small fossorial toad is pink and brown in color, which makes it appear sickly. It is unusual also in that it is completely toothless, and its tongue is similar to the mammalian tongue in regard to its method of protrusion.

Adaptations in breeding habits are not especially striking in our native burrowers. It is true that many of them have an extended breeding period enabling them to delay egg laying until suitable weather occurs. Suitable weather for the burrowers is generally a warm rainy night. With many species, the mating and egg laying occur in a single night, and after it is over the animals retire to their burrows to be only rarely seen for another year. Others, living in places where heavy rains occur more frequently, may extend the breeding season to several different favorable nights.

If we wish to find really striking modifications in the breeding habits of the burrowers, we must go to Africa, where we shall find two different adaptations.

We mentioned the headfirst burrower, Hemisus, earlier. The female excavates a nest underground in the bank of a pool. In it she lays her eggs and broods them. When the eggs hatch, she digs a tunnel from the nest to the pool, and the hatchling tadpoles wriggle their way down the passageway into the pool and complete their development there. You may wonder what would happen if the female had trouble digging the tunnel. Nothing at all would happen; the female has plenty of time for her excavations, for Dr. Rose has found that the tadpoles of at least one species, *Hemisus marmoratum*, can live for eighteen days out of water.

Other unusual breeders are members of the genus *Breviceps*. Breviceps presents the opposite extreme in body form to Hemisus, for it is as broad as it is long, and the body is usually kept well inflated with air. The front of the face is very flat, and there is no snout to speak of. Many toads are poor swimmers, but Breviceps is unable to swim at all, and never enters the water voluntarily. When placed in a pool by Dr. Rose, the subject of the experiment swelled himself up and just floated on the water, making little or no attempt to swim.

It becomes obvious from the above that Breviceps is a dry-land layer. This is a great advantage, for some species live in situations where the distance to the nearest water is fifty miles or more. Though the life cycles of only two species of the genus *Breviceps, Breviceps gibbosus* and *Breviceps parvus,* are known, it is probable that others of the genus have life cycles similar to theirs. *Breviceps gibbosus* lays 30 large eggs in a burrow about a foot below the surface. These eggs are attended by both parents, and when they hatch, fully transformed little Breviceps emerge. The entire tadpole stage is carried on inside the egg capsule. The length of time between laying and hatching is not yet known. Dr. Rose feels that the eggs of Breviceps may not develop and hatch when exposed to sunlight. It is also unlikely that they would develop if submerged in water, for land-laid eggs very often will not.

Now that we have examined the adaptations that make life underground possible, we shall describe the lives of some of our native burrowers.

Our first example of a burrower is the Eastern Spadefoot, *Scaphiopus holbrooki holbrooki*, found along the Atlantic coast from Massachusetts to South Carolina, throughout most of Georgia, Florida, Alabama, Mississippi, and Louisiana, parts of Arkansas, Tennessee, Kentucky, and the lower tips of Ohio, Indiana, Illinois, and Missouri. The Eastern Spadefoot ranges in size from 2 to 2¾ inches when adult, and has a stout body similar to that of the American Toad. Its skin is fairly smooth, but there are small warts scattered over the surface. The parotoid glands are round; the tympanum is distinct and smaller than the eye. The bulging eyes have a vertical pupil. The hind feet are large, fully webbed, and the inner-sole tubercle is well developed into a black horny spade. There is also a black horny cap covering the tip of the first toe. No outer-sole tubercle is present.

The Eastern Spadefoot is brown or greenish-brown in color on the back. Usually there are two yellow lines starting at the middle of each eye and curving down and in toward each other, then flaring out and curving in once more and meeting just above the insertion of the hind legs. These lines look like two parenthesis marks facing the wrong way and two parenthesis marks facing the right way and joined by a parenthesis mark at the bottom. There are also yellow squiggles along the upper jaws and lower sides and back. The underparts of the hind legs and lower venter are grayish; the underparts of the forelegs and upper venter and throat are white. Males may be distinguished from the females by their broader fingers, the first three of which have dark horny excrescences on them. In addition, the markings of the males are usually of a more vivid hue than those the females.

The voice of the male is low-pitched, very nasal, and is similar to the noise made by young crows. This sound may be approximated if one holds one's nose and says "aaanh" with the accent on the *a* and without pronouncing the *n*. The males usually call when lying on the surface of the water, but there are instances when underground calling has been heard. The vocal sacs swell to form an enormous glistening white throat bubble.

The Eastern Spadefoot generally migrates to the breeding ponds at night during a heavy rain. It has been found that a lowering of the atmospheric pressure is a necessary stimulus in laying. In order to get a spadefoot to lay in the laboratory, the animal must not only be sprinkled with water; she must also be in a special cage where the pressure can be lowered. Water alone will not persuade her to lay.

Usually, the breeding activities are over within a day or two at the most. But there may be successive waves of breeders, especially in the warmer portions of its range. Mrs. Goin mentions one year in which the Eastern Spadefoots mated in April and again in August. Furthermore, apparently there are years when it does not breed at all. What determines whether the spadefoot will or will not breed? Are favorable weather conditions the prime factor? And if so, just what temperature of water, earth, and air and what humidity level and pressure readings constitute favorable weather for this burrower? Or do breeding years go in cycles governed by sunspots or other such phenomena? No one knows, but finding out will be difficult and rewarding. For, as we must emphasize, the breeding season is limited to one or two evenings once or twice a year during weather that the toads like but humans don't.

The Eastern Spadefoot chooses temporary pools in which to lay, just as the American Toad does. The male spadefoot grasps the female inguinally rather than pectorally. The eggs are deposited in short strings less than 12 inches in length—they may be as short as 1 inch—along the stems of water plants. The vitellus is approximately 1.5 to 2 mm. in diameter, and is surrounded by 1 envelope. The entire egg complement in all bands deposited by one female is a little over 2,000—not a very large number for a temporary pool layer. However, the short incubation period of 2 days or less helps to compensate for this, as does a relatively short larval period of from 2 to 8 weeks.

The tadpoles are small—about an inch in total length when mature. They are dark and of an iridescent bronze sheen. The spiracle is on the left side, and the anus opens in the middle of the tail

Eastern Spadefoot Toad
Scaphiopus holbrookii

Eastern Narrow-mouth Toad
Microhyla carolinensis

Tiger Salamander
Ambystoma tigrinum

Some of the burrowers

crest, not to one side of it. The tail crests are transparent, and the tip is well rounded.

The newly transformed spadefoot is ½ inch long or less. These little fellows, like the newly transformed toads, evidently do not start to burrow until they have become larger. At just what size or what age do they begin to lead a subterranean existence? Mrs. Goin states that for two months after transformation she found them in her yard during the day. For ten months after that she found them almost every night. On the basis of her observations, then, we may say that the young ones do not burrow for two months, and for ten months after that, burrows are excavated but not occupied at night. However, this is only an observation at one particular locality in

Florida. Would the conclusions hold good in exceptionally dry years or very wet ones, or for spadefoots found in the colder climates of the North? We do not know.

We know even less of the adult life of the Eastern Spadefoot than of the less fossorial young. Many authorities state that the adults are found only during the breeding season or occasionally at night during periods of heavy rain. Mrs. Goin, however, has found them on dry nights in the summer also. Are they perhaps more common in the more southerly portions of their range? Possibly, not only because of warmer temperatures but also because of higher humidity.

The burrow of the Eastern Spadefoot is an unbranched tunnel slanting downward. Its depth varies, and depends, I imagine, upon the temperature and humidity of air and soil. These tunnels may be from 5 to 10 inches long or they may be much deeper, for spadefoots have been found 3 feet beneath the surface. There is little to indicate the entrance of a burrow when its occupant is inside, for as the animal burrows down, the earth at the mouth falls in, blocking the doorway.

The position of the Eastern Spadefoot within the burrow is best described as a crouching one. The legs are well drawn up under the body, the head is bowed, and the "chin" rests on the forefeet. This means, of course, that in a slanting tunnel the bony top of the head blocks the mouth of the tunnel. Perhaps it not only helps to protect the spadefoot but also serves as a cork, preventing dirt from falling in and around the nostrils of the sleeping animal.

The form of the burrow would seem to indicate that perhaps the Eastern Spadefoot is abroad more than we realize. Their homes are not like the subterranean dwellings of the mole where long tunnels radiate out in many directions from the central dwelling chamber. Therefore, unless it be found that the spadefoot leads a more or less vegetative existence, emerging only to breed and sleeping in its burrow the rest of the time, he must emerge from his tunnel in order to eat. For it seems unlikely that there would be enough worms, ants, and termites within the narrow confines of the shallow burrow to keep an adult spadefoot well fed. Undoubtedly he is secretive, and not frequently seen even at night. But I do not believe that we can assume that he seldom leaves his burrow. Intensive study of this animal may well reveal, as Mrs. Goin's observations seem to indicate, that the spadefoot comes out to feed oftener than was formerly believed.

Couch's Spadefoot, *Scaphiopus couchi*, is a southwestern species and is found in the western part of Texas, the southern part of New Mexico, Arizona, Lower California, and along the Mexican border. Its skin is rougher than that of the Eastern Spadefoot, and is covered with small warts. The parotoid glands are small, flat, and difficult to distinguish. The tympanum is also indistinct. Couch's Spadefoot is between 2 and 3 inches long, with the females slightly larger than the males. The animal is greenish on the back with bands or blotches of dull yellow. The tops of both fingers and toes are light. The underparts are white except for the rear of the belly around the vent and the undersurface of the hind legs, both of which are brownish-purple.

The females generally show a more distinct spotting, while the male coloring is muted. The males also have dark excrescences on the top of the fingers. While both sexes can make sounds, the male's voice is the more resonant. He alone possesses vocal sacs that expand into a throat bubble broader and less round than the one of the calling Eastern Spadefoot. The voice has been described as a gutteral *ye-ow*. During the breeding season, which extends from April to August, the males call to the females. They may sit on land while singing or they may lie stretched out on the surface of the water.

As with most Spadefoots, Couch's Spadefoot chooses temporary pools in which to lay its small black eggs. The eggs are enclosed in short bands of jelly and are surrounded by 1 jelly envelope. The complement ranges from 1,000 to 3,000. The development is rapid, as it must be, the eggs hatching in 1½ days. The tadpole may be fully transformed in as little as 15 days or as long as 40 days.

Several species of Spadefoots are found in the West. Most do not differ markedly from the species we have described. One, however, *Scaphiopus hammondi intermontanus*, found throughout Idaho, Nevada, the western three-quarters of Utah, and the eastern half of Oregon and Washington, must be mentioned briefly. This species is evidentally less fossorial than most Spadefoots, for a number of different observers have found them above ground not only at night but also during the day, even on dry days. The individuals thus observed were young—about a year old—but it is possible that even adults of this species are seen abroad in drier periods.

The Narrow-mouth Toads of the family Brevicipitidae are very small animals with a small mouth, narrow head, and a pointed snout. Unlike the burrowing spadefoots, their toes are either completely or almost completely free of web. On most of them you will find a fold of skin just behind the beadlike eyes. This skin fold looks much like the skin fold on a turtle's neck.

The Eastern Narrow-mouth, *Microhyla carolinensis carolinensis*, has the broadest distribution of all our native Narrow-mouth Toads. It is found along the Atlantic Coast from Virginia to South Carolina, throughout most of Georgia and Louisiana, all of Florida, Mississippi, Alabama, and Tennessee, the southern half of Kentucky and the eastern edge of Arkansas.

The Eastern Narrow-mouth is small, ¾ inch to 1 inch long, with the females slightly larger than the males. The head, with the skin fold back of the eyes, is small and pointed; the body is stout with a very wide waist. It is dark gray, brown, or black above, with two dark stripes slanting inward from the eyes back to the hind legs. The underparts are dark—although somewhat lighter than the back—and are heavily speckled with black. The skin is smooth and there is no tympanum or parotoid. The legs are short and stout, the arms slender. The fingers and toes are long, slender, and completely free of web. The foot has an inner-sole tubercle, but this is small and is not cornified.

The males are smaller than the females and have a darker throat. They breed during or after heavy rains from May through August. The male's call is a very nasal bleat, much like the sound a young lamb or kid makes. The vocal sacs swell out to a throat bubble similar to that of the American Toad. Usually the males sing while in the water; the front part of the body is supported by the hands on vegetation or rocks at the pond's edge.

They choose temporary puddles and shallow water in which to lay their small black eggs. These are deposited in surface masses of from 10 to 100 eggs, the total complement being around nine hundred or less. The egg itself is about 1 mm. in size, with 1 very distinct jelly envelope.

The Eastern Narrow-mouth tadpole is black above with very fine gray speckles. Underneath, it is whitish with yellow blotches. The body is wide, and much flatter than the ordinary tadpole body. The spiracle is very near the anus on the venter. The tadpole mouth has no labial teeth, no warts or papillae, and no horny beak. It is quite unlike almost all other tadpole mouths. The tadpoles transform after a larval period which may be as short as 3 weeks or may extend to 2 months, at a body size of ½ inch or less.

So far as we can ascertain, the Eastern Narrow-mouth does not seem to burrow very much, and hides under logs, boards, rocks, debris, leaves, or other similar cover, usually in moist situations. When one goes hunting for them, one needs to be alert, for despite the fat body and short legs, the Eastern Narrow-mouth is an agile little fellow, quick to jump away and hide when disturbed. They are generally found in the open only at night during periods of heavy rainfall. Even when they are breeding, they usually hide among vegetation at the water's edge.

The Great Plains Narrow-mouth, *Microhyla carolinensis olivacea*, is similar to the Eastern Narrow-mouth, and is found throughout most of Nebraska, Oklahoma, and Texas.

In the southern tip of Texas and down into Mexico is another Narrow-mouth, the Sheep Frog, *Hypopachus cuneus cuneus*. This species is a little larger than the Eastern Narrow-mouth, adults ranging from 1 to 1½ inches in size. It is more fossorial in habit than either of the two preceding species. The skin fold on the head, so characteristic of many Narrow-mouths, may be very prominent or so slight as to almost escape notice. The feet have small webs connecting the base of the toes. Both inner- and outer-sole tubercles are well developed, cornified, and equipped with cutting edges.

The upper parts of the Sheep Frog are brown or greenish-brown. There is a narrow stripe of white or orange or yellow running down the middle of the back from snout to vent. Furthermore, a black broken line in inverted V shape extends from the middle of the back down to the insertion of the legs, which are barred with black. The lower part of the back is irregularly spotted with dark. The undersurfaces are grayish-white mottled with black. A narrow white stripe extends from snout to vent in the middle. There is also a broad white band extending from just below the eye to the front of the arm insertion. The throat of the male is black, that of the female lighter. Besides these markings, there are various other stripes that correspond to the places where the skin splits during a molt.

The breeding season extends from March through September in periods of heavy rain. The males float on the water while voicing their lamblike bleats, which are lower than those of the Eastern Narrow-mouth and with the interval between each call more widely spaced.

The eggs, numbering about 700, are black above, white below, and are laid in a floating mass on the surface. The individual egg is approximately 1 mm. in size and is surrounded by 1 envelope of about 2 mm. in diameter. These eggs are a little smaller than those of the Eastern Narrow-mouth, and the envelope is considerably smaller. The eggs may hatch in as little as 12 hours.

The tadpole resembles the Eastern Narrow-mouth tadpole, and completes transformation in about a month. Detailed measurements of the tadpoles of the Sheep Frog have not been made, and therefore these tadpoles are "unknown" (quotation marks mine), according to the Wrights.

Very little is known of the habits of the Narrow-mouths in general, and this is especially true of the Sheep Frog. Because they are so secretive and so small, they are usually difficult to find even for the experienced herpetologist.

The Spadefoots and Narrow-mouths are not the only burrowers. Some true toads, genus *Bufo*, are also fossorial, and at least one of our native frogs, *Rana capito*, of the southern states, lives in the burrows of the Gopher Turtle.

There are many burrowing salamanders. The greatest number of these are found in the family Ambystomidae, the Mole, or Blunt-mouthed, Salamanders. The Eastern Tiger Salamander, *Ambystoma tigrinum tigrinum*, has a wide range over most of the eastern half of the United States. It is absent from New England, most of New York (Long Island excepted), Pennsylvania, West Virginia, Tennessee, and the southern half of Florida.

The Eastern Tiger Salamander is a very large creature, and specimens 10 inches in body length are not unknown. The males are larger than the females, and are about 8 inches long; the females are about 7 inches in length. The body of the Tiger Salamander is stout, with a blunt snout and wide head. The gular fold, a fold of skin at the base of the throat, is prominent. The upper parts are dark brown or black-spotted or blotched all over with greenish-yellow. The throat is yellow; the rest of the underparts are greenish-yellow marked with brown.

The males may be distinguished from the females by their larger size, longer, more powerful legs, and in the breeding season by the protuberant vent. The Eastern Tiger Salamander is an early spring breeder, and comes to the ponds in March, or even January or February in the more southerly portions of its range. The courtship consists of the animals of both sexes nosing and pushing each other.

The eggs, about 50 in number, are attached in a mass to weeds underneath the surface of the water. The egg is large, about 3 mm., brown above, tan below, and is surrounded by 3 jelly envelopes. These eggs may be confused with those of the Spotted Salamander, but in general there are fewer eggs in the mass of the Tiger Salamander, and the egg and each of its envelopes are larger. The eggs hatch in a month or more, depending upon water temperature.

The larva has neither claspers nor legs on hatching. The body fin extends in an unbroken line from the back of the head to the tip of the tail. It is greenish-yellow in color, with darker markings. Usually, there is a dark line or row of spots along either side of the backbone, and a light line from each eye along the sides. After a larval period of 2½ to 4 months, the young transform, and assume a terrestrial life.

Do the newly transformed Tiger Salamanders immediately start to lead a subterranean existence? Or are they, like many of the salientian burrowers' young, less likely to burrow until they are older? No one knows. The problem is made more difficult by the fact that newly transformed ambystomid salamanders are hard to identify, for the adult coloration is not attained immediately.

Dr. Bishop states that the Eastern Tiger Salamander spends most of its life underground, except in the breeding season. However, Dr. Noble stated that the Tiger Salamander is frequently found in ponds in the summer and is more aquatic than many other ambystomids. Furthermore, some herpetologists feel that this salamander is a land hibernator, while other investigators have found them in pond detritus in winter, which would seem to indicate that it sometimes or often hibernates in water. These divergent opinions by eminent herpetologists serve to emphasize how little we really know about the burrowers, especially the fossorial salamanders.

Many other species of the Ambystomidae also spend the greater part of their lives underground. We shall list some of them very briefly. The California Tiger Salamander, *Ambystoma tigrinum californiense*, is found in central California in a very dry region. The Mole Salamander, *Ambystoma talpoideum*, found in northern Florida and along the Gulf coast of Mississippi and Alabama, digs extensive tunnels many feet long. The Small-mouthed Salamander, *Ambystoma texanum*, found in Texas and parts of Oklahoma, Kansas, Arkansas, Missouri, Illinois, Indiana, and Ohio, burrows in hilly regions under logs well sunken into the ground. The Barred Salamander, *Ambystoma tigrinum mavortium*, is found throughout Texas, Oklahoma, Kansas, and most of New Mexico and Colorado.

These, then, are some of the burrowers. Much much more needs to be learned about their habits. We know less about them than we know about many other amphibians because of their secretive nocturnal ways.

CHAPTER *13*

Tree Dwellers

Though tree dwellers in other countries belong to many different families, our native tree-dwelling frogs are all confined to the family Hylidae. Not all of the Hylidae are true tree climbers. Many live on the ground or on low plants and shrubs. There seems to be a certain relation of the size of the animal to the height climbed, though precise ratios have not been worked out. In general, the larger treefrogs climb higher than the smaller ones. This is a very broad generalization, and it does not mean that all large treefrogs climb high. For instance, the Green Treefrog, *Hyla cinerea cinerea,* found in many of the southern states, does not climb so high as either the Squirrel Treefrog, *Hyla squirella,* or the Pine Woods Treefrog, *Hyla femoralis.* The last two species are both smaller than the Green Treefrog, though all three are larger than the Spring Peeper, *Hyla crucifer,* and other nonclimbing hylas.

The fact that larger species do climb higher is all the more amazing because many of the small nonclimbing species could climb with greater ease. For instance, the largest of treefrogs, *Hyla vasta,* climbs high, but is unable to remain on the sides of a glass jar, thus proving that as a climber it is less efficient than the Spring Peeper, who can remain clinging to glass for days or even weeks.

It is true that smaller animals have a proportionately greater surface than larger ones. This may be one answer as to why the smaller

173

treefrogs do not climb so high as the larger, heavier ones. Because of the greater area of skin exposed, the smaller species are more prone to desiccation, and must therefore remain close to the ground, where humidity levels are higher, in order to satisfy their natural requirements in this respect.

There are not very many salamanders that climb trees, and we are fortunate in this country to have one species that does. Remembering that tree-dwelling amphibians are more prone to desiccation than those living on the ground, it is surprising to learn that our tree climber is a member of the Plethodontidae, or Lungless Salamanders. This family, as we mentioned earlier, obtains most of its oxygen through its skin, or through buccopharyngeal respiration. The Lungless Salamanders are extremely susceptible to desiccation—just how very easily they succumb we learned to our regret this summer. We were photographing a Two-lined Salamander. It was a hot, humid day and we were in the shade. We were probably not over ten minutes posing and photographing the animal, but at the end of the time the poor creature's eyes glazed over and he died. Thereafter, we were more careful. The Red-backed Salamander, photographed under similar conditions, suffered no ill effects.

Why have the Lungless Salamanders, some of whom are so prone to desiccation, produced tree dwellers? Our own Aneides is not the only Lungless tree climber. The genus *Oedipus*, found in the neotropics, also belongs to the Plethodontidae, and some of its members are climbers. Of course, it must be remembered that of all the families of salamanders, the Plethodontidae are the most widely diversified, so perhaps this in part helps to explain why some of them, rather than species of some other family, took to the trees.

Since an arboreal existence is very different from an aquatic, terrestrial, or fossorial one, adaptations that make life in this habitat possible and successful are numerous. The most obvious of these adaptations are the toe pads present on all tree dwellers, though not confined to them alone. The pads of treefrogs are round, but they are not, as many people believe, suction disks. They are far more complex than that. The undersurface of a toe pad is made up of many wedge-shaped cells, each separate from the others. These cells penetrate the cracks and irregularities of the surface to be climbed. In addition, glands in the toe pad excrete a sticky substance that increases their efficiency. It would seem as if some treefrogs have stickier toes than others. For instance, when one holds a peeper one is not aware of any stickiness on the toe pads at all. How different are the toes of the Eastern Grey Treefrog! If this amphibian wishes to cling to your finger, it is quite difficult to disengage his toes. Incidentally, it should be mentioned that after the animal is removed one's fingers do not feel sticky.

Most tree dwellers depend almost entirely upon their toe pads to climb or maintain their position on the tree. But there are some, such as the African *Chiromantis xerampelina* and the South American genus *Phyllomedusa*, that grip the branch on which they sit. To make gripping easier and more efficient, Phyllomedusa has no (or very little) web between fingers and toes. In addition, both Chiromantis and Phyllomedusa have, unlike most Salientia, an opposable "thumb." Other treefrogs have some webbing between the toes and usually some between the fingers also—how much depends upon the family or species.

Arboreal amphibians usually have relatively long legs and a rather flattened body. Both are of value. The long legs aid materially in climbing. The depressed body presents a large ventral surface to the object to be climbed. If you watch a treefrog climb a perpendicular surface, you will see that he does indeed press his belly to the surface and that it helps him to edge his way up.

Though all amphibians are able to modify their color to a certain extent, the tree dwellers show a remarkable ability in this respect. Many species are able to change from green to gray to brown and all shades in between, obliterating or modifying the markings present on the ground color.

The way in which the skin coloring is produced and changed in the amphibian is both complicated and technical. Since, however, color change is one of the outstanding characteristics of the amphibians, the treefrogs in particular, we must try to explain in a brief and simplified manner just how color and color changes occur. The skin of most amphibians contains three different types of chromatophores, or pigment cells: the lipophores, the guanophores, and the melanophores. The lipophores are yellow, and they form the first layer of pigment cells. Next come the guanophores, and below these are the melanophores, or black pigment cells. The red color of some amphibians may be produced by the lipophores, or, more rarely, by a fourth type of pigment cell, the allophore.

Actually, when we speak of these pigment cells as being in three layers, we are giving the wrong impression. The cells and the pigments they contain may expand or contract, may become round or elongate. In addition, the cells may, in young amphibians, move amoeba fashion, either up or down. In fully mature individuals the chromatophores evidently lose this power of movement and remain stationary, but parts of each cell extend up and around other pigment cells, regardless of their type. Though the cells themselves cannot move in the mature amphibian, the pigment they contain can and does move.

Where the melanophores are many and close to the surface of the skin, black or brown coloring is produced. Many lipophores near the surface produce either yellow or red. White is produced by a predominance of guanophores near the skin surface. Green or blue are not produced by specific pigment cells. When a frog appears green, the arrangement of the pigment cells is lipophores, guanophores, and melanophores, with the latter cells at the bottom. Light passes through the lipophores, but only the green rays are reflected back, the other rays being absorbed by the various pigment cells. Blue is produced in the same manner, but in this case the lipophores are absent and the guanophores reflect back only the blue rays, the others being absorbed either by the guanophores or the melanophores underneath them.

Color change is produced by movements of the different pigments within their cells and the branches or processes of these cells. The plasticity of the color cells, their relative numbers, and their distribution vary from species to species, and determine not only the animal's coloration but also the amount of color change that can be produced. This variation in distribution and plasticity of the chromatophores occurs, though to a much lesser degree, in individuals within the same species. For instance, most Eastern Grey Treefrogs are able to change from light green to gray to brown to black. Others, however, evidently can change from gray to brown to black but are unable to become green.

The length of time required for color change varies with the species. With some, such as the Pacific Treefrog, *Hyla regilla*, and the Squirrel Treefrog, *Hyla squirella*, the change is effected in as little as ten minutes. Others, such as the Barking Treefrog, *Hyla gratiosa,* found in Florida and along the coasts of the southern states, may take half an hour or longer to change color.

The reasons for color change in amphibians are many. Low temperatures, high humidity, and darkness—any one or all of these factors tend to stimulate the amphibian to assume a darker coloring, while the opposite factors produce lighter colorings. In addition, certain treefrogs, such as the European Treefrog, *Hyla arborea arborea,* turn dark on rough surfaces, light on smooth ones. Probably this type of reflexive color change occurs in other treefrogs as well, for we often find a green treefrog on a green leaf and a gray or brown one on bark. Proof that any given species does or does not change on smooth or rough surfaces is not easy to obtain, but it can be done, and might provide an interesting challenge to those who like treefrogs and live where they are numerous.

Color change is not wholly the result of reflex action. Diet and possibly even emotions may cause a color change. Furthermore, the eye plays an important part in effecting a color change. Some amphibians lose their power to change color when blinded, or color change may be much slower on animals thus affected.

Color change in tree dwellers needs to be more flexible than with other amphibians, for they are exposed to more light, less humidity, and other conditions that in general are inimical to the amphibian's physiology and ontogeny. Therefore, in order to survive in such surroundings, the tree dweller needs to be more adaptable than the average amphibian.

Although many treefrogs can adopt different colors, it must not be assumed that they are constantly making use of this ability. Color change is most rapid and extreme in periods of maximum activity—as in the breeding season—and during periods when food supply is plentiful. At other times the treefrog tends to assume his characteristic color and maintain it with only the slightest of variations over long periods of time.

It has been proved that certain individuals among the tree dwellers have more or less permanent homes or resting spots. A Brazilian treefrog, *Trachycephalus nigromaculatus,* was found to occupy the same spot for four months. Mrs. Goin has observed Squirrel Treefrogs. (She calls them Rain Frogs.) One individual could always be found on the underside of a particular leaf. Another was not so fussy. He sometimes changed leaves but could be found in the same general vicinity each morning. During the evening these treefrogs left their "beds," but how far they roamed in search of food Mrs. Goin could not determine.

Little has been discovered about which species of treefrogs have a definite "bed" and home range. Perhaps some species do, or perhaps individuals among certain species do. Here is a field where the interested amateur can score. But, as with so many scientific discoveries, the way will not be easy, for many different individuals of the same species must be marked and their resting places and foraging areas observed over several years and in different localities before one can definitely state that such and such a species does or does not have a home range or resting place.

It would obviously be to the advantage of the tree dwellers if they could remain in their arboreal habitat all the time, and if they did not have to leave it for breeding and egg laying. Our native treefrogs all must go to water for mating and egg laying. Many foreign frogs, however, as we mentioned briefly in Chapter 3, have evolved methods whereby they need not leave the trees to lay. Breeding adaptations for an arboreal life vary, but we find that many different families have evolved similar methods.

For instance, some of the South American hylids, some of the Asian Rhacophoridae, and the African tree dweller, *Chiromantis xerampelina,* all make foam nests on branches of trees overhanging the water. Fluid is secreted among the leaves and beaten into a foamy mass by the hind legs of the female, the male, or both, depending upon the species. The eggs are laid, and more fluid is excreted and beaten into a foam. The eggs are thus protected from desiccation during their development. The *Chiromantis xerampelina* parents evidently guard the nest, squirting water upon it occasionally to ensure sufficient moisture. The aerial egg masses of other species do not require this care, and are usually unattended by the parents. As the larvae hatch, the foam nest disintegrates and the larvae drop into the water below to complete their development.

Other South American treefrogs of the genus *Phyllomedusa,* remarkable for the opposable thumb and their eyes with vertical pupils and red iris, also lay in the leaves of branches overhanging the water. They do not make a foam nest, but merely glue the leaves together around the eggs.

Adaptations for an arboreal life: 1. The Asian Mount Omei Treefrog, *Rhacophorus omeimontis*, showing (*a*) the enlarged digital disks. 2. An aerial egg mass. 3. Enlarged drawings of (*b*) the sole of the foot and (*c*) the palm of the hand of *Rhacophorus omeimontis*. Adapted from drawings of I. S. Wang in *Amphibians of Western China* by C. C. Liu, with permission from the Chicago Natural History Museum.

The Brazilian *Hyla resinifictrix* is said to use wax obtained from the nests of stingless bees to line cavities in trees to make them watertight. Upon the advent of rains, eggs are laid in the water caught in this wax-lined cavity and develop there. Just how *Hyla resinifictrix* goes about robbing the bees, how it carries the wax, and many other details, we have been unable to find out.

Adaptation for an arboreal existence is best exemplified in those species of treefrogs that have developed a dorsal brood pouch or marsupium. The marsupial frogs are all found in South America. Among them are *Gastrotheca marsupiata*, which has a brood pouch with a small opening. As the eggs hatch, the small tadpoles emerge from the marsupium and complete their development in the water collected in bromeliad leaves. The genus *Nototheca* is also noted for its marsupium, which covers the entire back from shoulder to coccyx. In this genus, the marsupium has a Y-shaped external opening. *Gastrotheca ovifer* has a brood pouch similar to that of *Gastrotheca marsupiata*. The eggs are large and few in number. Development is completed in the pouch, and the young emerge as fully transformed frogs.

These, then, are some of the adaptations made by amphibians to equip them for an arboreal existence. Let us now go on to describe the lives of a few tree dwellers.

Found throughout the eastern half of the country, northern Maine and southern Florida excepted, is the Eastern Grey Treefrog, *Hyla versicolor versicolor*. This animal is fairly large for a treefrog, the adults ranging in size from 1½ to 2¼ inches in length. The body is intermediate in build between that of the true toads and the frogs. It is compact, with a blunt snout like the toads, but it has the narrow waist and long legs of a frog. The fingers and toes have large round adhesive disks at their tips. The fingers are slightly webbed; the toes are webbed to the base of the disks.

The usual color of the Eastern Grey Treefrog is gray above, grayish-white below. Between the shoulders there is a darker marking vaguely starlike in shape. For some reason this characteristic marking is generally absent in the treefrogs found in our immediate vicinity. In most of ours, the star is replaced by two long irregular markings on either side of the backbone. When the legs are folded, one sees that they have two dark bars on them, and there are two on each forearm as well. When the animal is taken in the hand with the hind leg extended, it will be seen that the undersurfaces of the legs are orange, reticulated with black or dark brown. This brilliant coloration may also be glimpsed if one stands below a climbing treefrog. One further characteristic is usually present. Beneath each eye there is often a white spot. The eyes themselves complement this amphibian's appearance, much as a piece of jewelry complements a dress. The pupils are black and shining, the iris grayish-green with a fine network of black lines.

The skin texture of the Eastern Grey Treefrog is granular without being warty, and is slightly rougher above than below. This feature, together with the coloration, makes this animal look like a piece of bark with bits of lichen growing on it. Even when one has a specimen in the hand, one can see how well its markings, color, and skin fit it for an inconspicuous existence in the trees.

Color change in the Eastern Grey Treefrog is extreme, but, as we mentioned, not all individuals are able to assume the green color. A complete change of color takes about half an hour in this species. The change takes place in definite sequence. Let us take a treefrog who is almost black and watch him change color. He is so dark that none of the markings except the light spot beneath the eye shows. Gradually, the skin lightens, and the dark star and leg bars begin to show up. As the ground color continues to lighten, the markings too begin to bleach out until they are almost the ground color and are merely outlined with black. If the animal is going to change to white or grayish-white, the fading continues until even the outline of the

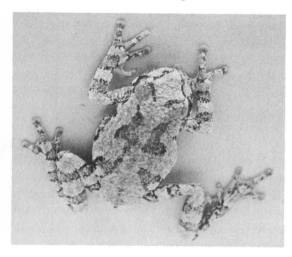

The Eastern Grey Tree-frog, *Hyla versicolor versicolor*, climbing

markings fades. If green is to be assumed, the outlined markings gradually take on a greenish hue first, followed by the rest of the body until a plain green shade is attained.

The male Eastern Grey Treefrog is distinguished from the female by the darker-colored throat. The voice of the male is a trill. It is lower-pitched and more full-bodied than the trill of the American Toad, and of much shorter duration. The vocal sac of the male swells into a large throat bubble similar in form to that seen in the American Toad.

The mating season does not begin until the nights are warm, May through July, depending upon the climate. The calls are at their loudest on those nights when the humidity is high. Indeed, just before rain, if the afternoon is warm, scattered individuals may be heard trilling during the late afternoon. This does not mean that you can find them on the ground if you go to the pond, for usually they do not descend from the trees until darkness falls. They have, however, come down to lower tree branches, where if you are clever and patient, you may find them. But do not think that you can hear a trill, head for the spot, and catch the singer. You can hear the trill, but some time and experimentation are often required before you can trace the sound to its source, for the voice of this treefrog is ventriloquial, and appears to emanate from several points.

The eggs are laid in the pond in small surface masses of about 30 eggs each, the total complement of all packets being around 1,800. The eggs are small, a shade over 1 mm. in diameter. They are brown above and cream-colored below. The jelly in which these eggs are enclosed is sticky to the touch, and adheres to the surface vegetation where it is deposited. Sharp eyes and much time and patience are required to find these eggs in the pond. The incubation period is short, 4 or 5 days being about average for pond-laid eggs. We have had eggs laid in the aquarium start hatching 36 hours after deposition.

The tadpole is medium in size and has a very high dorsal crest that extends on the body up to or beyond a point perpendicular to the spiracle, which is found on the left side. The tail is usually a bright orange-red, spotted with black, and makes the identification of this tadpole by the amateur fairly simple. However, though any tadpole with a black-blotched scarlet tail may be assumed to be *Hyla versicolor versicolor,* the reverse statement—that is, that a tadpole without this characteristic is not *Hyla versicolor versicolor*—is not true. Treefrog tadpoles we raised never assumed this brilliant coloration on the tail. Furthermore, a pond tadpole with a brilliant red tail lost this coloring within two days of living with our home-raised tadpoles. Whether these tadpoles lacked the natural coloring because of different dietary conditions, or whether it was due to differences in light, temperature, mineral content of the water, or some other condition, would be hard to say. We suspect that perhaps in this case light may have been an important factor, for our tadpoles were in a very dark spot. But since we carried on no experiments, we cannot state this as a fact.

Since some adult Eastern Grey Treefrogs are unable to assume a green color, and since all of them are more often gray than any other color, it comes as a bit of a surprise to learn that these treefrogs are green when they transform after a larval period of 1½ to 2 months. How long after transformation they retain this green uniform has never been determined. Evidently it is to the froglet's advantage to be green as it journeys from the pond through green grass to the tree. But it does seem miraculous that a species noted for its ability to effect extreme color changes should emerge from the water dressed in the color it least often assumes.

Does the Eastern Grey Treefrog have a definite sense of home? Does it sleep on the same branch or leaf each day? Does it forage over a wide area for food at night or does it confine its food-getting forays to a single tree? No one really knows, though there is some evidence to indicate that it is a home body and does not range far from its chosen tree.

How high up this treefrog is commonly found depends very much on the temperature and humidity. We have found that during the mating season at dusk the treefrogs begin to call. But their position in the tree is, in every instance we have witnessed, just within reach of an extended arm, or slightly above it. This makes the height at 6 feet 9 inches or higher. We suspect that during the day they rest considerably higher, though just how high we cannot say, for we have not, despite frequent tree climbing, been lucky in finding these frogs during the day. There are so many leaves and branches and twigs on one tree, and so many of them are beyond close scrutiny. In addition, a treefrog is admirably dressed to escape notice.

These treefrogs have a personality that makes them ideally suitable as pets if proper food can be obtained. They are not nervous and agile, but are rather "confiding" and clumsy. Eastern Grey Treefrogs jumping from limb to limb often do not land squarely. Instead they may "miss" their objective, merely adhering to it by one sticky toe. This is sufficient, however. Though one would hardly believe it possible, this treefrog can pull his full weight up with one finger or toe. Jumping from one twig to another is their normal means of travel. Only when ascending a perpendicular surface do they resort to climbing. They even catch their prey by leaping at it as it flies by; no treefrog stalks insects walking along a branch in the manner of a toad. In the vivarium they will starve to death amid plenty unless their food is on the wing.

The Eastern Grey Treefrog is very rarely found sitting crosswise on a limb. They prefer instead to sit lengthwise. Furthermore, you will never find them sitting with their heads downward. Always, when on a leaf or on a perpendicular "tree" in the vivarium, they so orient themselves that their snouts are facing up. In the vivarium they usually climb to the highest point. Though good climbers and well able to adhere to the round sides of a glass jar, they have difficulty in maintaining a stationary position on a vertical pane of glass. They can climb it without any trouble, but if they pause in their ascent they start to slip down. It must be the weight of the body that causes this. Surely it is not the climbing adaptations that are at fault, for the Spring Peeper, whose toes are not so sticky, can remain in one place on a vertical pane of glass for as long as it cares to do so.

In the North, early in the fall, before the first frost, the Eastern Grey Treefrog descends from his leafy summer abode and burrows into the ground for a long hibernation period. In the South, of course, the hibernation period is greatly abbreviated, or may be nonexistent if the winter temperatures remain warm enough.

Two other subspecies of *Hyla versicolor* exist—or may exist. Both are limited in range, and one at least may not be a valid subspecies, for essential differences between it and *Hyla versicolor versicolor* are slight. The problem is complicated by the fact that in certain parts of its range, *Hyla versicolor versicolor* interbreeds with both *Hyla avivoca*, the Bird-voiced Treefrog, and *Hyla femoralis*, the Pine Woods Treefrog. In addition, some *Hyla versicolor versicolor* have a slow trill rate; others have a trill rate that is almost twice as fast. This does not occur in all parts of its range, but where it does occur it influences breeding. Some females respond more readily to the males whose voices have a slow (normal) trill rate, while in others the opposite reaction is found. This response to a certain call rate may, in time, produce another subspecies.

For our next example of a tree dweller, we shall leave America and go to Asia—western China, to be exact. Because the flying frogs have made a better adaptation to an arboreal existence than our native hylids, it is interesting to examine in some detail the ways of one of the better known of its members. This is *Rhacophorus omeimontis*, found in the mountainous region west of Chungking at altitudes of between 3,000 to 6,500 feet. This flying frog ranges in size from 2 inches to a little over 3 inches. The arms and legs of this heavy-bodied treefrog are long, with large hands and feet. The tips of all digits are expanded into enormous friction disks, those on the fingers being larger and more fully developed. In addition, both fingers and toes are partially webbed. The form of the hands and the form of the feet are very similar to those found on the mountain-brook-dwelling *Staurois*, and it is believed that the treefrogs of the genus *Rhacophorus* have developed from *Staurois*.

Rhacophorus omeimontis is green in color, with large brown markings on its back and on the upper surfaces of the legs. The brown markings are in turn marked with spots of a darker brown, and these brown spots are also found on the sides. The venter is cream-colored, with the throat speckled with black or dark brown. The general appearance of this treefrog with granular skin is that of a piece of moss-covered bark, and they evidently match their surroundings so well that Dr. Liu says that it is extremely difficult to find them.

The males may be distinguished from the females by their much smaller size—they are at least ¾ of an inch smaller—and by white nuptial pads on the first and second fingers. The male voice is described by Dr. Liu as being similar to a cricket's chirp; the sound does not carry far. The males call from the branches of trees overhanging pools or from the bank of the pond.

Unfortunately, no one has ever seen exactly how *Rhacophorus omeimontis* makes its nest. Since the process has been observed for other related species, we may assume, without taking too great liberty, that *Rhacophorus omeimontis* produces its foam nest in a similar manner. In species observed, a small amount of fluid is produced, and this is beaten by the feet of the female or the male or both, depending upon the species, into a foamy mass. Then, as the eggs emerge, they are accompanied by more fluid and are fertilized by the male. The egg mass and its fluid is beaten until the fluid is foamy. When egg laying is finished, the pair disengage and manage, each separately, to free their legs from the foam, which has become very sticky. In general, this is how a foam nest is made.

The Mount Omei Treefrog prefers to lay on tree branches overhanging the water, but if there are none available it will make its nest among vegetation on the bank of the pond. The tree nests are made at the very tips of twigs. The egg mass is attached to several twigs, and their leaves partially cover the nest.

The benefit of a foam nest to eggs deposited in trees becomes apparent when we learn that the outer foam hardens while the inner foam liquefies, so that the eggs develop in a watery medium that has been well aerated when deposited. But unless the eggs are sufficiently moistened by heavy dew or rain, they may dry up despite the protection of the foam. After a week or less, the outside membrane begins to soften, and the now developed tadpoles wriggle vigorously, and hatch, dropping into the water below to complete their larval life. About 40 days after hatching, the tadpole has completed his development and is ready to assume an arboreal existence.

The arboreal Oak Salamander, *Aneides lugubris lugubris*, is a large salamander, 5 to 6 inches in size, found in the western part of California. It is brown on top, with scattered flecks of pale yellow or dirty white. The underparts are light yellow or white. The throat and undersides of the legs are sometimes flesh color, or they may be the same color as the rest of the venter.

There is little to distinguish this tree dweller from other salamanders that are not arboreal. It is true that the arms and legs are long and well developed, but so are those of many other terrestrial salamanders. The tips of the toes are only slightly expanded into adhesive disks; their development is not nearly so pronounced as the disks found on another species, *Aneides aeneus*, which climbs but rarely.

If one counts the respiratory throat movements of the Oak Salamander, it will be found that there may be as many as 180 a minute —a very large number even for a Lungless Salamander, to which

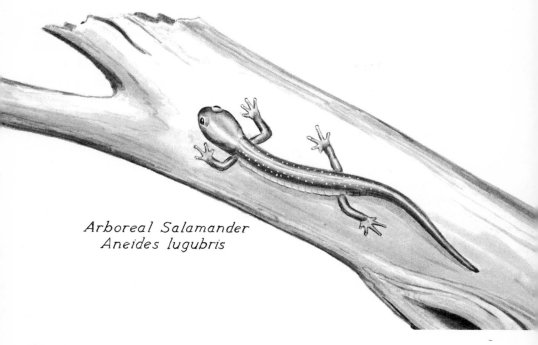

*Arboreal Salamander
Aneides lugubris*

The arboreal Oak Salamander, *Aneides lugubris lugubris*

family Aneides belongs. But does this rapid throat pulse mean that
other species of the Plethodontidae are incapable of breathing so
rapidly? And is the throat pulse slower when the Oak Salamander
is found on the ground than when he is high up in an oak tree? In
short, is the rapid throat pulse an adaptation for arboreal life especially developed in this salamander to enable it to spend all or part
of its life in trees?

The Oak Salamander is found in trees as high up as 60 feet, but
it is also found in rotten logs or under logs, stones, bark, and so
forth. The questions this statement prompts are many. Does one
salamander take up a permanent abode in a tree, while another
prefers to make his home on the ground? Or is one salamander
sometimes found in a tree, sometimes on the ground? If one is looking for these salamanders on any given day, does one find equal
numbers in trees and on the ground, or are they more numerous on
the ground when certain conditions of temperature and humidity
are present, or in certain seasons of the year? Within their range, are

they more often found living in trees in one place than in another? There is no answer to these and similar questions at present.

Apart from their intrinsic interest, the answers might possibly indicate that the Oak Salamander is either in the process of becoming less arboreal or more so—we cannot know which now, though we might place the odds on more. Many species of the genus *Aneides* have slight tree-climbing proclivities, though in none are they so marked as in *Aneides lugubris lugubris*. For instance, the Clouded Salamander, *Aneides ferreus*, found in the western part of Oregon and the northwest of California, is also found in trees, though not so often nor, as far as we know, so high up. The Green Salamander, *Aneides aeneus*, found in West Virginia, and on the border of Ohio, Kentucky, Virginia, North Carolina, Tennessee, and Georgia, though not so arboreal as either of the two preceding species, is sometimes found underneath loose bark of standing trees.

The large unpigmented eggs of the Oak Salamander are laid in July, August, and September. The vitellus is about 5 mm., and the entire egg and its capsules may be as large as 9 mm. Each egg is deposited singly and attached by a long (8 to 20 mm.) stalk to the roof of the cavity. If the laying site is a cavity in a tree, many salamanders of various ages may be found there. The female broods the eggs until they hatch 1 to 2 months after laying. She may even eat a few of them while brooding. The total egg complement is small —19 or less. However, despite her habit of eating an occasional egg, the female Oak Salamander is a wonderful mother. She is almost unique among salamanders, for she stays with the young even after they have hatched.

These, then, are some of the tree dwellers. In some ways they display the ultimate in amphibian evolution away from the original mode of life. Though their habitat, nocturnal ways, and protective coloration make them more difficult to observe intimately than many other amphibians, this only serves to make them the more interesting.

The Robber Frogs

The Leptodactylidae, or Robber Frogs, are a large family of amphibians found on the American continents and in Australia. Most of its representatives here are in South America—Dr. Cochran lists 55 species and subspecies for southeastern Brazil alone— but some of its members live in the West Indies, Central America, and Mexico, and this country has six species. Where the popular name of Robber Frog came from we cannot imagine. Not from the scientific name, which means slender-fingered, or because of any habits these amphibians may have, for they do not, like many insects, steal anything from man or any other animal. The alternate popular name of Barking Frog may be more appropriate, for certain members of this family are said to have a voice similar to that of a dog.

Before we tell about our native species of Robber Frogs, let us scan some of the genera which make up this family; like the Hylidae, their ways are varied and we find no such homogeneity of habits as are found among the members of the genus *Rana* for instance. In general, the Robber Frogs are woodland inhabitants and spend much of their lives under the leaves of the forest floor. But some of them prefer the banks of streams, others caves and rocky regions. Some have even taken to an arboreal life. *Eleutherodactylus inoptus*

189

of the West Indies is generally found high up in tall trees, just as are so many of the large foreign hylids.

Some of the Robber Frogs are large and powerfully built. This is especially true of some members of the genera *Leptodactylus* and *Ceratophrys*. The bigger members of these genera, *Ceratophrys* in particular, are noted for their cannibalistic tendencies and even the tadpoles of *Ceratophrys* are equipped with many labial teeth indicative of their carnivorous diet. Other Robbert Frogs are tiny; our own *Syrrhophus campi* may be only ⅝ of an inch long.

The principal reason that most of us are interested in the Robber Frogs is that they are our only land-laying Salientia. All of the members of the genus *Leptodactylus* (we have only one in this country) lay their eggs on land in a mass of foam. The members of the genus *Eleutherodactylus* also deposit their eggs on land, but with them there is no foam nest and they lay in situations drier than those frequented by the laying Leptodactylus. The entire development of the genus *Eleutherodactylus* takes place within the egg capsule, and the young hatch as fully developed froglets— miniature replicas of their parents.

What adaptations make land laying and transformation within the egg possible? To begin with, the eggs, while few in number are very large—up to 7.5 mm. in *Eleutherodactylus augusti latrans*. These eggs are unpigmented, and we wonder of what value an unpigmented egg might be. Does it perhaps serve as a temperature regulator? Light-colored eggs would absorb less heat, and possibly this helps to prevent desiccation of the eggs. But this is theory pure and simple, for no one has ever proved whether or not the unpigmented egg has any advantages over the pigmented one.

Eggs require a certain amount of oxygen for proper development. Tadpoles require even more. A tadpole enclosed within an egg capsule must have either superior gills or must utilize other existing organs for respiration or develop new ones. Naturally, the oxygen in the egg capsule is not—could not be—as high as would be available were the tadpole swimming in a pond or stream. In the land-laying Robber Frogs, where the entire development is within the egg, we do find an existing organ has been modified to serve as a respiratory organ. This is the tail, which is long, thin, and well supplied with blood vessels. Through it the developing tadpole receives much oxygen, and it supplements the gills while they exist.

As the latter are absorbed during transformation, the tail supplies the necessary oxygen until the froglet hatches and the lungs can take over the respiratory function. The incubation period required for these direct-developing Robber Frogs is very short; only about fifteen days elapse before a tiny froglet emerges from the eggs laid by *Eleutherodactylus ricordi planirostris,* for instance.

The tadpoles of most amphibians are able to free themselves from the egg capsule because the secretions of glands on their snouts help dissolve the jelly. In aquatic eggs, the fact that the jelly absorbs water and thus becomes less dense is an additional aid in hatching. The eggs of Eleutherodactylus are not laid in water, and though it is possible that they may absorb a little moisture from the soil in which they are deposited, this alone will not enable the Robber froglet to hatch. Nor does he ever develop snout glands. Instead he has what is unique among the Amphibia but common in reptiles and birds—an egg tooth. The egg tooth of Eleutherodactylus is located on the premaxillary bone in the middle of the upper lip. With it, the little one frees himself from the capsule. Soon after hatching, it is shed.

Now that we have looked at the Robber Frogs in general, let us examine a few species in detail. Of all our native Robber Frogs, none is so common as the Greenhouse Frog, *Eleutherodactylus ricordi planirostris,* found in the southern part of Florida as far north as Jacksonville. It is also found in Cuba, from which country it was evidently accidentally introduced into the United States. It has done well here and is gradually extending its range northward. Residents of states bordering Florida may make the first discovery of it in their state—if not now, then in the near future. But sharp eyes are needed, for this little frog's maximum size is only a little over 1 inch and specimens of ½ an inch are not uncommon. Mrs. Goin feels that smaller ones are frequently found in very dry years, and she suggests that there is a possibility that drought may be the reason for this. Perhaps, if this supposition is proved correct, it may be found that a dry season is an indirect cause of stunting. In periods of extreme heat and aridity, these small frogs evidently aestivate and do not, in all probability, ingest their normal food supply. This may be the prime cause of the smaller size. Or again, it may be that lack of moisture in itself has an adverse effect on growth.

The Greenhouse Frog is reddish brown in color with two pink, red, or orange stripes running along the sides on some individuals. On others, these stripes are lacking. The snout is of the same red or orange as the stripes, and the back is also irregularly marked with this color. The legs are barred with dark, and the venter is whitish spotted with brown. The iris of this small frog is red with very fine dark wormlike markings. The tympanum is distinct, about half the size of the eye, and may be either white or reddish. The joints of the fingers and toes are enlarged, and the tips of the digits have T-shaped disks. The digits are completely free of web.

There is little external difference between the sexes. The male's call is a cricketlike sound, but the vocal sacs are internal and do not swell into a large bubble, as in so many other species of frogs. Mating takes place on land at night during rains, and few have ever witnessed it. The breeding period is an extended one from April to August. The number of eggs laid ranges from 12 to 24. These eggs are unpigmented, with a vitellus of about 2 mm. surrounded by a jelly envelope of 4 mm. The incubation period ranges from 10 to 15 days.

As we glance over this breeding data, we can realize how difficult finding the frogs mating and laying their eggs must be. To begin with, these creatures are very tiny. They are secretive, evidently breeding in the darkest of places on the rainiest of nights. The eggs, though large for so small an animal, are relatively few in number, and are laid not in a pond but in concealed spots on land. However, despite this, a number of people have been fortunate in finding the eggs of this beautiful little creature. They have found them under moss or in the dirt of flower pots kept outside. This, indeed, is why it is called the Greenhouse Frog, for it frequently resides in gardens and greenhouses.

The Greenhouse Frog is largely nocturnal, and spends the day hiding under boards, rocks, or leaves. When searching for them during the day, one needs be alert, for they are very agile and leap away with great speed when the cover under which they are hiding is overturned. The Greenhouse Frog does not hibernate, and may be found throughout the year. Its northward spread will, in all probability, be limited by the climate, for it is doubtful whether it could survive in places where the temperature falls very low.

We humans are apt to regard hibernation as an act of voluntary intelligence, which it most certainly is not. Though one might not care categorically to state that intelligence plays no part, it is certain that the greater force in governing hibernation is instinctive, with falling temperatures and possibly duration of light also playing an important part. Species who have no need to hibernate in their original habitat often will fail to adapt themselves to a colder climate. They may fail to hibernate at all, or they may emerge too soon.

A very amusing but pathetic account of *Rana adspersa*, the African Bullfrog, is given by Dr. Rose, and illustrates this point very well. This specimen, whom Dr. Rose christened Bartholomew, not being a native of South Africa, was unaccustomed to the rapid changes of weather from cold to warm normally occurring during a Capetown winter. When it was cold, Bartholomew burrowed down into the earth. On the first warm day he emerged, only to be forced to hibernate once more. This behavior continued until a very hot

Greenhouse Frog
Eleutherodactylus ricordi

Barking Frog
Eleutherodactylus augusti

Two of the Robber Frogs

day was followed by a very cold night. The next morning Dr. Rose found poor Bartholomew dead—he had failed to retreat to the bottom of his burrow.

Such a thing would never happen to our own American Toad, for before the first frost occurs this creature burrows into the ground to hibernate. Nor does Indian summer fool it, for it will not emerge until spring is here. Not all frogs and salamanders are such cautious hibernators as the American Toad is, but at least they "know" (not necessarily with conscious thought) what hibernation is. The Greenhouse Frog does not, and its range north will be limited by the temperature unless it can adapt to the colder climate and "learn" to hibernate.

Another Robber Frog, the Barking Frog, *Eleutherodactylus augusti latrans,* is found in central Texas from Waco west through the southern part of New Mexico into the southeastern tip of Arizona. Its range also extends into Mexico. It is closely related to another subspecies found in Mexico.

The Barking Frog is considerably larger and stouter than the Greenhouse Frog, and ranges from 2 to a little over 3 inches in size. It is tan or brown in color, with scattered irregular brown markings. The venter is a light tan, and there is a ventral disk. This is a fold of skin encircling the middle part of the belly. Whether this disk is of any value in climbing would be interesting to know. Though the Barking Frog is not a tree climber, it does spend most of its life among limestone ledges, cliffs, and rocks. As with the Greenhouse Frog, there are expanded *T*-shaped disks on the digit tips, and the toes are webless. The males may be distinguished from the females by the thicker lower arm.

The Barking Frog gets its popular name from its call, which, when heard from a distance, is similar enough to a dog's bark to be mistaken for it. What kind of dog—for dog's barks vary considerably from breed to breed—we are not told, though it would have been helpful. Close up, the voice of this species is more like a *whurr* sounded in the throat, according to the Wrights. Breeding probably occurs during rainy nights from February through April. We must say "probably," for as yet no one has seen this frog mating nor have the eggs been found in nature. Through dissection of a gravid female, it has been ascertained that the eggs of the Barking Frog are the largest laid in this country. It is likely that these eggs are deposited on land and that the entire larval period is spent within the capsule, just as in the Greenhouse Frog.

Though this frog is not tiny, it is very secretive. Few people have ever seen it and fewer still have investigated its ways. The Barking Frogs evidently prefer a rocky limestone habitat, and are sometimes found in caves, as well as in cracks in the rocks.

Though most frogs are able to swim—some better than others—the Barking Frog is not very gifted in this respect. Dr. Wright tells us that one observer put a specimen in a pan of water while attempting to identify it. The poor animal soon "passed out." Artificial respiration was given (that, we would have enjoyed seeing), but though the frog revived for the moment, it expired during the night. All of this would seem to indicate that the Barking Frog can't swim. However, much more evidence is needed before this may be stated as a positive fact. We understand it is possible to drown even an aquatic frog if he is placed in an aquarium of deep water from which he cannot climb. How long this would take (if it be true) we do not know—nor have we any stomach for such experimentation.

The Robber Frogs of the genus *Syrrhophus*, of which there are three species in this country, are found in restricted localities in Texas. They are small animals, and their breeding habits are believed to be similar to those of the eleutherodactylids.

Though the Mexican White-lipped Frog, *Leptodactylus labialis*, is not really a native species, we shall discuss it briefly because it *is* found in the extreme southern part of Texas from Rio Grande City, Edinburg, and Brownsville south into Mexico and Panama. It is a small agile frog of 1¼ to 2 inches in length. It is grayish-brown in color, with scattered darker irregular spots. The edge of the upper lip is white or cream-colored. The underparts are white. A ventral disk is present, though there are no digital disks.

The Mexican White-lipped Frog is a frog of marshy fields and is often found near ditches and small streams. It has also been captured inside burrows in sandbanks and among cliffs.

The male digs a shallow hole in the bank of a ditch or stream with his nose. There he sits and voices his sea-lion bark. The female is attracted, and lays her eggs in the nest he has made. Though no one has witnessed the mating and laying, the frothy egg mass containing about 86 eggs has been found. One may assume that either the female or the male or both beat the jelly into foam, much as some of the treefrogs do. The eggs hatch in less than 2 days. Upon the advent of rains, the tadpoles are washed into the stream.

We mentioned that many of the leptodactylid tadpoles were carnivorous. The tadpole of the Mexican White-lipped Frog begins its diet with plant material. But after about a week, it starts to vary its diet with animal matter, and as it grows, animal food is accepted in increasing amounts. After a larval period of about a month, the tadpole transforms and takes up a more or less terrestrial existence.

CHAPTER 15

The Blind Cave Dwellers

Caves of some sort are found in almost every state in the union. But southwestern Pennsylvania, West Virginia, western Virginia, southern Ohio, southern Indiana, Kentucky, Tennessee, southern Missouri, northwestern Arkansas, and eastern Oklahoma abound in caves because this is a limestone region where conditions are ideal for cave formation.

Caves contain three different ecological niches, one gradually merging into the next. First, there is the mouth of the cave, fairly open and with almost the same amount of light and roughly the same temperature as is found just outside the cave. Gradually, as one penetrates farther, there is less light until one reaches the twilight region, where the light is dim, just as it is at dusk. As one descends still farther, one reaches a zone where there is no light at all—a zone of eternal blackness, darker than night. Here the temperature remains almost constant the year round.

Caves would appear to be ideal homes for amphibians, and so they are for certain salamanders. We find very few frogs in caves, and none in the region described above. Why this should be is a mystery as yet unsolved. Many salamanders are found in the mouths of caves. Among them are the Green Salamander, *Aneides aeneus,* mentioned earlier, the Kentucky Spring Salamander, *Grinophilus*

197

porphyriticus duryi, Wehrle's Salamander, *Plethodon wehrlei,* and the Slimy Salamander, *Plethodon glutinosus glutinosus.*

Farther inside the cave, in the twilight zone, we find that the numbers fall off sharply. In this niche we find only the Dark-sided Salamander, *Eurycea longicauda melanopleura,* and the Cave Salamander, *Eurycea lucifuga.* As we look over this list, we notice that without exception, all these salamanders are of the family Plethodontidae. All have large eyes, the better to see with in the failing light of the cave. But these salamanders cannot really be considered true cave dwellers. The ones found inside the cave mouth are as often or oftener found outside it. The two cave salamanders of the twilight region are also found frequently outside, though during certain months they are evidently more numerous in the cave.

Dr. Oliver tells of investigations carried on concerning the seasonal occurrence of *Eurycea lucifuga* in a cave in Tennessee. The cave was visited once a month. No salamanders at all were found in March, June, November, and December. From 1 to 10 were found in January, April, May, July, and October. From 10 to 20 salamanders were found in February. It is impossible to draw any conclusions at all from these figures. If, on the same day, the investigator had also made a search outside the cave for this salamander, and recorded all he found outside each month, together with temperature and humidity readings inside and outside the cave (he may well have done these things, but they are not reported by Dr. Oliver, and we have not found the original article), we should be better informed and might learn many things.

The true cave dwellers of the world may be named on the fingers of one hand, and we are fortunate in having three of them in this country. They are the Olm, *Proteus anguinus,* found in the eastern Alps; the Grotto Salamander, *Typhlotriton spelaeus;* the Texas Blind Salamander, *Typhlomolge rathbuni;* and the Georgia Blind Salamander, *Haideotriton wallacei.* All are salamanders; all are blind when adult; all are white or very pale in color; all but one are neotenous; all but one are plethodontids; all live in the deepest recesses of the cave; and all are rare and extremely restricted in their range.

The Olm, *Proteus anguinus,* belongs to the family Proteidae and is of the same family as, but of a genus different from, our native mudpuppies. Proteus is neotenous, as are the mudpuppies, but, unlike them, he has lost his color and his eyes—or rather the eyes do not develop sufficiently to enable him to see. When Proteus is exposed to light, its skin becomes pigmented. This pigmentation is retained even if the specimen is subsequently returned to darkness. This fact, as innocuous as it may appear, led to one scientist's suicide. A fascinating account of how the arguments over Proteus culminated in Dr. Paul Kammerer's suicide is contained in the first chapter of Willy Ley's *Salamanders and Other Wonders* (Viking Press, New York, 1955).

Normally Proteus produces one or two young ovoviviparously. But in captivity, if the temperature of the aquarium water rises above 50° F., eggs may be laid. One or two young may hatch from these eggs; however, to date, any such young have not survived for more than a few days. In nature, of course, the water temperature remains constant, and young born alive are the rule. The Olm makes his home in the subterranean waters of the eastern Alps, and is rarely found outside them.

The Grotto Salamander, *Typhlotriton spelaeus*, is found in limestone caves of the Ozark Plateau of Missouri, Arkansas, Kansas, and Oklahoma. Nothing is known of the breeding habits, and the eggs of this species have never been found. Does the Grotto Salamander lay on land inside the deepest recesses of caves with the young entering the water upon hatching or shortly afterward? The adults are often found (when they are found at all) on the cave floor, and it is felt by Dr. Bishop that they are more terrestrial in habit than other blind cave dwellers. Or are the eggs laid in the subterranean waters of the cave? This is possible too, for the Grotto Salamander is also found in these underground streams. Or is it possible that the adults leave the caves and go to streams just outside its mouth and deposit their eggs there? This may seem farfetched, but it is not so ridiculous as it sounds, and it cannot be ruled out as a possibility. For it is strange but true that the larvae of the Grotto Salamander are most frequently found in streams outside the cave, though a few larval specimens have also been captured in subterranean waters. Do the larvae hatch from the egg in the cave and then leave it to spend their larval life outside? If this be so, why do they leave the cave at all? And since it is known that their larval life is frequently spent in surface streams, why do they, when adult, leave the world of light and retreat to the complete darkness of the cave?

One answer to the last question lies in the adult Grotto Salamander's requirements. Inside the deepest recesses of the cave, the temperature remains constant year round, varying only by a degree or two. In addition, this air has a higher oxygen and moisture content than that of surface air. It is known that the Grotto Salamander cannot tolerate high temperatures. Perhaps, too, it cannot tolerate fluctuations in temperature either, and in order to survive it retreats to the only place in this region which meets its requirements in these respects—namely, the cave.

The larval Grotto Salamander is grayish-white above, with dirty white legs and belly. It has well-developed eyes that see as well as the eyes of any other salamander larva. When the time for metamorphosis approaches, the larva enters the cave and transforms there in utter darkness. As it transforms, or soon after, the eyelids close and grow together; the rods, cones, and eye muscles degenerate until the adult can no longer see. Of course, in the complete darkness of its environment eyes are of no use at all, but it seems curious that blindness is not an inherited characteristic in this species. Larval Grotto Salamanders do not lose their sight during metamorphosis if they are kept in a lighted place.

What does the adult Grotto Salamander look like? It is small, averaging about 3½ inches long, though larger and smaller specimens have been found. The head and body are long and slender, as are the legs. It is a pale flesh color with small orange spots scattered on the top of the tail. The eyes show as small dark spots, and are completely or almost completely covered by the fused eyelids. The Grotto Salamander is the only non-neotenous blind cave dweller known.

This summarizes what is known about this rare species. And since so very little *is* known, many questions occur to us—questions that will have to wait to be answered until some persistent scientist has done more research on these salamanders.

Rarer and more restricted in locality is the Texas Blind Salamander, *Typhlomolge rathbuni.* It has been found only in the area around San Marcos, Texas, about thirty miles southwest of Austin. In the Grotto Salamander, we have seen a species that has not, as yet, become completely adapted to cave life, for the larval period is spent at least in part outside. But the Texas Blind Salamander is a true cave dweller, for neither adults nor larvae have ever been found except in deep wells and the subterranean waters of caves.

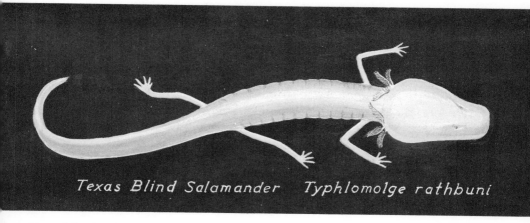

Texas Blind Salamander Typhlomolge rathbuni

One of the blind cave dwellers

Nothing is known of the breeding habits in nature, and the eggs have never been found, though one captive specimen did lay eggs in the laboratory.

Dr. Noble stated that the thyroid "may be absent" from this salamander. Whether this phrase means that it is absent from some specimens and not from others, or whether it means, as is probable, that sufficient data is lacking to make a positive statement, is not entirely clear to us. Be that as it may, the Texas Blind Salamander is neotenous with permanent gills. The larvae resemble the adults closely in form, but they are, of course, of a smaller size.

The average length of the adult Texas Blind Salamander is 3¾ inches, though individuals over 5 inches in length have been found. The general color of these animals is white, but parts of the head, body, and tail are suffused with iridescent shades of pale pink, blue, and lavender, which must give this rare creature a beautiful but strange appearance. The legs are very long—much longer than those of the Grotto Salamander—and slender, with long fingers and toes. Probably its most outstanding feature is its head, which is very broad in front of the gills and gently tapers to a long snout. The outline of the head viewed from the top resembles the outline of a dog's head. In a side view, however, this salamander's head looks not at all doglike, for from this angle it may be seen that the snout is very greatly flattened (herpetologists term it "depressed"). The eyes show as small black spots, but they are covered with skin. The eyes are completely useless, for not only are there no eye muscles or rods and cones, but even the lens is nonexistent.

Our remaining salamander is the Georgia Blind Salamander, *Haideotriton wallacei*. It is the rarest of them all, for only one specimen has ever been found and described. This individual was an adult female that came from a well 200 feet deep in Albany, Georgia, a town about 150 miles south of Atlanta. It is a small salamander, 3 inches in total length, neotenous, with permanent red gills. The head is broad, the snout equally broad and very gently rounded. The viscera and larger blood vessels may be seen easily through the thin white skin of the body and legs. There are no eyes at all, nor are there any dark eye spots that might indicate where they once were.

These are the blind cave dwellers of the amphibian world. Before leaving them altogether, let us consider for a moment the possible reasons for their rarity. Caves make ideal homes for many salamanders. They are primarily nocturnal creatures, and the cave with its darkness, even temperature and humidity, and high oxygen content would seem to be ideally suited to their needs. Why, then, are there so few of them? It may be because relatively few amphibians are able to tolerate the high concentrations of limestone found in many caves. It may be that most species require some light in order to survive. Perhaps they need more temperature variation than is present in most caves. And most important of all, perhaps there is an insufficient food supply to support great numbers of salamanders in the cave. We may wonder about all these things, but until we learn more about amphibians we cannot know why more of them do not make the darkest inner recesses of a cave their home.

It seems surprising that those salamanders who are true cave dwellers have not become highly adapted to the darkness, as have those other creatures of eternal night, the deep-sea dwellers. Instead of the huge eyes and phosphorescent bodies of many deep-sea fishes, the cave-dwelling salamanders have only pigmentless bodies and blindness. Nor have any extrasensory organs been developed on these cave creatures, though it is felt that sensory perception is greatly heightened. And since no green plants grow where there is no light, animals who live in the darkness are, of necessity, carnivores. The deep-sea fishes have evolved all kinds of devices for more efficient food getting, ranging from large teeth to elaborate "lures" to entice their prey within grabbing distance. But the blind cave-dwelling amphibians have none of these, and are the same as noncave salamanders.

Perhaps we are too impatient. Deep-sea fish were in existence millions of years before there were any amphibians or any caves. Is it possible that the blind cave dwellers may become as highly adapted in time? No one can know, for in nature all things are possible, but it is interesting, we think, to speculate.

CHAPTER 16

Our Unique Amphibian

The Tailed Frog, *Ascaphus truei,* is a unique animal in many ways. It is found in a belt about 100 miles wide along the coasts of Oregon, Washington, along the southern border of part of British Columbia, and down into Idaho and Montana about as far south as Weiser, Idaho. Its area of distribution when seen on a map resembles a reverse question mark with the tail of the mark running along the Pacific Coast line of Washington and Oregon. Within this region the Tailed Frog is found in wooded areas in or near small but rapidly flowing very cold mountain brooks.

It is considered to be an extremely primitive frog, with skeletal characteristics more like those of the salamanders than any other frog now living. Because of this, it is placed in the family Ascaphidae, of which it is the sole species. Recently the species has been divided into three subspecies, but we shall consider it as one species, and not bother about the small differences involved in the subspecific division.

All this, though nice to know, does not really greatly interest most of us, for we do not know enough about pectoral girdles and vertebral types to become wildly excited about the differences between them. We are most interested in the Tailed Frog because he represents an outstanding example of perfect adaptation to his environment. We mentioned the adaptations of the mountain-brook-dwelling frogs of Asia earlier. The Tailed Frog, though in no way related to them, has made similar adaptations for mountain-brook dwelling, but he has carried them much farther than have they.

What does the Tailed Frog look like? He is small. The maximum size recorded is 2 inches, but adult individuals have been found that are only a little over 1 inch long. This small creature has a very depressed body covered with a skin that may be either smooth or covered with widely scattered warts or wrinkles above. There is no tympanum, but a long brown parotoid gland is found on either side. The eyes with their vertical pupils are large. The Tailed Frog is brown on top, irregularly spotted with black. There is a bar of green or yellow between the eyes, and in front of this the snout is greenish or tan. The underparts are yellowish-white marked with a darker color of purplish hue. The fingers are long and thin and completely free of web; the toes are only partly webbed.

The outstanding external feature of the Tailed Frog is the "tail" possessed by the male. It is not, as we mentioned earlier, a true tail, for it has no bones, and extends, not from the spinal column as do all true tails, but from the underside. It is an extension of the cloaca and an intromittent organ. Incidentally, when a male Tailed Frog is measured, the "tail" is not included in the body measurement but is measured separately. The female Tailed Frog has a short anal tube, but this is not very long and is not readily visible unless one has a specimen in the hand.

Internally, the Tailed Frog has a number of interesting features. Unlike all other frogs, it has short ribs attached to some of the vertebrae. Its lungs are very much reduced, for in the mountain-brook habitat large lungs are a disadvantage rather than an advantage. Its tongue is nonprotrusile. A protrusile tongue—or a tongue at all—is not, as we noted earlier, of any use as a food-getting device in water. Though the Tailed Frog has no true tail, it is surprising to learn that he (and she) have two tail-wagging muscles, as do the salamanders.

The males may be distinguished from the females not only by their "tails" but also by the horny excrescences on the inner side of the first finger, forearm, and even sometimes on the chest. The male arms, legs, and feet are larger and thicker than those of the female. But he has no vocal sacs and no voice. A voice would be of little use to him, for though some frogs do call under water, it is generally

The Tailed Frog, *Ascaphus truei,* **showing the adult male and female and the tadpoles**

in a quiet pond that they do so. If the Tailed Frog did have a voice, the sound would be inaudible, or very nearly so, in the rushing water of the brook.

Correlated to the lack of voice and the mountain-brook habitat is the fact that the ear of the Tailed Frog is not like that of most frogs. He lacks not only a tympanum—a condition quite frequently found—but also lacks a Eustachian tube and a stapes. It would seem that the hearing of the Tailed Frog is not very keen, though experiments to determine just what sounds he can hear are lacking. Since he lacks a tympanum and a stapes, it is difficult to imagine how any sounds at all could be transmitted to the inner ear inside the brain case.

Since the male Tailed Frog lacks a voice with which to attract his mate, and since she lacks ears to receive air-borne sounds, they have developed other means by which they come together. During the breeding season, which extends from May through September, the male crawls along the bottom of the stream looking for a female.

He does not, as do other frogs, wait for her to come to him. As he crawls along, he grasps any frog that comes near him, but unless it is a female swollen with unlaid eggs he releases his grip. Upon finding a female, he grasps her, not just behind her forearms, but just in front of her hind legs. This is termed inguinal amplexus as distinguished from pectoral amplexus. The male then bends the hind part of his body down between the female's extended hind legs and inserts his "tail" into her anal tube. The sperm goes into the female's oviducts, since there is no spermatheca or separate chamber in which to store the sperm, such as is found in all salamanders that practice internal fertilization.

We know that external fertilization is uncertain in swift-running water, a fact that helps to explain why so few frogs lay their eggs in such a habitat. The Tailed Frog has admirably solved the problem by practicing internal fertilization.

The eggs of the female are very large—about 5 mm.—and are surrounded by a capsule of 8 mm. in diameter. These eggs are unpigmented. They emerge from the female's oviducts in two rosary-like strings, and are deposited in a circular mass attached to the underside of rocks in the stream. The total egg complement does not exceed 50. This is a small number; but that should not surprise us, for not only is the Tailed Frog a small animal and the eggs large, but internal fertilization makes large numbers unnecessary.

The incubation period of the eggs is about one month. The Tailed Frog tadpole is much like those of the Asian mountain-brook dwellers of the genus *Staurois*. It has a rather wedge-shaped body when viewed in outline from above. The tail is long, but the tail crests are low and never extend up onto the body as do those of many pond-dwelling tadpoles. The spiracle is located near the anus on the underside of the body. These tadpoles are dark in color, speckled with black. The tail is similar in color to the body, and may be speckled with either black or white. The tip of the tail is white.

The mouth of the tadpole is very large and round. On the upper labium we find two or three uninterrupted rows of labial teeth. There is an upper mandible. The lower labium has anywhere from seven to ten rows of labial teeth—a very large number when we consider that most of our native frogs have only two or three rows. There is no lower mandible at all.

The tadpole of the Tailed Frog lives principally on the algae growing on rocks. It clings to these rocks with its large suctorial lips and scrapes its food from their surface with the labial teeth and upper mandible. Such is its nature that it prefers the rocks found where the water runs at its swiftest, and most of its larval life is spent attached to these boulders. The tadpoles are able to swim even against the current, but they do not do so very much, preferring to move by inching their way along by the movements of the lips.

The exact time between hatching and metamorphosis has not been precisely determined, but it is about a year in most places, though in Canada, where the mean annual temperature of the water is slightly colder, a two-year-old tadpole was found.

The adult Tailed Frog spends much of its life in the water hiding under rocks. It is extremely solitary in habit, and one evidently does not find numbers of them in a small area. Occasionally, after periods of heavy rain, they leave the stream and enter the forest for a change of scenery, so to speak. How far from the water they could be found would be interesting to know. We wonder also just how long they would stay away from the stream. What prompts them to leave it? Study of this species should be very rewarding for those who live in its vicinity, for few details concerning its everyday life are known.

Enemies

The number of enemies that prey on animals in the wild is astounding. No animal is completely immune to depredation. The porcupine with his sharp quills has a weapon that few animals care to tangle with. But bears and martens have learned how to turn the porcupine on its stomach, and thereby kill it with ease, for the underside is unprotected by quills. Since the amphibians are relatively small and comparatively helpless, they seem to have more than their fair share of enemies. From the moment the egg leaves the mother's body until the day the adult amphibian dies, life is fraught with danger. Toads have lived for thirty years in captivity, but I imagine that the toad that is able to survive this long in the wild is more myth than fact.

The Michigan Department of Conservation recently issued a booklet entitled *Red Foxes of Michigan*. We usually think of the fox as an animal without many enemies, and with a life span similar to that of a dog—about ten to fourteen years. The Michigan Department of Conservation discovered, however, that the average life of a fox in the wild was about one year! Despite the fact that foxes produce between four and eight young, the fox population remains stable from year to year.

What is the average life span of a toad in the wild? We don't know, but it has been estimated that less than 5 per cent of a toad's eggs live to attain adulthood. Since the toad may lay as many as 20,000 eggs, this would amount to about 1,000 little toads. You may think that this is a fair number, and so it is. Within a year, however, only about 100 of the 1,000 will still be living. As you can see by these figures, the mortality rate rises with age. Some investigators seem to feel that the mortality rate is greatest during "egghood." We have two diametrically opposite views here, and there are good arguments for both sides. It is almost impossible to obtain accurate figures in nature to settle the matter conclusively. But it really isn't important to most of us. Suffice it to say that the mortality rate is high at all stages of development.

As we have seen, the amphibian eggs have no shell and are protected only by the jelly surrounding them. Insects and other animals that could not hope to feed on the hard-shelled egg of reptiles or birds are therefore able to eat frog's eggs with ease.

The insects that prey on the eggs are usually aquatic, for eggs laid on land are frequently protected by the parent. Besides, terrestrial eggs, whether guarded by the adult or not, are not all laid in the same spot. Whereas almost any pond will have many millions of eggs in it during the beeding season, land-laid eggs are well hidden under logs or stones. Occasionally, several individuals of like species lay in a common nest, but as a general rule each female makes her own nest apart from others of her kind.

Because there are so many aquatic eggs laid in the pond, with little attempt at concealment, it is not surprising that these defenseless eggs should constitute a convenient food supply for the many different kinds of larvae that make their home in the pond. The larvae of many different kinds of water beetles eat aquatic eggs, as do dragonfly nymphs. The Giant Water Bug may resort to a meal of eggs if nothing larger presents itself. The black sheep of the earthworm family, the leech, also enjoys eggs for breakfast. Dr. Liu reports that Planaria, a class of nonparasitic flatworms, common in cold-water streams all over the world, eat the eggs of *Staurois chunganensis* and *Rana boulengeri*. In fact, eggs of the former species placed in cloth cages in the stream for rearing were picked clean of Planaria twice a day. In spite of this care, over half of the embryos were destroyed by these carnivorous animals. Though we have never read of it, or seen it, we wonder whether the eggs of our stream dwellers are not also often destroyed by planarians.

Furthermore, the eggs of amphibians are often eaten by the adults. The Bullfrog and the newt both like eggs, as do many others. Amphibians, of course, prefer other food, such as insects; if they didn't, they would rapidly eat themselves into extinction. When, however, other prey is unavailable, they are not above eating their own eggs or those of other species.

You might think that aquatic eggs watched over by the parent would be relatively safe from enemies. The male Hellbender, who fiercely fights off all intruders, would seem to be more than a match for any insect or other amphibian that might come along to disturb the eggs. He is; but he has a weakness for eggs himself, and does not hesitate to eat some of the eggs he so carefully guards from others. However, since the eggs take about 2½ months to hatch, and since the male Hellbender does not leave them until after they are hatched and the little ones are ready to leave the nest, undoubtedly the pangs of hunger drive him to it. When we judge animals from a human standpoint, we must not fail to take into account all the factors in the case. It is doubtful if the Hellbender knows why he is guarding the eggs or even what the eggs are—namely, the next generation of Hellbenders. Instinct tells him to guard the eggs—but not why he should—and guard them he does against all interlopers. Instinct does not tell him that it is wrong to eat a few eggs if he is hungry. As far as Nature is concerned, it is far more important that a few eggs be sacrificed to keep the watching male alert and healthy than that he become lethargic from starvation and leave all the eggs without protection.

As we mentioned earlier, the hylas on the island of Jamaica all lay their eggs in the rosettes of bromeliads. Frequently, one plant will contain the egg complement of several females. The tadpoles hatch out, and may find themselves short of food and space. Consequently, a large part of their diet consists of unhatched eggs. Many species are equipped with a special egg tooth enabling them to cut through the tough egg capsule and eat the nourishing vitellus.

Those amphibian eggs that live long enough to develop and hatch out into tadpoles and larvae do not live the carefree life that some of their antics might lead us to believe that they do. Far from it. The older the amphibian gets, the more enemies it seems to accumulate. The tadpole and larva must fear not only all the enemies of the egg, but some new ones as well. Fish, which do not bother with

the eggs, are voracious in their appetite for tadpoles. Among the worst offenders are pike, bass, and catfish. Reptiles also, such as snakes and the aquatic turtles, love a meal of tadpole.

The Giant Water Bug prefers tadpoles to eggs. This brown, flat-bodied insect is 2 inches long, and about ¾ of an inch wide. He would give all but the most ardent entomologist the shudders. This ogre lurks among the water weeds, hanging by his hind legs head downward. His front legs extend ready to grab any unwary tadpole that ventures too close. Once he has captured the soft-bodied animal in his powerful forearms, he transports it to his mouth, inserts his beak, and begins sucking a liquid meal. Soon nothing is left of the tadpole but a husk. Not a very pleasant way to die, but the Giant Water Bug is not a very agreeable sort of creature. If you tangle with him, you will regret it almost as much as the hapless

Left above: **Dragonfly nymph with the labium extended**
Left below: **The Giant Water Bug, *Lethocerus americanus***
Below: **Larva of the water beetle *Cybister* eating a tadpole**

tadpole. Though you will not pay for your carelessness with your life, for several days afterward you will have a very painful swelling where you were bitten.

The aquatic larvae of dragonflies probably eat a few tadpoles when the latter are in the earlier stages of development.

The large Diving Beetles, *Acilius*, *Dytiscus*, and *Cybister*, as well as many smaller beetles, prey on tadpoles. These do not hesitate to attack animals much larger than themselves. They are no mean size, for they range from 1 to almost 2 inches long. Their larvae, known as Water Tigers, are even more rapacious than themselves. The Water Tigers have long bodies with two sharp curved hollow mandibles. The mandibles are used both for grasping the prey and for sucking out its body juices. The appetite of the Water Tiger is almost insatiable, and the number of tadpoles they eat must be prodigious. Not having any precise scales, we have never weighed a Water Tiger and the food it consumes in a day. However, judging by bulk, I do not believe it would be an exaggeration to say that they probably eat their own weight in food every day. It is nothing for a Water Tiger to eat three or four tadpoles in an hour or two. After such a meal, they are satiated, though when in the aquarium they will often kill other tadpoles even though they do not eat them. However, a meal of three or four tadpoles does not satisfy them long, and they are ready to eat again after a few hours.

One would never think of spiders as enemies of tadpoles and larvae, and it is true that they are not major enemies. However, there are two families of spiders, the Lycosidae, or Wolf Spiders, and the Pisauridae, or the Nursery Web Weavers, certain members of which do eat an occasional tadpole or larva. Both Pirata (belonging to the Lycosidae) and Dolomedes (belonging to the Pisauridae) are large spiders that live near the water. They are able to run on the surface of the water and even dive underneath it for a moment or two, it is said, though we have never been so fortunate as to witness this. These spiders do not weave webs to catch their food. They depend instead on their swiftness to enable them to run down their prey, like their namesake, the wolves. Indeed, they can move almost faster than the eye can follow them. When they spy a tadpole, they dart out onto the surface of the water, and insert their poison fangs; the tadpole is immediately anesthetized by the bite, and dragged out of water to be eaten.

Certain tadpoles, such as the Wood Frog tadpoles, and all salamander larvae are carnivorous. They do not hesitate to eat any smaller or weak members of their own or different species. Some years ago, when we were beginning to learn about amphibians, we had an aquarium in which were housed some newly hatched Spotted Salamander larvae, and one fair-sized newt larva. After a few days there seemed to be considerably fewer Spotted Salamander larvae than there were in the beginning. We thought it must be our imagination, but after a week it became quite apparent that the newt was eating them. In the wild, we don't believe that small tadpoles or larvae make up a very large percentage of the larger carnivorous tadpole's diet—obviously they couldn't, or the species wouldn't survive—nonetheless, some of them *are* eaten by their stronger brothers.

There are many microscopic crustaceans, relatives of the lobster, that prey on the young amphibian. One of the most common of these is a copepod that attacks salamander larvae, first eating their external gills, so vulnerable because of the thin skin, and so nourishing to the predator because of their rich supply of blood. No more efficacious method could be devised for a minute animal to kill one so much larger than itself.

And now, we come to the enemies of the adult amphibian. It may come as a surprise to many people to learn that frogs, toads, and salamanders suffer from diseases and parasites just as we do. Because a complete list of all these would be lengthy and boring, we shall confine ourselves to glancing at just a few of them.

Amphibians, especially frogs and toads, suffer from several fungus skin diseases, which are usually fatal. Since the amphibian depends on his skin as a respirator and internal-temperature regulator, as well as for protection, it is no wonder that any damage to it is followed by death. One of the most common of these diseases manifests itself by feltlike blotches on the skin. The fungus soon spreads all over the animal's body. It is highly contagious, and if one amphibian in a small pond is stricken the others will soon contract it also.

A serious bacteria-caused disease is "red leg." This disease produces hemorrhages under the skin of the belly. The frogs become edematous. That is, their skin absorbs more water than their kidneys can discharge, and they are bloated or waterlogged. "Red leg" is also contagious, and any diseased animal that touches a healthy animal transmits his affliction. "Red leg" is the bane of the laboratory frog's existence. It is common in the lab, but you will be happy to learn that if your frogs contract it you can cure them by putting them in your icebox for a while.

That is, maybe you can. We had an experience that was inconclusive, but we shall relate it for reasons that will become apparent. We had, in an aquarium, two Green Frog tadpoles. Both had well-developed legs and one had arms as well. We noticed that a small area on the underside of one hind leg on the more advanced specimen was quite red. This looked suspicious to us, and we watched this individual carefully. The red area, which was a gorgeous cherry color, spread to include the underparts of both legs and the lower half of the belly. The animal appeared quite bloated as well. As the days passed, we found this frog on a rock frequently, though his long tail still remained. At this point, we felt that the animal was now depending on his lungs to supply his oxygen and that we should try the icebox treatment. Accordingly, we popped him in. A day passed, then two, then three. No change was apparent in his bloated condition, nor did the color of the red underparts fade to the normal yellowish white. On the morning of the fourth day, we found that the poor creature had expired during the night. Did he die of a respiratory failure of his perhaps insufficiently developed lungs? Or did he die of "red leg"? If the latter was true, why didn't he show some improvement after three days in the icebox? How did he contract "red leg"—if that's what it was—in the first place? The other inhabitant of the aquarium never developed "red leg." Why not, if it is so contagious? And if it was not "red leg," what caused the bloating and red underparts of the first unfortunate? We don't know any of the answers, but the facts as they stand and the questions they invite make one suspect (with all due respect, of course,) the scientists' pronouncements on the causes, effects, and cure of "red leg."

Unfortunately, in nature, there is no icebox cure the frog can take, unless by some miracle he gets the disease in the fall, when it is beginning to get cold. Probably in nature, however, the disease is not so common as in the laboratory, though a number of authentic cases of "red leg" in ponds have been recorded.

Not too long ago, one alert amateur observer of amphibians found a male toad grasping a dead female. Since the male toad has a tremendously strong nuptial embrace, the man attributed the female's death to an excess of ardor on the part of the male. He returned to this pond a day later and found more dead females, some with live males embracing them. He thought this unusual. Upon returning on the third or fourth day, he found not one toad alive. Most of the dead were couples, for the clasping reflex is so strong in the male toad that even death does not relax it, and usually release comes only when the female feels slimmer—after she has laid her eggs. Since these females had "red leg," they kept getting fatter from water absorption, and naturally the males retained their holds. Soon they too caught the disease, and died still grasping their dead mates in their arms.

Many microscopic parasites have been found in frogs and toads.

Among them are the tubercule bacillus; *Trypanosome inspinatum*, a relation of the trypanosome that causes African sleeping sickness in humans; Hemosporidia, other species of which cause malaria and tick fever; and amoebas, causing dysentery in man. Many of these undesirables are transmitted to the amphibian by the bites of leeches. But whether all of the many species of leeches transmit all these parasites, or whether just certain species transmit certain parasites, no one knows. Research on leeches could be tremendously rewarding for those who have the equipment and the necessary desire to work with them. We, personally, admit that we do not care for them, and we can never repress an indignant shudder when we see a leech attached to a frog. This happens quite frequently, incidentally, especially in the spring and early summer. Whether this is because there are more frogs around the ponds, or because we catch more then, or because of the leeches' habits, we cannot say. Perhaps all three are factors. Be that as it may, during the amphibian breeding season, three out of every five frogs we catch have leeches on them.

Little is known about the results of parasites transmitted by leech bites and a myriad of other tiny parasites on their amphibian hosts. Some are believed to cause disease in their host, but the precise symptoms and the results of these diseases have not been fully investigated. Others of these parasites have not been proved innocent or guilty. They may or may not be pathological. Diseases of animals in the wild are difficult to trace, for wild animals usually crawl off to a hidden spot to die. And once dead, Nature's scavengers, leeches, planarians, crawfish in the water, burying and carrion beetles on land, soon consume the body so that little if anything remains for a post-mortem.

Nor is much known about the effects of larger parasites on amphibians. They have roundworms and hookworms, tapeworms and flukes, all of which attack our domestic animals, and even man, with results that are always unpleasant and often disastrous if the affected animals are not wormed in time.

There are flies that parasitize frogs and toads in much the same way that the botfly parasitizes horses and mules. Some species of these flies lay their eggs in the nostrils of toads. Upon hatching, the larvae or maggots crawl into the nasal and body cavities. We imagine that death ensues, for when lungs and other organs are riddled with maggots, all voraciously feeding on them, their efficiency must be impaired, to say the least.

Mrs. Goin, in her charming book *World Outside My Door*, reports seeing the lizards known as Anoles dropping to the ground dead. Shortly afterward white maggots ate their way out of the dead Anoles, burrowed into the ground, and soon transformed into tiny flies. It is doubtless the same with the amphibians, though the same species of fly does not parasitize both amphibians and Anoles, for many parasites manifest considerable host specificity. For example, none of the other kinds of lizards found by Mrs. Goin were bothered by the Anole fly.

Another species of fly, known as *Batrochomyia*, lives in Australia. This fly lays its eggs under the skin of frogs. As the eggs hatch, and the larvae grow, they make huge lumps under the frog's skin. The maggots eventually bore their way out to pupate in the ground. Usually the frog does not die, though he could hardly be in the best condition to fight off other enemies and disease. In fact, he must be all the more vulnerable, and personally, we would be willing to hazard that most of the frogs that have suffered maggot infestation of *Batrochomyia* do die—if not directly from the maggots, then indirectly because of their lowered resistance to disease and predation.

When we come to larger enemies, there are many of them also. Probably frog Enemy Number One is the snake. Not all snakes eat amphibians; many prefer a diet of rats, mice, and other warm-blooded prey. But the water snakes, garter snakes, blacksnakes, hognose snakes, and even the poisonous copperhead all love a meal of frog or toad. The salamanders are less often caught by them because they are smaller and more secretive. The Mud, Musk, and Snapping Turtles take their share of aquatic amphibians. Even the alligator eats frogs.

Herons and domestic ducks prey on aquatic species, crows on terrestrial species. The screech owl eats numbers of nocturnal salamanders.

Weasels, skunks, raccoons, rats, cats, and dogs all enjoy frogs. But the mammal that does more damage than all the others put together is man. This should come as no surprise. Man is the most destructive of all of Nature's children. Man kills amphibians in many ways. First of all, he does so by draining swamps and polluting water with garbage, sewerage, insecticides, and "planticides." Many of the amphibians thus trapped do not survive a trip to other waters, but die of desiccation on the way. Amphibians are not so fussy about water as many tropical fish are, but they cannot withstand powerful chemicals that are often added to ponds and swamps to kill insects or noxious water plants.

The toads are attracted to street lights at night for much the same reason that we are attracted to a softly lighted restaurant. They know that they will not fail to secure a fine variety of delicious food. They sit under the lights on the street, snapping up moths and other night-flying insects drawn to the light. Unfortunately, cars also go under street lights, and many toads are run over as they sit peacefully eating their dinners.

Frogs' legs are considered a great delicacy. It used to be that they could be ordered only in the finest restaurants. Since the advent of the freezer and frozen foods, frogs' legs may be bought in almost any store or·supermarket. This means, of course, that more frogs are caught than ever before.

Frogs are used by man in school, college, and medical laboratories everywhere. Anyone who has ever taken a course in biology in school has dissected at least one frog. They are also widely used in medical research. But we shall discuss this and also tell more about frogs' legs in another chapter.

Natural causes or "acts of God" are not usually considered enemies. But since they reduce the number of animals that survive, we shall discuss them briefly here.

Drought kills millions of amphibians, from the egg up to and including the adults. The greatest mortality rate is in the egg and larval stages. In a dry spring the water line of ponds and swamps recedes rapidly, leaving many eggs high and dry. Toad eggs are particularly vulnerable, since they are always laid in very shallow water—often in a mud puddle that may well evaporate even in a year of normal rainfall. During the summer one usually finds a few frogs dead from desiccation. They have misjudged the distance to another spot of water, or they go onto a plowed field or road, not realizing how hot and dry it is. Frogs can endure quite a bit of desiccation if it is gradual—up to 30 per cent—but speedy dehydration kills quickly. A frog's skin absorbs water when the animal requires it. A frog's skin also evaporates water quickly when the air is dry, and if he is exposed to hot dry air for long it is not surprising that he should die. The rough-skinned toads are not, of course, so likely to become desiccated, partly because they are not, as a rule, diurnal, and partly because their skin, being thicker and dry, does not lose water by evaporation so rapidly. Salamanders, too, are less vulnerable because they are secretive, and keep well under cover for the most part, and the majority are nocturnal.

Spring freezing kills many eggs. Some species of frogs and salamanders appear at the breeding sites to lay their eggs when the nights are very cold and there are thin films of ice on the water. Wood Frogs, and some of the Mole Salamanders are among those that lay early. If they do not lay their eggs in deep-enough water, the eggs may freeze and will not develop. The adults and larvae themselves are not affected by the ice, for they can go to deeper water and remain there until it warms up. But the eggs are stationary, and until they hatch they have no defense at all against freezing.

Though the amphibians have many enemies, Nature is not so cruel as to leave them completely at the mercy of these foes, and has endowed frogs, toads, and salamanders with some defenses. Let us now look and see what they are.

CHAPTER 18

Defense

Amphibians have many enemies, as we have seen, and few of them have any active defense. Nevertheless, there are a number of ways in which the amphibian is able to ward off predators.

Probably the most valuable protection the amphibian possesses is his skin. All amphibians have mucous glands in their skin. These serve primarily to keep the skin lubricated, but they are also a defense, for a struggling moist-skinned amphibian is almost as slippery and difficult to hold as the proverbial greased pig.

But by far the greatest protection comes from the granular glands in the skin. These occur on various parts of the body. The parotoid glands of toads, those largest of warts located behind the eyes, are granular glands, as are the dorsolateral folds of frogs. The granular glands of salamanders are distributed over various places on their backs. All the tadpoles of the Asian genus *Staurois* have two pairs of poison glands. One pair is on top, behind and below each eye. The second pair is located on the belly on either side of the anus. (See illustration, page 96.) These tadpoles are unique in possessing poison glands. Do these glands serve as a defense against insects, Planaria, leeches, or other enemies? Experiments are needed to prove this, for as yet we do not know the answer.

The granular glands of adult amphibians function only with outside pressure or from injury. If you press the parotoid glands of a toad, you will see that a thick mucous spurts from them. This secretion is, in many species, extremely poisonous when swallowed. It also acts on all mucous membranes. If you rub your eyes after handling an amphibian, your eye will immediately begin to water and sting. Put your hand in your mouth, and your tongue will start to burn, and after touching at least one species your tongue and lips may, after the burning sensation has passed, become as numb as they do after an injection of novocain.

Not all amphibians have strongly poisonous skin secretions, but most of them will cause irritation to the mucous membranes of man and beast. Some, however, are sure death to an animal that eats them, and in some cases they are lethal to an animal that even bites them.

The amphibian with one of the most virulent poisons known is *Bufo marinus,* one of the biggest of all the true toads. A large specimen of this animal may have a body and head length of 8½ inches. *Bufo marinus* is found in southern Texas and southern Florida, but specimens found here do not attain the maximum size. For the really big ones you must go into Central and South America. The enormous triangular-shaped parotoids of this toad eject a stream of thick milky venom when pressed, and this is the principal poison. However, a dog who bit a Giant Toad on the leg became paralyzed less than a minute later, which proves that the mucous glands of this species are also poisonous. Fortunately for the dog, he recovered after an hour or two. Had he seized the toad in his mouth, or snapped the parotoid, the outcome would have been less fortunate.

Since the secretions of *Bufo marinus* are, at present, being used in the medical laboratory, it is necessary to "milk" the toads, just as poisonous snakes are "milked" to obtain their venom to make the serum for snake bite. The workers who extract the poison of *Bufo marinus* must be extremely careful not to get any of it in their eyes, for it causes temporary blindness and excruciating pain.

Bufo marinus feeds largely on beetles and cockroaches, and so is of great benefit in the tropics where cockroaches, as one friend of ours insisted, grow as large as rats. She exaggerated a little, we suspect, but we can see her point. We once saw a cockroach on Third Avenue in New York that must have been fully 1½ inches long, and *he* looked as large as a rat to us.

A little closer to home is the American Toad, *Bufo americanus,* found throughout the northeastern part of the country. His secretions are also poisonous, though not quite so virulent or as lethal as those of the Giant Toad. Nevertheless, if your dog grabs one, you will see him quickly release it, and he will be in considerable pain until the next day.

Dendrobates is a South American amphibian distantly related to our treefrogs. Many species are brilliantly colored in vivid green or pink with darker spots, and most of them are forest dwellers. The South American Indians make good use of the poison from these small frogs. They smear their arrows and blowgun darts with the poison. Small animals hit by such treated weapons are said to die immediately, so virulent is the venom when thus injected into the bloodstream.

The Pickerel Frog, *Rana palustris,* of the eastern half of this country, has a strong poison. It is said that other types of frogs carried home in the same jar with it will die, though we have never tested this statement. Snakes living in the same territory as the Pickerel Frog are able to tell the difference between it and the Leopard Frog, *Rana pipiens,* which looks so much like it. *Rana pipiens* is harmless, and snakes enjoy it; *Rana palustris* they shun. Snakes that do not live in the same territory as *Rana palustris* can be induced to eat it. The result, however, is death to the snake within a half-hour.

Most of the secretions of amphibians work only on the mucous membranes, or on the internal organs or the bloodstream. No toad can give you warts, for instance, nor does it harm your skin in any way to handle amphibians. There is but one possible exception to this. The largest of treefrogs is an animal about the size of our Green Frog, *Rana clamitans.* This treefrog, known as *Hyla vasta,* lives on the island of Haiti. Its skin secretions are known to burn the hands—like acid, according to one reporter, though others say one feels only a stinging or burning sensation. Be that as it may, collectors of *Hyla vasta* would do well to wear gloves.

Since amphibians make up part of the diet of many animals, what are the results of the poisons on them? First of all, it must be remembered that amphibians differ in the virulence of their poisons. Possibly the amphibian eaters are able to differentiate between the more poisonous and those that are innocuous. We know definitely that certain snakes are able to do so; perhaps all of them can, though this has not been proved. Just as certain snakes that eat rattlesnakes are immune to the rattlesnake's venom, so some amphibian-eating snakes may have a certain immunity to the effects of the amphibian's poison.

Skunks and raccoons are very fond of amphibians. Skunks seem to have a special love for the terrestrial nocturnal toad, while the raccoons eat principally the aquatic frogs. Now the American Toad, as we know, is poisonous. The skunk, however, when he captures a toad, has been seen rolling the unfortunate creature over and over in the dirt. This makes the toad express the venom on the ground, and not in the skunk's mouth. Not until the skunk has rolled his prey thoroughly does he eat it. Perhaps skunks possess a certain immunity to toad venom. They have a certain immunity against the effects of rattlesnake venom.

It should be emphasized here that the venom of rattlesnakes is not poisonous when swallowed. Nor is rattlesnake venom the same type of poison as those of the amphibians. Therefore, it does not necessarily follow that because an animal is immune to the effects of the bite of a rattlesnake that he is also immune to the effects of the various amphibian poisons.

So far as we know, the raccoon possesses no immunity to either the poison of snakes or of amphibians. But when raccoons are near water, they usually wash their food before devouring it. A frog or salamander is deftly caught by the strong little black hands, squeezed, washed, torn apart, washed again, and then eaten. Perhaps it was to protect them from eating harmful amphibian poisons that this habit of washing food caught near the water arose. Raccoons are very fond of corn, and will quickly destroy a stand of corn, pulling and shucking far more than they can eat. They do not carry the corn away with them to the nearest stream to wash before they eat it, as we have heard some people suggest. They eat it in the field, without washing it. Owners of pet raccoons report that, contrary to popular opinion, they do not wash all their food, but only some of it, even though the water pan is close by.

Cats and dogs are also enemies of amphibians. But a cat is like a skunk in the way it plays with a frog or toad before eating it. A dog usually drops a toad when he mouths it. But should he gulp it down, he will be nauseated, and his muscles will become paralyzed.

When the paralysis reaches the respiratory centers and the heart, he will die.

Actually, it is difficult to generalize about amphibian poisons and still be accurate. First of all, the secretions of both mucous and granular glands may be unalike; furthermore, they are different in different species. Then too, relatively few of the secretions have been chemically analyzed. A few examples will serve to illustrate our point. The South American frog, *Dendrobates tinctorius,* has a skin secretion that is of the neurotoxic type. It acts in a manner similar to the venom of cobras and our native Coral Snake, paralyzing the nerves. Secretions from the mucous glands of certain amphibians may act as does the venom of the vipers and pit vipers, such as our rattlesnakes, destroying the blood. The parotoid and other granular glands of many toads produce secretions that act in much the same way as does an overdose of the drug digitalis, paralyzing the muscles so that the heart is unable to beat, the lungs to inhale and exhale, and so on.

Biting is an active defense, and not one that we usually associate with amphibians. Frogs and toads do not bite, with a few exceptions. Most frogs and toads lack teeth large enough to make biting efficient. Some have teeth only on the lower jaw; some only on the upper jaw; while a few have no teeth at all. One of the outstanding exceptions to this no-biting rule is the Horned Frog, *Ceratophrys dorsata,* of South America (page 226). This is a large broad-bodied frog with a brilliant green back and dark markings. He gets his popular name from the two triangular "horns" just above his eyes. The Horned Frog possesses sharp teeth on his upper jaws and sharp bony processes on the lower jaw; what is more, he does not hesitate to use these teeth. Not for him is the strategic retreat. As an enemy approaches, the Horned Frog hops toward him, and snaps. If the enemy decides an approach from the rear is the better maneuver, the frog jumps around to face his adversary rather than attempt to escape. More than one collector has been bitten painfully as he extended a hand to capture the Horned Frog. Once this frog has a hold, he is as difficult to shake loose as a snapping turtle or a bulldog, for he hangs on just as tenaciously as they do.

The salamanders use biting as a defense more than the frogs and toads, and with good reason. In general, salamanders have better teeth and more of them than do frogs and toads. They have teeth not only on both upper and lower jaws, but most of them have some teeth on the roof of the mouth as well. These teeth are often slanted back toward the throat, making it difficult for food and enemies to wriggle loose from a salamander's grasp.

Naturally, the bite of the smaller salamanders is effective only against small enemies. The Mole Salamanders bite at small snakes that attack them, but we have never had one offer to bite us. With some of the larger salamanders, however, it is another matter. The large neotenous salamander, Amphiuma, bites fiercely. It is noted for its quick temper and viciousness in attacking when disturbed. Siren, however, seems to be harmless. The other large neotenous salamanders, the Mudpuppy and the Hellbender, do, we understand, bite occasionally, but they do not assume such an aggressive attitude as do the more eel-like salamanders.

Horned Frog
Ceratophrys dorsata

Gampsosteonyx batesi

Two frogs with unusual methods of defense

There is an African frog with the imposing name of *Gampsoste-onyx batesi,* who uses scratching as a defense. Now amphibians, as we know, do not have true claws as do lizards and some mammals. But in *Gampsosteonyx batesi,* the last bone of all the digits protrudes through the skin. This "claw" development is not confined to this frog alone; others, such as the Platanna, *Xenopus laevis,* have this type of "claw" development to a lesser degree, though they do not, that we have ever heard, use their claws for anything. But when *Gampsosteonyx batesi* is caught, his claws dig in and give very painful scratches. Herpetologists have wondered to what other use he puts his claws, for they feel that the defense that the claws offer is only incidental and not their principal reason for being. Some think that they may be useful in cracking open the shells of crabs on which this frog is reported to feed. But, like many foreign species, relatively little is known about his life.

Most amphibians, when seized, immediately eliminate the contents of their bladder. If you are not expecting this flood of water, you may be startled into dropping the toad you have picked up to examine. This elimination serves two purposes. It makes the animal lighter, and thus facilitates a speedier escape. It also provides a water "smoke screen" to divert an enemy's attention momentarily from the animal's flight. It is interesting to note that the urinary bladder is largest in the true toads of the genus *Bufo* and in the neotenous salamander Amphiuma. A large bladder is of considerable value as a protection against desiccation in the terrestrial toads. Whether it is of any use to the aquatic Amphiuma is questionable.

All frogs and toads are able to scream. The noise that they make is quite unlike their normal singing voice, and in some species it is similar to a baby's cry. This scream is uttered when the amphibian is pinched or squeezed, and is primarily a cry of pain and not a defense reaction. But it is not without its protection value against humans. Have you ever pulled a wild rabbit out of a stone wall? The loud scream coming from an animal normally so silent is startling, and you may let it go. Animals that prey on rabbits or frogs, of course, are not usually surprised by the rabbit's cry, nor are they likely to pay much attention to a frog's scream, but some people may be astonished or moved by pity into releasing a screaming animal. One scientist has suggested that the frog's pain cry may serve as a warning of danger to all other frogs in the neighborhood.

Garter Snake and Green Frog, showing the frog's defense reflex

We have noticed that quite frequently the scream reflex is only partially induced in the Green Frog. Many open their mouths when captured by a snake, but no sound emerges. In fact, only one Green Frog ever actually screamed. The sound it made was much like the crying of a newborn baby. The scream started as soon as the frog was seized, and continued even after it was completely swallowed and until it reached the snake's stomach. Salamanders, incidentally, have no vocal chords, and therefore are completely silent when caught or handled roughly.

Frogs and toads with their short bodies and long legs have another defense mechanism the salamanders lack. When threatened by an enemy, they inflate their lungs, bow their heads, and extend both fore and hind legs, lifting the body well off the ground. Dr. Noble tells us that this defense reflex is, as a general rule, better developed in the more terrestrial salientians. We have found that the Pickerel and Leopard Frogs do not assume this defense reflex so rapidly as does the Green Frog. When confined with a snake, they spend a much longer time trying to escape than does the Green Frog, who quickly tires and assumes this defense posture.

Somewhat similar to this inflation is the warning attitude assumed by many foreign frogs and toads, especially those aquatic toads of the genus *Bombina* found in Europe and Asia. They arch their backs and heads and extend the arms and legs over their backs, taking a position similar to the one a person takes when executing the exercise known as the "rocking horse." In addition, the eyes are closed, respiratory movements are retarded, and skin secretions are increased. This is known as the *unken* reflex. Since many of the frogs and toads who adopt this defense reaction have brightly colored underparts and poisonous skin secretions, herpetologists think that the display of chest, palms of hands, and soles of feet is intended as a warning to enemies to keep their distance.

If the frogs and toads can assume different shapes and postures with their bodies, it seems only fair that the salamanders should be able to defend themselves in some way by using their tails. And they can. The long thin salamander squirms desperately when captured, and this often enables the animal to free itself, or at least to free the body from an enemy's grasp, which in many species is the same thing. Many of the Lungless Salamanders snap their tails off when grasped by this appendage. The enemy is momentarily distracted and interested in subduing the tail, which wriggles violently, and the now short-tailed salamander makes good his escape. He is not incapacitated in the least, for, strange as it seems to us, there is no pain involved and little or no blood. The salamander will soon

Two-lined Salamander with its tail broken off

grow a new tail, not quite so long as the original, but just as useful.)

Most people have, at some time, seen a startled frog make tremendous leaps away from what he considers a source of danger. Toads, though shorter-legged, can also jump—and farther than you might expect would be possible for such a heavy-bodied animal. Curiously enough, the Platanna, *Xenopus laevis,* of South Africa, can actually even jump backward, and, according to Dr. Rose, frequently does so to escape enemies. But when you try to capture some of the Lungless Salamanders, you are in for a real surprise. Cautiously you lower your hand; then you make a grab. You put your hand right where he was, and he didn't wriggle out of your grasp. You must have him. But you don't. There he is. You try again. You miss. What's wrong? You must use both hands, one to grab at the front, the other at the rear. But his whole body isn't as long as one hand, you may insist. That is perfectly true, but what happens is this: Just as you grab, the salamander slaps his tail on the ground, pushes off with all four feet, and jumps away. This maneuver is a very common one with the Dusky Salamander; the Two-lined Salamander also employs it, though not so frequently. The thing that makes this jump so effective is that it is done more rapidly than the eye can follow it. Time and time again we have tried to see just how high the salamander jumps, and never yet have we succeeded in even seeing him move from beneath our descending hand.

It is commonly believed that amphibians, especially the treefrogs, change their color as they change their surroundings, and that if a treefrog is on a green leaf, he will be green, and if on a brown leaf, brown. This idea is false. An amphibian's ability to change color is primarily an internal-temperature regulator. On a hot dry day an amphibian will be lighter in color than on a cool wet day. Light colors reflect more of the sun's rays, whereas dark ones absorb most of them. The frog knows this scientific principle instinctively, and changes his color to suit the temperature and humidity of his immediate surroundings. The Wood Frog, who breeds so early in the spring, even before those harbingers of spring the peepers do, is at that time a very dark reddish-brown. He is so dark, in fact, that

Above: The protective coloration of the Pickerel Frog. Can you see him at first glance?
Below: The protective coloring and skin texture of the American Toad

unless one picks him up and looks carefully, one is apt to think that here is an anomaly, a Wood Frog without a dark mask. The chances are that he has his mask but that it is so nearly the color of the rest of his body that it is not noticeable. But catch a Wood Frog on a warm summer day after he has left the pond and taken up life in the forest, and you will find that he is an altogether different-looking fellow. Now he is tan, and the dark mask below his eyes stands out very strikingly in contrast.

All amphibians are able to modify their color somewhat. Wood Frogs, Green Frogs, peepers, Bullfrogs, salamanders—all change from light to dark. But only a very few can actually change from one color to another.

Even if an amphibian never changed color, the way he is marked is a protective device. When we see a frog as strikingly marked as the Leopard Frog or the Pickerel Frog, we are inclined to disbelieve this, just as it doesn't seem possible that the leopard or the brilliantly striped tiger would ever be difficult to see. But those who know tell us that the leopard's spots and the tiger's stripes blend in so well with the light and dark of the jungle that careful searching is required to find them. So it is with the Leopard Frog. His pattern of spots make him almost impossible to find in the grass, and usually we see him only when he makes a startled leap out from under our very noses. Early in the spring, however, when the Leopard Frog comes out of hibernation and begins to lay his eggs in the pond, he is darker in hue. His spots are still there, but they do not stand out in such bold relief. That is because of the cool temperature of the water; nevertheless, his color does protect him, for he nearly matches the pond bottom in ground color, and the spots serve to break up the general frog outline, making discovery more difficult.

Many tree-dwelling frogs have a strong protective device in their ability to "fly." There are no frogs that "fly" in this country, but South America has several. *Hyla venulosa,* found in the high tree-tops of Brazil, can leap to the ground without injury, as can *Hyla vasta.* But of all the treefrogs, none can surpass the brilliantly colored treefrogs of the genus *Rhacophorus.* They are called Flying Frogs because of their ability to volplane thirty or forty feet through the air from the top of one tree to the bottom of another. Nature has equipped these frogs most admirably for gliding by exaggerating some of the natural characteristics of all treefrogs. The toe pads of the Flying Frogs are enormous, and there are huge webs between all the digits. When the animal spreads its fingers and toes, it can glide with ease to escape enemies. Probably the best of the gliders is *Rhacophorus dennysi,* found in southern China.

As a defense against "acts of God," amphibians are prolific egg layers. Those species whose eggs and tadpoles are most vulnerable to desiccation lay a very large number of eggs, and the development of egg and tadpole is rapid. The American Toad, who always lays her eggs so carelessly in the shallowest water, lays up to 20,000 eggs. These eggs develop in about 4 days, and the tadpoles are transformed within a month. Contrast this with the Spotted Salamander, who lays in deep water. She lays about 125 eggs, and these take about 1 month to hatch and the larvae 2 or 3 months to complete metamorphosis. By and large, the salamanders lay fewer eggs than do the frogs because they are smaller, nocturnal, and more secretive, and therefore do not have so many enemies as do the larger and more diurnal frogs.

All amphibians have an instinctive knowledge of the weather. Just what receptors they possess to give them this information we do not know. But it is fortunate that something warns them of changing atmospheric conditions, for without this attribute they, with their naked skins, would have become extinct long before man came on the earth. How is the Spadefoot Toad of the West, living in a desert where it rains but once or twice a year, able to foretell rain? How is he ready to mate and lay his eggs at that moment, and not a few weeks later after the rain has passed and the puddle dried up? How does a frog know whether he can safely cross a plowed field, or whether he will become desiccated before he can gain the haven of a moist bunch of grass? They make mistakes in their judgment occasionally, but not often. How do the Wood Frogs, who hibernate far from water in the forests, know where there is a pond suitable for egg laying? Do they return to the pond of their birth? No one knows the answers to these and many other questions. But it is certain that Nature takes care of even the lowliest animal, equipping him with defenses and habits that will enable him to survive and maintain a more or less stable population level.

C H A P T E R *19*

Intelligence Versus Instinct

For some reason, people are apt to admire intelligence and look down on instinct. Because we are creatures of the intellect, it is difficult for us to understand how creatures that are governed primarily by instinct can get along. The animals that we love most are credited with superior intelligence, and the average person does not realize that much of this so-called intelligence is really instinct. Actually, though the line of demarcation is not always very clear, instinct and intelligence are two separate things. Most living things possess a measure of both. Man is, at times, governed by instinct, and the lowly earthworm can be taught to run a maze for food.

Before we examine the amphibians to see whether they are predominantly creatures of intelligence or of instinct, let us try to define what we mean by these two terms. Instinct is inborn knowledge. It consists of patterns of behavior that are not taught, nor are they learned through observation. The garden spider that weaves its beautiful orb web does not learn how to do so by watching its parent or by examining other orb webs. Even if it never saw an orb web or another spider, it would still weave its web. And the web will always have the same number of radii and the same number of spiral threads as do those spun by others of the species. Web weaving is an example of instinct, and surely it is no less wonderful than

234

a man's bridge just because every orb-weaving spider knows how to do it, while only a few men learn how to build bridges.

Though instinct is innate, it may not be fully developed at birth. The instinct to reproduce, for instance, though unlearned, is not present at birth, for the animals are not physiologically able to carry out reproduction at that time.

Furthermore, instinct is unquestioning adherence to set reactions. No questions are ever asked by instinct. The reactions it causes are automatic. Even though conditions may change so that the instinctive reaction becomes inappropriate, no change in these reactions comes about through instinct. As an example, let us look at the hunting wasp. The hunting wasp paralyzes its prey, excavates a nest, drags its prey into the nest, and lays an egg on the body of the paralyzed prey so that when the larva hatches it will have fresh meat on which to feed. The female hunting wasp then closes up the burrow. These are all completely instinctive actions. They are always carried out in the same unvarying order. What does the hunting wasp do when something interrupts or thwarts her? The great French entomologist Henri Fabre carried out many experiments to answer this question. One of the most startling of them was to remove the prey with the egg laid on it just before the wasp closed her nest. The wasp saw him do so, but unhesitatingly closed up the burrow just the same. No attempt was ever made to catch new prey and drag it to the nest and lay another egg on it before closing up the burrow. To human beings this seems like the height of stupidity. And perhaps it is. But it is a good example of our definition of instinct. And if we are inclined to judge, we must not forget that if it were not for Fabre's interference we probably would not be aware of this "stupidity," for in nature, the prey would not be removed from the burrow.

To illustrate this unquestioning adherence to set reactions, let us take one more example—this one without man's interference. The cowbird is a parasite. It is her practice to lay her eggs in the nest of another kind of bird and allow the other bird to hatch her eggs and raise her young. Let us say that a cowbird lays two eggs among the eggs of a warbler while the warblers are away. She may throw some of the warbler's eggs out to make room for hers. Her task accomplished, she flies away. The warblers return. They incubate the eggs—their own and those of the cowbird. The cowbird eggs hatch sooner than the warbler eggs. The young cowbirds grow faster, and soon starve or smother their nest mates, the warblers. The parent warblers have it in their power to get rid of the intruders. Why do they not do so? They do not because the nesting, hatching, and rearing of the young are instinctive actions, and no reasoning is involved; no questions are asked. It is their habit to feed birds in the nest. It is also their way not to waste time in pitying weaker specimens. And they follow their natural instinct even when the young are not their own.

There are certain species of warblers parasitized by the cowbird that illustrate how instinct has been modified to intelligence. Some kinds of warblers, when they find a cowbird's eggs in among their own, will floor over all of these eggs, and lay more of their own eggs above, thus foiling the cowbird's plan effectively.

Intelligence is the antithesis of instinct, for it is knowledge learned either through trial and error, by imitation, or through inference. Here we find different reactions to fixed conditions. Confronted with a crying baby, one mother will rush for the bottle, another will pick the baby up and play with it until feeding time, while a third will allow the baby to cry it out.

For intelligence to become the predominating factor in governing an animal's life, certain requirements must be fulfilled. The first of these requirements is a long life span and a sheltered youth. For the actions of all animals, even man, are completely governed by instinct at birth. There is a long period of learning necessary before intelligence can be developed and used advantageously and to its fullest extent. Second, the animal must possess a brain that is capable of reasoning and memorizing.

Let us now see to what extent the amphibians possess or lack these requirements for the predominance of intelligence. Have they a long life? Theoretically, yes. That is to say, captive specimens of toads have lived for thirty-six years; other species have a slightly shorter life span. But the amphibian who attains this age in the wild is undoubtedly very rare, if not unheard of. So to all intents and purposes, we think we may safely say that their life span is short.

How about a sheltered youth? They lack this too. Of course, there are the few examples, such as *Pipa*, *Rhinoderma*, and *Nectophry-noides*, where the larval period is spent in a safe place. But can the unborn baby learn inside its mother's body? No. No more then can these larvae learn. Pond-hatched larvae can learn to a limited extent. But it has been proved by several investigators that anything learned before metamorphosis is forgotten afterward, and must be retaught. This is not surprising, for learning is only a modification of instinctive reactions, and the instinctive reactions are different in a larva and in an adult.

How about the adults? Can they learn? Yes, to a certain extent. Toads have been found to be the most intelligent and to have the most retentive memories of all amphibians tested. Though scientists insist that no amphibian can distinguish one person from another, we are inclined to doubt this. We have kept salamanders that would look at us fixedly at the accustomed feeding time, though they would hide from a person to whom they were unaccustomed if he came over to their aquarium instead. We might also add that we fed the salamanders in the evening. They seemed to have a definite time sense, for at other times they took not the slightest notice of us. Scientists may feel that this does not prove intelligence, and may argue that the salamander's natural feeding time is at night. We cannot argue, for we conducted no lengthy experiments. We must grant that the average person is all too apt to endow a pet with superior intelligence. This is most natural, for though examples may be given to show the striking differences between instinct and intelligence, in practice it is usually difficult to differentiate clearly between the two types of behavior.

Though amphibians show a certain amount of intelligence and are capable of learning certain things, and of retaining the impressions thus received for a limited period of time, they are primarily creatures of instinct. But let us not look down upon them for this, unless we are prepared to look down upon all animals below man, for the behavior of all except adult man is predominantly instinctive. Instinct is a very wonderful thing, and when man with his experiments does not intervene it is virtually foolproof. Those animals whose instincts work to their disadvantage soon modify them through natural selection, or quickly become extinct.

Since the amphibians are primarily creatures of instinct, we shall discuss it and its various reflexes in greater detail. The three basic drives in the life of any animal are the satisfaction of its hunger, protection of its life, and reproduction of its kind. The problems

Unken reflex   *Defense reflex*

Examples of two different protective reflexes

that arise in trying to satisfy these urges are complex, and two or more instincts may vie with each other as to which will take precedence.

The snapping reflex is characteristic of all amphibians. This is to carry out their instinct of hunger satisfaction. Small objects that move are snapped at. The object usually is an insect or something edible. But try blowing a small feather toward a toad, and you will find, in all probability, that it too evokes the snapping reflex. The fact that the amphibians are attracted to moving objects makes their feeding by the amateur herpetologist more difficult than with many other types of animals. It is probably impossible to teach frogs and toads that stationary objects may be food also; they will starve to death amid plenty unless their prey moves. Salamanders will snap at quiescent objects more readily than will frogs and toads. With the salamander, smell and shape, as well as movement, evoke the snapping reflex. Treefrogs will not feed on insects in close proximity to them. We have temporarily kept both Spring Peepers and Eastern Grey Treefrogs in a small aquarium. Gnats we captured and liberated in the aquarium could crawl right before the noses of these amphibians with impunity. But as the gnats crawled farther away, the frogs leaped at them and snapped them up.

Now let us assume that we slowly push a very small rubber hose toward a toad. What reflex is called into play? Does the toad snap at it? Not at all. The defense reaction is called into play. The body is inflated with air; the legs are stiffened out behind, the head is bowed. The toad may even attempt to butt the hose. If the toad is in a corner where he cannot escape, the defense-fight reaction will be called into play more rapidly than if he can escape. Thus we see that moving objects of a small size evoke the snapping reflex, while larger objects arouse the defense reaction. No amphibian recognizes specific food or specific enemies. They are only aroused to snap at moving objects of the same size as food, and they retreat or assume the defense-fight or *unken* reflexes upon the approach of a moving object of the same size as their natural enemies.

But just because they do not ordinarily distinguish between inanimate moving objects and those that are alive does not mean that they cannot learn. Toads may snap at a moving feather once, but they will not do so a second time unless some time has elapsed. It is felt that toads may learn some things almost as rapidly as mammals. However, they are able to remember what they have learned for only a very short time.

Salamanders can easily learn to distinguish between a piece of wood and a piece of meat, but since they normally nose their food to smell it before snapping, this does not prove that they are more intelligent than toads.

With the Horned Frog, *Ceratophrys dorsata,* we find the snapping reflex has become not only a means of satisfying hunger but also a method of defense, for, as you will remember, this frog bites fiercely when approached.

With the mating instinct, we have, perhaps, the best illustration of an instinct that we can find. The urge to reproduce is strong, and one reflex is stimulated into play, followed by another, until finally —sometimes many months later—the urge to reproduce is satisfied for that year.

The Hellbenders, as well as those most primitive of all salamanders, the *Hynobiidae* of Asia, fertilize their eggs externally. During the breeding season groups of these salamanders congregate together in the "breeding grounds." The males excavate their nests in the water. A female enters the nest and prepares to lay her eggs. The male pays little attention to her. But the moment her eggs start to emerge from her cloaca, all is changed. The sight of the eggs stimulates the male to rush forward and seize the eggs with the forelegs. He pushes the female away with his hind legs, thus facilitating the withdrawal of the eggs from her oviducts. As he makes these movements, he rubs the eggs with his cloaca, and fertilizes them with his sperm.

A little less primitive are the Mole Salamanders. The males congregate at the breeding site before the females arrive. As soon as females are present, the males start their *liebesspiel,* or love dance. They twine in and around each other and the females, wafting their perfumes toward them. The culmination of the dance is followed by the deposition of the spermatophores, and the females then pick up one of these spermatophores.

All this is similar to a play. Each sex has its own part to play, but, unlike human players in a play, amphibians do not forget their proper actions, for these actions are not memorized and therefore easily forgotten, but are inborn knowledge—instinctive patterns of behavior as natural as breathing. Without a female to evoke the reflex, there would be no dance. Without a dance the males would be unable to deposit their spermatophore, and the females would not be stimulated into retrieving it. Thus we see that, as in a play, each sex is absolutely dependent upon a previous action of the opposite sex in order that he or she may make the next proper move.

We have spoken in very general terms of the courtship of the Mole Salamanders. It must be remembered that within the family, each species exhibits variations of this pattern. For instance, in the *liebesspiel* of *Ambystoma jeffersonianum,* the male holds the female with the hind legs. The male of the Spotted Salamander, *Ambystoma maculatum,* does not seize the female at all. And so we begin to see one of the reasons why crossbreeding between species and subspecies is impossible. Naturally, sometimes it is physiologically impossible because the sperm of one species may not fertilize the eggs of another species. But often, especially in closely related species, there can be no interbreeding because the different species smell differently, act differently. The correct stimuli are not present to evoke the various reflexes, and therefore no courtship and mating can take place. Without being held by a male, the female Jefferson Salamander would not be stimulated to pick up the spermatophore; and without being able to hold a female the male would be unable to deposit the spermatophore.

Courtship and mating in the salamanders is followed by egg laying, but several days or several months elapse before egg laying takes place. Is there a special stimulus that determines when the female shall lay her eggs? Is the time that elapses between mating and egg laying constant within the species or does it vary by several weeks or months? So far as we know, there exists no precise gestation table for the salamanders as there does for domestic and many wild mammals.

With frogs and toads, the instinct to reproduce is satisfied quite differently. Warmth and humidity and physiological factors stimulate the males to congregate in suitable breeding sites and commence their calling. The calls are mutually stimulating, and serve to attract the females. The clasping reflex is evoked by various means in different species. The American Toad, for instance, must be nudged. Once the couple is paired, it may be anywhere from 1 hour to 26 days before the female lays. She evidently requires the stimulation of clasping before she can discharge her eggs in the characteristic mass. Unmated females resorb most of the eggs before they are laid, and the few eggs that are not resorbed are allowed to drop from the oviduct singly.

When the female begins to lay her eggs, the male is stimulated by the movements she makes to force them from her oviducts, and as the eggs emerge from her body he discharges his sperm over them, thus fertilizing them.

Though the instinct of self-preservation normally takes precedence over all others, it does not take precedence over the clasping reflex. Paired animals rarely separate voluntarily to escape danger. Indeed, it has been found through what is, to us, a gruesome and brutal experiment, that a male frog may be cut in two, and the forepart of the body will still remain clasped to the female for several hours.

Much as we may discuss intelligence and instinct, and much as the psychologists experiment, we really know very little about either one. Though most educators believe that the I.Q. test is a reliable indication of a child's intelligence, there are others, equally prominent, who feel that it is not. Since we know so little about the workings of our own minds, it is apparent that we know even less about the workings of a mind as different from ours as is that of the amphibian. But whether an animal's reactions are primarily governed by instinct, or whether these instincts have been modified by reasoning and memory, one thing is certain. Both of these governing forces work adequately for their possessors, and are equally mysterious and wonderful.

CHAPTER 20

Economic Importance

When we speak of an animal's economic importance, we are inclined to think only of how it directly benefits us and exactly how many dollars this benefit is worth on the prevailing market. This, to most of us, is what economic importance signifies. Actually, economic importance implies much much more, and blends into ecology —but we shall discuss this later. For the present, let us try to list some of the direct uses of the amphibians.

Frogs' legs used to be considered a Continental dish. It is true that the European countries, France, in particular, do consider frogs' legs a great delicacy. Lately, however, especially since the advent of frozen foods, one can find packages of frogs' legs in most supermarkets. These are not all domestic frogs, for we import frogs' legs from Japan and before recent restrictions, from Cuba. Our imports from Cuba alone were in the neighborhood of 800,000 pounds a year. How many frogs would it take to make up just a pound of frogs' legs? It would depend upon the species, of course. In this country, Bullfrogs, Green Frogs, Pig Frogs, and Leopard Frogs are the principal species used. Bullfrogs (introduced) were imported from Cuba. What species Japan sends us we personally do not know. We have weighed a very large Bullfrog and found it was about ½ pound or 8 ounces in total weight. Never having cut off a frog's legs, we don't know what they weigh. But in an eight-ounce Bullfrog, the two probably would not weigh more than two ounces. This arbitrary figure would mean that for every pound of Bullfrog's legs, eight Bullfrogs are needed. In order to supply this country, Cuba needed to kill 1,600,000 Bullfrogs if each pair of legs weighs only two ounces.

Most of the frogs that supply the market are wild frogs caught while they are breeding. Although there are many advertisements extolling the advantages of starting your own frog farm ("one dollar for complete instructions"), it still remains a risky endeavor wherein few succeed.

Although there are no salamanders commercially available in this country, many people in the South do eat the eel-like salamanders Siren and Amphiuma. In Mexico, the Axolotl, a permanently neotenous form of the Tiger Salamander, is widely used for food. Dried toads and frogs are used for food in the Orient.

The Australian burrowing toad *Chiroleptes,* who inflates his body with water, provides the natives with water in case of need, and doubtless has saved many a human life while forfeiting its own.

The South American Indians use certain species of small forest frogs—*Dendrobates tinctorius* and others of the genus—as a source of poison for their arrows. The poison is of the neurotoxic type, acting on the central nervous system. Unfortunately, the poison of this frog is not concentrated in one spot so that it may be expressed by pressing on a set of glands. In order to obtain it, the Indians hold the poor frog over a fire, and the poison is then exuded by the animal in its agony. Not a very pleasant thought, but let us not condemn the Indians. It was not so long ago that we were burning *people* alive, and not for food either, but merely for their beliefs.

In the Oriental countries of China and Japan, toad skins are a source of fine leather. How durable this leather is, or to what uses it is put, we do not know.

Amphibians are used as fish bait in parts of this country, and although we do not see column upon column of frogs and salamanders advertised for bait in the hunting and fishing magazines, as we do of worms and crickets, for instance, nevertheless, the amphibian bait market is larger than you might suppose. Dr. Oliver tells of one southern dealer who sold $20,000 worth of salamanders in one year!

Amphibians are popular as pets and are used also as part of the amusement trade. The annual Bethlehem, Connecticut, Fair each year offers a prize of five dollars to the individual bringing in the largest Bullfrog. Various other fairs probably have similar contests and prizes. Of course, the Frog Olympics, held at the Calaveras County Fair in California, are world famous. Frogs from all over the world are sent to compete in the jumping contest. The prize for the winner is $200. If the winner should break the existing record, he will be awarded an extra $1,000 as well. Don't get your hopes too high, however, for our native jumpers are easily outstripped by the foreign athletes. According to Dr. Rose, *Rana fasciata* of Africa can jump 14 feet. Imagine how much ground this animal could cover in the three successive leaps required by the contest.

In various countries amphibians are worshiped or used in magical rites. Certain African tribes have magical rites involving the femur of *Rana goliath,* the largest known salientian. The South American Indians have stories and superstitions revolving around indigenous species. The Flying Frog, *Rhacophorus dennysi,* of southern China, is closely related to *Rhacophorus omeimontis,* described in Chapter 13. *Dennysi* has a green back with round dark spots rather than the large, irregular blotches of *omeimontis. Dennysi's* fingers are more fully webbed, and it is considerably larger. This animal is worshiped and is carried around in a chair! (We assume the chair is enclosed so the god won't take off at an inopportune moment.)

Mount Omei in western China has many temples on its slopes. One of them has a small frog about two inches in length, known as *Rana adenopleura,* living in a pool within its walls. The frog is called the Fairy Musician because of its sweet three-note call. Here, these frogs are protected, and may not be collected or molested in any way.

At the very top of Mount Omei is the Temple of the White Dragon. The White Dragon is the salamander known to science as *Bratrachuperus karlschmidti.* The temple is consecrated to these salamanders, and the monks believe that a terrible storm will occur if one of these creatures is killed.

The White Dragon, *Batrachuperus karlschmidti,* is not, as its popular name implies, white. It is dark gray, black or olive green above, with a belly of lighter hue. It is a heavy-bodied animal much like the Mole Salamanders in general appearance. Actually, though, it is more closely related to the Hellbenders, for both belong to the same suborder, the Cryptobranchoidea. *Batrachuperus karlschmidti* belongs to the one family of salamanders not found in this country, the Hynobiidae. Though generally a protuberant vent is a male salamander characteristic, in this species it is the female that has the protuberant vent instead. As with the Hellbenders, the eggs are fertilized externally. The egg case is a curious one, but typical for the family as a whole. It is between 3 and 3¾ inches long, with a diameter of about ⅝ of an inch. Inside this rounded curved tube are from 7 to 12 unpigmented eggs. The case is attached to the underside of rocks in small brooks. The total complement is unknown. The bottom of the tubelike egg case is of jelly rounded in much the same way as is a test tube. As the embryos develop and the inner jelly liquefies, jelly and young drop to the bottom of the egg case. The rounded bottom ruptures, and the young start their larval life in the stream. How curious that the case is so constructed and constituted that the young always hatch through the bottom, never through the sides!

Despite its worship on Mount Omei, other western Chinese consider that the White Dragon is an excellent cure for stomach trouble. The salamanders are collected and dried. When a stomach-ache occurs, one should pulverize the animal, dissolve the powder in boiling water, and drink the mixture.

Dried salamanders are used as a vermifuge in Japan, but whether on people or on animals we do not know. More to the point, do they rid the animal of its worms? We don't know that either. It may be an old cure, and worthless, or it may be an old cure and of value. No experiments that we are aware of have been performed to prove the matter either way.

It is a mistake to scoff at ancient and seemingly quaint uses of amphibians without prior investigation. Dried toads and skins of toads have been used as medicine by the Chinese and others, for centuries. There has been a recent upsurge of investigations of the skin secretions of various frogs and toads, of which we will say more in a moment. Scientists have discovered that many amphibians produce skin secretions with properties that are similar to many of our modern drugs. They have conceded that many of the old remedies using toads, formerly believed worthless, were of some value after all. They are not so good, perhaps, as treatment by a doctor with refined drugs, but they are far cheaper, more readily available to the masses, and of definite value.

The demands of science are a considerable drain on amphibians.

In this country the Leopard Frog is probably used to a greater extent as a laboratory animal than any other. Biology students in schools and colleges throughout the country regularly dissect preserved specimens. One large scientific supply house offers a set of 40 different species of amphibians, and also states that a complete listing of all their preserved amphibians is too large to enumerate in the general catalogue; a separate list is issued for those particularly interested in this field. Embryology is easily studied in the shell-less amphibian egg. Tadpoles are used for studying problems of endocrinology.

Pregnancy tests to determine at an early stage whether or not a woman is pregnant are of various types. There is the Aschheim-Zondek Test, using immature female rats, and the Friedman variation, using immature female rabbits. However, these tests have two disadvantages. The first is the length of time needed to obtain results. The second is the expense of the animal involved. It takes five days for the A-Z Test, two for the Friedman. Rats are not very expensive, but rabbits, being larger, are more so. The next step in the story of biological pregnancy tests came with the Hogben Test. This test took but twenty-four hours. The test animal was the South African Clawed Frog or Platanna, *Xenopus laevis*. Because this frog is an unusual creature, let us digress for a moment to tell something about it.

Xenopus laevis is related to *Pipa pipa*. Both belong to the family Pipidae. The Platanna is a large animal with heavy muscular hind legs and huge fully webbed feet. The first three toes on the hind feet have "claws"—that is, the bones of these digits protrude beyond the skin. It is so well adapted to an aquatic life that it is almost helpless on land.

Though the adults have no mouth tentacles as does Pipa, their tadpoles do. The tadpole feelers are two in number, and project from the snout. They have large soft mouths and a curious method of feeding that is more like that of the baleen whales or certain fish than like a frog. The tadpoles suck in water and the small animals that live in the water. The water is passed out through small slits on the side of the head, while the animal matter is retained and swallowed. This not only rids the ponds of noxious insects and other invertebrates, but helps to clarify the water.

We remarked in the chapter on the burrowers that *Hemisus mar-*

moratum was the only known headfirst burrower. And so he is on land. But the Platanna burrows into the pond muck headfirst when it aestivates.

The Platanna uses its long fingers to feed itself—like others of the family, it is tongueless. Being of a large size, its appetite is voracious, and it consumes many harmful aquatic insects. It was a sorry day for the South Africans when the Platanna was used for pregnancy tests, as we shall see in just a moment.

In the Hogben Pregnancy Test, the female Platanna is injected with the urine of a supposedly pregnant woman. If the woman *is* pregnant, the Platanna extrudes her eggs within twenty-four hours. Unfortunately, other species of female frogs are not so obliging. For a while, a brisk international trade in Platannas went on. The Platanna, which had been numerous in its native ponds, became more and more scarce. Mosquitoes and other aquatic-breeding Diptera increased. Attempts to raise Platannas in captivity were unsuccessful for the most part.

The Platanna was well on the way to becoming extinct when Galli-Mainini, experimenting with a South American bufonid, found that if the male were injected with the urine of a pregnant woman, spermatozoa would be found in his urine. This was in 1947. In 1948 Wiltberger and Miller successfully experimented on the male Leopard Frog, and found that it would respond equally well.

The Galli-Mainini Pregnancy Test can be used with almost any adult male frog as a test animal. In this country the Leopard Frog is the commonest frog and therefore the one usually employed. But other species have been used, including the male American Toad.

Two or three frogs are generally employed for each test so that as high a degree of accuracy as possible may be obtained. Five cubic centimeters (cc) of urine are injected into the dorsal lymph gland lying just underneath the skin of the back. The frogs are then confined in a large funnel so that all their waste products may be collected. Two to four hours later, the frog is released and his urine examined microscopically. If it contains spermatozoa, the test is positive and the woman is pregnant.

Some workers filter the urine and inject 10 cc's; others concentrate the urine and use only 1 cc. Some allow the frogs to rest for two or three weeks before using them again; others feel that one week's rest is sufficient; still a third group feels that fresh frogs should be used for every test. But these are minor details.

In the hands of experts, the Galli-Mainini Pregnancy Test has now become fully as accurate as the earlier A-Z and Friedman tests, and 99 per cent accuracy is achieved. The frog test has the advantage in that it is more rapid, the test animals are not usually sacrificed, and they are inexpensive and easy to obtain. Unfortunately, the savings are not passed on to the consumer—at least in our locality. Pregnancy tests in a local laboratory are $10 no matter whether rats, rabbits, or frogs are used. Unless otherwise specified by a doctor, they use toads almost exclusively in this laboratory.

How does a pregnancy test work? Briefly stated, the human placenta secretes a substance known as chorionic gonadotropin, and this is voided in the urine of a pregnant woman. When injected into a frog, this substance stimulates the gonads and the frog then ejects his sperm.

Perhaps the most important research now being conducted using amphibians concerns investigations and experiments with serotonin. Serotonin is a hormone-like substance found in the secretions of the parotoid gland of the Giant Toad, *Bufo marinus*. It is also found in mammalian lung and intestinal tissues, in brain cells, in blood serum, and in artery walls. The presence of serotonin in the Marine Toad was discovered only a few years ago. Until that time tons of beef blood were needed to extract even a minute quantity of this substance.

What does serotonin do that makes it so important? We do not yet know just how it acts on all parts of the body, though many things have been learned. It is known that serotonin is produced by certain cells in the brain. Some investigators feel that schizophrenia may result from a failure of the brain cells to make enough serotonin. Other investigators believe that too much serotonin in the brain produces schizoid hallucinations—that this is so has been proved in normal individuals. Whether serotonin is or is not a key factor in the cause of schizophrenia has not been proved, but several different investigators are carrying on intensive studies in the hope that they may discover in serotonin a cure for schizophrenia.

Too much serotonin in the lungs, bronchial tubes, and bloodstream has much the same results as histamine. It produces allergic reactions such as asthma and anaphylactic shock. Hitherto such allergies had been blamed on hystamine alone, but we now know that serotonin may play a part. Antiserotonins have been discovered to combat these allergies when they occur.

Serotonin is contained in the blood platelets. It is released in minute quantities when a cut occurs. It causes the blood vessels to contract, and thus helps to stop bleeding. Serotonin works on all smooth muscle where it occurs—in the heart, lungs, bronchial tubes, and gastrointestinal tract. It is believed that it may also play a part in regulating blood pressure and body temperature. Certain types of cancer, heart disease, mental illness, and allergies may be overcome through the investigations now carried on with serotonin obtained from the Giant Toad.

We can see that the direct economic value of amphibians is considerable. Actually, the direct value is but the smallest drop in the bucket compared to the indirect value. Of course, the amphibian's worth as an insect destroyer and as food for many other useful animals cannot, unfortunately, be measured. If we could equate an animal's indirect use in terms of dollars and cents, many species now extinct, either because of ignorance of their role in nature or because of avarice for the dollar, might still be living today.

Fortunately, the part that various amphibians play in eating noxious insects is better known than it used to be. When the Platanna was reduced in its native South Africa, a hue and a cry was raised by the citizens who were overwhelmed by mosquitoes. *Bufo marinus* has been introduced into many different countries all over the world, for it loves the large beetles and cockroaches found in tropics the world over. Toads are welcomed in most gardens, for their value as destroyers of insect pests is now almost universally recognized.

But though we know of the amphibian's indirect value, because certain species are so numerous, we are apt to think that we can have our cake and eat it too. How long can we go on collecting millions of frogs annually for food and laboratory and still have the numbers we need for pest control? Unfortunately, frogs are generally captured as they migrate to the ponds to breed. This is killing the goose that lays the golden egg.

Dr. Wright feels that laws should be passed so that certain of the most frequently used species could not be captured until after they had finished breeding. He suggests the season open on the following dates to ensure that breeding be completed:

Leopard Frog—May 15
Pickerel Frog—May 20
Bullfrog—July 15
Green Frog—August 1

His booklet was written for the Bureau of Fisheries in 1919. What legislation has since been passed to protect the amphibians?

Twenty of our states (Alaska, where there are few amphibians, is not included in this survey, but Hawaii is) have no regulations at all concerning amphibians. Five states require a license for frog hunting but have no other restrictions. The remaining twenty-four states have laws of various degrees of stringency. Some states protect all frogs; others protect only certain species, notably the Bullfrog and the Pig Frog, *Rana grylio*. No salamanders are protected in any state, and very few states make mention of any amphibian except the ranids. In many states there is a small daily bag limit, ranging from 8 to 24, a closed season, and the selling of frogs caught within the state is not permitted. The legislation in these states is a step in the right direction, but not nearly stringent enough if we go by Dr. Wright's standards.

It is to be hoped that eventually all the states will pass laws protecting amphibians. It also would seem that the laws of all states should be stricter, but the same might be said for the laws protecting many other animals. Conservation and Fish and Game Officials do their best to conserve our fauna, but the truth of the matter is that we know pitifully little about conservation as a whole, and it often happens that we become aware of the impending extinction of a species when it is too late. Once population levels fall below a certain minimum, the animals often cannot reproduce at a sufficiently rapid rate to flourish and multiply. And, unfortunately, we do not really know just what these minimum population levels are for any given species.

Amphibians are a small group of animals; there are but eight families of salamanders, twelve or fourteen families of frogs (depending upon how they are classified), and one family of caecilians. The number of species of all amphibians is variously estimated at between 2,000 and 2,500. Compare this to the 850,000-odd insects known to science, and you will realize that the class Amphibia is not large. It would be a shame if these useful, harmless creatures, never a large group even in prehistoric times, were to become completely extinct. Such a thing is not in danger of occurring at present; proper legislation, rigidly enforced, will ensure, in so far as it is in man's power to do so, the continued presence of our frogs, toads, and salamanders.

CHAPTER 21

How to Learn More About Amphibians

Not everyone will be sufficiently interested in the amphibians to wish to learn more about them. We hope there are a few, however, whose interest in, and affection for, these harmless and useful creatures will urge them to desire more knowledge than this book offers. It must be granted that if one wants something badly enough, one will find a way to obtain it. The very effort required to learn about things often makes the results achieved all the more appreciated. But when we first became interested in amphibians, we wished that there were someone who could tell us how to go about studying them. And, lest we be accused of conceit, we freely admit that we still wish there were someone who could guide us in many of the simple experiments we should like to carry out. Therefore, we are offering a few suggestions to those who would further their understanding of the amphibians in the hope that it may help smooth the beginning of their study.

The best way to learn more about amphibians is by personal observation. It is obvious that the knowledge gained from watching one frog in nature is worth many times more than the reading of several books on the same frog. We learn best by seeing, doing, and hearing. We are reminded of a young boy who was a great reader, and had a phenomenal book knowledge of birds. He could recite by the hour on the various colors of birds, their habits and

253

habitats. He impressed everyone who heard him. Unfortunately, he felt that he knew the birds so well that observation in nature was quite unnecessary and superfluous. He once pointed out a towhee to us and identified it as a robin. If he had pointed out a warbler and told us that it was a nuthatch, he would have been quite safe, and we would never have been the wiser. It was his misfortune wrongly to identify a bird which we knew and had observed; his mistake was our gain, for it impressed upon us at an early age that book learning to the exclusion of field observation is not to be greatly admired.

Field trips are pleasant. Sometimes it seems as if there isn't time, or one doesn't feel like going to the bother, but once started, enthusiasm takes over, and the prospect of new sights and experiences excites one.

The equipment to take is simple, and much of it can be made at home. First on the list are the nets. One small net such as is sold for removing goldfish from an aquarium may be purchased or made at home. In addition, a long-handled net is a must. The materials required to make it are an old broom handle (saw the broom off), a heavy wire coat hanger, and an old curtain. Anyone above the age of ten can construct such a net, and the end product, though nothing exceptional in the way of beauty, will be completely serviceable. The procedure is as follows. Bore a hole in top of the broom handle diagonally down until the drill emerges on the side about one and a half inches from the top. Straighten the hook part of the hanger, push it through the hole at the top and then twist the end that emerges around the broom handle. Shape the rest of the hanger into a circle, and the frame is finished. Sew the net made from the curtain firmly both at the seams and around the framework, for the water exerts considerable pressure on it. If you make the net part very deep, large aquatic frogs are easier to catch and less likely to escape. A couple of small cloth sugar bags are handy for carrying adult amphibians home, and a jar or two for larvae and eggs are necessary.

A small notebook and pencil to record what you see on the spot is also important equipment. You would be surprised how much you can forget, and how garbled your impressions can become within a few minutes. Then, too, we believe you will find that you will observe more if you record your impressions on the spot. The untrained naturalist is apt to overlook important details, but as you start to write up your observations, questions will occur to you, which may be able to be answered on the spot by observation. If you wait until you get home to record your experiences, and questions arise, you have no way of answering them accurately until such time as your experiences are repeated, which may be this year, next year, some time, or never.

The hours between dark and midnight are the ideal ones for amphibian watching. More species can be seen at that time. Courtship, mating, and egg laying are best watched then. If you go at night, a flashlight is another addition to your equipment. One that fastens to the head is best, since it leaves the hands free. But where there's a will there's a way, and we have yet to own a head flashlight, so you see that it's not indispensable. The stronger your flashlight, the better you will be able to see, but any flashlight will show you much that you don't see in the day.

One reads that amphibians depend on their eyes to warn them of danger, and at night they cannot see you. This, we believe, is true in the main. Certainly no one can deny that amphibians are much more easily approached in the dark. But our experiences lead us to believe that hearing and the stage of the breeding activities also play some part in silencing the calling males. At the beginning of the breeding season for any given species, amphibians are much more wary of danger, for the mating instinct has not yet completely assumed precedence over the instinct of self-preservation. Therefore, it is not always quite so simple as loudly crashing through the brush and scooping up your frog as he sings away. A certain amount of stealth is required, especially in situations where the going is rough, as over uneven rocky ground and through bushes. Upon your arrival at the spot where you think you heard your frog calling, switch off your light, stay absolutely still, and he will soon start singing again so that you can locate him. Light does not seem to disconcert the amphibians very much; most trill away or lay their eggs as unconcernedly as if there was no spotlight shining on them.

Most of us cannot take night field trips as often as we might wish. Do not think that there is nothing to see during the day. Indeed, daylight field trips have the advantage in that you can see well, and though you cannot move about so freely as at night, and you will not see so many things, what you do see will be more clearly perceived.

Where should you go? Ponds, swamps, slow-running brooks are all excellent. The smaller bodies of water offer more advantages than the larger ones because you can see across them, walk around them, and even wade to a certain depth if you have boots on. Different species like ponds in different settings. Some prefer woodland ponds. Others prefer ponds in the open. There is one pond near us that seems as if it would be an ideal breeding site for amphibians. Though we have watched it carefully day and night over several seasons, and have gone over every inch of it frequently, we have never yet found an egg or even one live amphibian or larva in it. We do not know why.

Do not concentrate on the water alone. As you circle the pond or swamp, look over the ground, too, and you may see salamanders going to and fro. Rocks and logs should be overturned (and carefully replaced), for there you may find many of the more secretive species hiding. Swift streams are a fertile discovery ground for plethodontids and some neotenous salamanders. Search under logs, bark, and stones in the woods. Watch your lawn and garden. Look on the lower branches of trees and shrubs. All these are hiding places for amphibians. The most seemingly unlikely place may surprise you.

A child is a valuable ally. If trained to handle specimens gently, and praised for bringing them to you, you will find, we are sure, that he or she will reward you with many interesting species. We wouldn't see half of what we do if it weren't for our daughter, age eight. She has more time to look for amphibians; she is nearer the ground; and she has that blessed singleness of purpose we adults to a great extent have lost.

What is there to look for on these field trips? First of all, you will want to see the many different kinds of amphibians: how they look, how they act, what the male's call sounds like. Does he call from under water, above water, or on land? What do the various kinds of eggs look like? How long does it take the tadpoles to hatch? How do they act? What do they eat? When does metamorphosis start and how long does it take before completed? How large are the newly transformed adults? How do their actions differ from those of the older adults? The more you study amphibians, the more questions will occur to you. We never go out that questions don't arise in our minds, and as they arise they are duly noted down. It is surprising that quite a number of these can be answered by observation later in the season, or another year, or as one's knowledge increases. It must be admitted, however, that the questions always outnumber the answers. But if they did not, the subject would no longer be a challenge and an absorbing interest.

Valuable as is personal observation in the wild, many things are better watched in an aquarium or vivarium. The development of eggs and tadpoles can be seen clearly in the aquarium, and a comparison may be made of the different types of eggs and larvae— their rates of development, behavior, and so on. The eggs of the Spring Peeper, being so tiny, and laid singly, are almost impossible to find in a pond. But you have only to capture a mated pair, place them in your aquarium, and leave them alone until they lay their eggs. You may find the eggs laid the next morning. Or you may not, for frogs and toads may remain clasped anywhere from 3 to 26 days before laying. The chances are that you will not have to wait the full 26 days, but if you do, don't be discouraged. Your peepers require no food at this time, and all you need do is change the water every two or three days. After the eggs are laid, you can liberate the male and female, study the eggs, and, if you like, keep them until the tadpoles transform.

Aquariums may be as simple or as elaborate as you please. Square-sided fish aquariums, stone crocks, wide-mouthed gallon jars, dishpans, mixing bowls are all satisfactory receptacles. Do not use a metal container unless it is overlaid with enamel. Chemicals in some metals make the water unfit for the growth and development of eggs and larvae.

Any water that is not chemically treated either by chlorine or water softeners is satisfactory. Chemically treated water must be aged for several days, or neutralized by tablets sold by pet shops. The water should be cold, and the aquarium should not be set on a radiator or in the sun.

These simple rules should be observed for maximum success with hatching eggs:

1. Eggs need room to hatch. Do not keep too many in a small container. Break the egg mass if pressed for space.

2. Change the egg water every three days.

3. Do not allow the eggs to freeze.

4. Surface-film eggs should be barely covered with water. If they

sink to the bottom of a jar filled with water, they are less likely to hatch.

If you follow these rules, you should have no trouble hatching any eggs you collect, unless by some misfortune you happen to get some eggs that have been previously frozen in the pond. Though it is claimed that eggs can withstand a certain amount of freezing, how low a temperature they can endure, or how long they can remain frozen, is known for the eggs of only a very few species. Any frozen eggs that we have collected have not hatched for us.

It must be remembered that the length of time that elapses between laying and hatching varies with the temperature of the water and from species to species. Some salamander eggs have an incubation period of over a month. These, since they are larger than most frogs' and toads' eggs, are ideal for observing the development of the egg. A strong magnifying glass or pocket microscope is very useful, and if you decide to watch the smaller toad and frog eggs in detail, it is an absolute necessity.

It is unlikely that you can raise stream-laid eggs and larvae in the manner suggested above. The chances are that most of them will not develop without an aerator to increase the oxygen content of the aquarium water. Dr. Liu tells how he tried to raise the eggs of *Staurois chunganensis* in the aquarium. Though he provided water from streams, changed it daily, and took care not to overcrowd the eggs, none of them developed beyond the morula stage. When he placed the eggs of this stream-dwelling frog in a cloth cage, where water was slow-moving, he had better success, but many of the embryos died because the jelly hardened in later stages of development. Eggs placed in a cloth cage in a swift stream developed normally.

Never having attempted to raise the eggs of our native streamlaying salamanders, we have no idea whether or not they would react in a manner similar to Dr. Liu's Staurois eggs. It seems a likely possibility, though. Could they be raised in a well-aerated aquarium rather than in a cloth cage in the stream? We lack the equipment to experiment, but it would be interesting to find out.

Tadpoles, being "more alive," if we may be permitted to use such a term, require a little more care than the eggs. If the following rules are adhered to, your success is ensured with them also:

1. Do not overcrowd. They need plenty of space. Overcrowding invariably results in disease and death.

2. Change the water frequently—every two or three days.

3. Feed outside lettuce or spinach leaves boiled until soft (about half an hour in an enamel pan. Do not use a metal pan for boiling.

4. As the hind legs emerge, provide a rock out of water and cover the aquarium top with cheesecloth or screening.

Carnivorous tadpoles and salamander larvae present a feeding problem. They must have small insects or entomostracans in order to survive. You may buy live daphnia and other suitable food. Or you may throw in daily a quantity of pond weeds, together with some mud scraped from the pond bottom, into the aquarium. This provides a good variety of food, for minute animals cling to the matted vegetation and bottom detritus. But this has the great disadvantage of making the aquarium difficult to clean without loss of your larvae. Or you may capture larvae when they are larger, and feed them with recently hatched larvae, and such night-flying insects as you can capture. We have tried to feed chopped earthworms and chopped meat. Though many books state that larvae will eat any or all of these foods, we have never succeeded in getting any of ours to touch them. They will eat raw liver agitated on a broomstraw, but this diet alone is deficient in necessary vitamins.

Growth in aquarium-raised tadpoles and larvae is apt to be rapid, though the animals do not seem to attain so large a size as those in the pond. Transformation generally occurs sooner, perhaps because the diet is not so balanced as in nature. This differential may be lessened by feeding pond weeds, and detritus to tadpoles, but, as we said, it makes cleaning more difficult, nor are they so readily observed.

In keeping adult amphibians, there is not only the problem of sufficient live food but also the necessity of providing a vivarium that conforms to the animal's natural environment. The smaller terrestrial salamanders may be easily kept in an aquarium planted with ferns and woodland plants with a log or rock provided for cover *if* suitable live food is available. But frogs and toads need more space than the glass aquarium can provide. Overcrowding results in discomfort, disease, and death. Unless an animal can be in a place similar to his natural environment, few interesting or valuable observations can be made.

The solution of the problem is the construction of an outside vivarium. This can be as large and elaborate a place as one desires and can afford. In its simplest form, it may consist of a boxlike frame approximately six or eight feet square and four feet high, made of 2″ by 4″ stock. This frame should be completely covered on all sides, including the top and the bottom, with hardware cloth of ⅛-inch mesh, with provision for a door on top. This box should be placed on a slight slope and the bottom covered with earth to a depth of one foot, and planted with ferns, moss, and other suitable cover. A large plastic dishpan or small plastic pool should be sunk in the earth inside the vivarium. The sides of this artificial pool should project an inch or two above the earth. Flat stones are used to provide a coping around it, and help prevent the water from becoming overly muddy. Stones and/or sand should be placed inside the pool to form a sloping ramp on one side so that the vivarium occupants will be able to climb out of it easily.

This vivarium may be used year round in frost-free climates, but in most parts of the country it will be advisable to free the specimens before frost comes, and restock the vivarium in the spring.

A small outside vivarium such as this is not a carefree proposition, though its proper maintenance may be made easier by placing it wisely. It is advisable to have shade in some part of the vivarium. Care must be taken that the earth is kept moist—but not soggy— for amphibians cannot escape to cooler or more damp spots. The water of the pool should be siphoned off and fresh water added occasionally, and the water at all times must be watched to see that it does not get overly warm. If it does, cold water must be added.

The feeding problem is greatly minimized by an outside vivarium, though not entirely overcome. If some rotten meat is placed in the vivarium, bluebottle flies will soon flock to it and be promptly eaten by the vivarium inmates. A colony of ants may be planted under a rock in a dry spot, for ants are greatly appreciated by toads. Defunct lettuce leaves placed in a cool damp spot will attract slugs and snails. A dull light—either a lantern or regular electrical bulb—turned on at night will draw many night-flying insects for the consumption of the nocturnal species of amphibians.

When stocking a vivarium of this size, care must be taken not to crowd it, and large species, such as the bullfrog, are better kept with others of their own size, for they are likely to eat small species of frogs and toads.

Too much emphasis cannot be placed on the fact that common sense, intuition, and attention to the faithful reproduction of natural habitat is required for success in keeping adult amphibians. As with all animals, hard and fast rules for their care are impossible to lay down. Depending upon your viewpoint, caring for them may be a simple pleasure or a time-consuming nuisance, not worth the trouble involved. Those who have the slightest doubt on how they will feel should not attempt to build and maintain a vivarium, but should remember that they can get far more pleasure out of watching uncaptured specimens in the wild.

While observation of live amphibians in nature and in the home aquarium and vivarium will give you a knowledge of the species found around your home, you will miss seeing species from other parts of the country and those from foreign countries if you neglect the museum and zoo. And if you would get the most benefit out of museum and zoo trips, take along a pencil and notebook. Read the legends about the various exhibits and take time really to observe all you can about the captive or preserved specimens, noting down all salient features. Most of the larger museums display only a small fraction of their collections. The rest are kept in the curator's offices. If, after you have examined the museum exhibit several times, and you feel that there is much that is not exhibited that you would like to see, you may write the Curator of Reptiles and Amphibians and ask to see certain specimens of the study collection. You may not be granted permission, for curators are busy people, but if your reasons for wishing to see a specimen or specimens of a study collection seem valid, you will probably be given an appointment. It never hurts to ask, and most curators are delighted to help and encourage a serious amateur.

Though personal observation teaches us best, one person's lifetime is not long enough to see all there is to see, nor have most of us the time to see all we might wish, or the facilities to perform all the interesting experiments that occur to us. Therefore, in order further to broaden our knowledge, we must turn to literature. Popular books on amphibians are the first on the list, for they are or should be what one person called "interest-pricking." Many of them give a general survey of the subject without going into specific details too deeply.

For those who would go further, technical or semitechnical literature will follow. This type of book is specific in the extreme; those who read them will be impressed at the thoroughness and exactness of the true scientist. Many technical words pertaining to herpetology will be unfamiliar, but will either be defined in the text or may be looked up in any good dictionary. The going may be slow and difficult for the first few days, but soon the terms will be mastered and you will forget that there was ever a time that you didn't know them.

At first glance, a key for identifying amphibians seems bewildering and impossible. However, it is far simpler than it looks, for the purpose of a key is to enable anyone quickly and accurately to identify the species. Keys are not complete descriptions of each species. They contain only the most important identifying characteristics. In order to identify an amphibian scientifically (or anything else, for that matter) from a key, it is necessary to have the animal before you in a bowl or jar. On one side of you you have your key, on the other your dictionary. A ruler marked in millimeters as well as in inches, and a magnifying glass, complete your equipment. Keys generally give alternate characteristics to choose from, and you keep continuing, choosing features that best fit your specimen, until you have keyed out, or found, your species. As a double check, it is well then to read the complete description of your species and check on its range to make sure of your identification.

Some keys seem better organized and easier to follow than others. Most are accompanied by instructions as to the best way to use them, and have diagrams illustrating unfamiliar technical terms. After you have identified a frog several times using a key, you will be able to make a spot identification, for you will rapidly become familiar with the salient characteristics of the species found in your area, and will not need the key except for specimens whose markings or other features seem aberrant.

"But why," you may ask, "is it necessary to differentiate between one species and another?" First of all, you will probably like to be able to do so. It bolsters your own ego if you can say to yourself, "I saw *Rana catesbeiana* this morning," instead of "I saw a frog of some kind." But far more important than this is the fact that each species is distinguished from every other not only by differences in appearance, voice, eggs, tadpoles, but above all in habits and habitat. Your observations and conclusions are accurate only for the species you observed. And so, though the Bullfrog and the Green Frog look similar and are, as a matter of fact, closely related, their appearance and ways are sufficiently different to make them separate species.

Technical and semitechnical literature should, in my opinion, be taken in small doses, especially at first, when the constant reference to a dictionary is necessary and makes reading slow and tedious. You need not necessarily start at the beginning of a technical book. Noble's book is good anywhere—read the chapter that most interests you first. Don't be afraid to do a little judicious skipping. You won't be able to understand it all the first time you read it without more formal education than a school or college biology course—or we couldn't, anyway. You will get most of it, and a great deal of the rest will come with further readings. Concerning the three handbooks listed in the Bibliography, do not fail to read the introductions first. These contain a great deal of important general knowledge.

Though books give a good general view of the subject, they do not contain the latest, most up-to-date studies on any aspect of science. Books, even technical ones, are for the most part a compilation and abridgment of the important scientific discoveries. For the latest word on what is being done in any scientific field, one must turn to technical magazines. It is here that the amateur finds himself at a great disadvantage, especially if he does not live in or near a large city. The small-town library cannot help him. Though many books may be obtained through them from larger libraries on an interlibrary loan, periodicals are not generally loaned on such a basis. They must be perused at the library that owns them.

A further complication arises when one learns that there is no one technical magazine that contains all or even most of the literature on herpetology. If there were, one could subscribe to it. Even scientists have trouble keeping track of the enormous bulk of technical literature published in many different journals all over the world. The *New York Times* noted that a Paris physician had recently remarked that in order to keep completely up to date on the medical literature of the world, a doctor would have to read 638 scientific articles a day!

What is the solution for the amateur who wishes to know the latest facts? There is no easy one if he does not live near a large library. Perhaps the best solution is to subscribe to one or two herpetological magazines (see Bibliography).

For many people, technical magazines will not be worth the bother of obtaining them or the expense of subscribing to them. But for a selected few who are passionately interested in the subject, their acquisition will be worth their weight in gold. In them, the amateur scientist will find the exact, well documented, detailed facts he has desired and which are lacking in books.

A few words concerning the color descriptions of amphibians as given in technical and semitechnical literature are in order. When we first saw such terms as "ochraceous buff," "light greyish vinaceous," "Dresden brown," and "pale Veronese green," our hair stood on end. Luckily, in most semitechnical literature, and in some technical literature as well, a general color description is given as well as this more precise one, so that we can manage without having to bother ourselves about these lovely-sounding but completely incomprehensible color terms. However, science is precise, and what a scientist does when he wishes to describe the color of his specimen exactly is this. He gets out a copy of Robert Ridgeway's *Color Standards and Color Nomenclature*. In our ignorance, when we first heard of this book, we thought that it was a small book of color charts such as painters have, costing a few dollars. We soon found out that it cost $20 back in 1908, and Heaven only knows what it costs now. Therefore, we can't give you all details on this work of reference. It does have color charts and descriptions, complete with fancy names. Our scientist matches his specimen's color with the charts and writes Ridgeway's color down in his description. Other scientists reading this description can refer to their copy of Ridgeway and know precisely what shade the specimen was.

The more you see and read about amphibians, the more questions you will have. Naturally, if you are absorbed in your subject, you will want to find the answers. Other books and further observation may help you. Or it may be that you have exhausted your library's resources and still cannot find the answer. If so, write to the curator of a museum or a zoo, or the author of the book (care of the publisher). Do not hesitate to do so for fear of a rebuff. These men are busy, it is true. But one of the reasons that they are is that they answer hundreds of questions from people they have never heard of. Whenever we have had occasion to ask questions of them, their reply has been prompt, courteous, and helpful. Of necessity, answers to questions must be brief and to the point and do not go into all ramifications. Therefore it helps if, along with your question, you inquire about any literature extant on the matter, and where it may be borrowed or purchased. Then if you find, as we often do, that the answer to your question raises others, you can read up on the subject.

But though scientists are helpful, they may not be able to answer some of the questions you pose. If so, you may have to say that no one knows the answers. For there are many things that are not known—yet. What are some of them? First of all, the eggs and/or larvae of many species of native frogs and salamanders have never been described, to say nothing of foreign species, especially in the tropics. There is a crying need for someone to find a better method of tadpole identification. As it stands now, they are primarily identified by differences in their mouth parts. These are difficult to measure uniformly, and the Doctors Wright feel that there may be many variations in mouth parts even within a species and subspecies. Someone with patience and much observation of tadpoles may someday find a method that is more accurate than, and superior to, the one now used. Perhaps there are identifying characteristics that would enable the layman, as well as the scientist, to differentiate betwen tadpoles without recourse to the mouth parts. At present, if the average layman is anything like us, his identification of tadpoles is not even a well-informed guess, and does not satisfy himself, let alone a scientist.

Not only are scientifically accurate descriptions of certain eggs and tadpoles lacking, but the life cycles of many species are unknown or known only fragmentarily. Then, of course, there is always a chance that a new species will be discovered, or, more commonly, that the range of a given species may be narrowed or broadened.

But most fertile investigations by the serious amateur will probably be in the realm of general knowledge. Such questions as how Siren courts and breeds and where, within what temperature and humidity ranges each species breeds most freely, and a host of others are of the type that may be answered by the nonscientist without laboratory facilities or a great deal of formal education. Throughout this book, questions have been raised for which there are no answers that we can find. Perhaps some of them may interest you sufficiently to arouse you to find the answers. Questions that you ask yourself are more likely to be productive of answers for the simple reason that only you know what problems interest you most. Without interest and a burning desire to find the right answers, nothing worth while can be accomplished. Besides absorption in one's problem, patience, continued observation, attention to the most minute detail and, above all, exactness are needed. In short, one must apply the scientific method and convert oneself into a scientist, although an amateur one.

True scientific research, whether done by a professional or an amateur, is not what many people imagine it to be. Reading existing or related literature on the problem under consideration, repeated observations, controlled experiments, careful records, and proper application of statistical methods—all these play an important part in scientific discoveries so that as much accuracy as is possible may be attained. Concrete examples may be obtained by reading various articles in a technical magazine. Two books on scientific research and statistical methods are listed in the Bibliography. These are helpful for those who wish to make contributions to science.

But whether you make a new discovery, or a discovery new to you, it should give you pleasure. When we first saw frogs and toads breeding—a thing we had read about—we were as thrilled as Balboa discovering the Pacific. That others had seen it before did not detract one whit from our pleasure. The main objective that most of us have in learning more about anything is personal pleasure and satisfaction. And since we have no one to drive us, we can learn as much or as little as time and inclination permit. Fortunate indeed is he who finds that his studies consume more hours than time permits but less hours than inclination dictates. This individual is a confirmed amphibian watcher and a happy person, for he possesses one of the most valuable of all intangibles, an avid and continued interest in something outside himself.

A Comparison of the Caudata and the Salientia

	SALAMANDER ADULTS	FROG AND TOAD ADULTS
Body	Long and thin	Short and squat
Tail	Long	No tail
Legs	4 of almost equal length	2 short front legs, 2 long hind legs
Locomotion on land	Runs or crawls	Jumps or leaps
Locomotion in water	Uses tail to swim	Uses hind legs to swim
Voice	Has no voice	Males croak or trill
Ears	Has none. "Hears" by feeling vibration through front legs or lower jaw	Hears as we do
Eyes	Not retractable, not very large	May be retracted into the roof of the mouth. Usually large and bulging
Recognition of mate	By smell and touch	By voice and touch
Recognition of enemies	Mostly by sight	Mostly by sight
Fertilization of eggs	Internal, with a few exceptions	External, with one known and two probable exceptions

267

	LARVAE	TADPOLES
Gills	External until transformation	External for a few days, then internal until transformation
Diet	Carnivorous	Mostly herbivorous, with a few exceptions
Teeth	Has true teeth	Has horny beak (absent from one family)
Other differences	Usually has balancers or claspers to hold onto plants when first hatched	Has sucking disks when first hatched

SALAMANDER TRANSFORMATION	FROG AND TOAD TRANSFORMATION
Front legs appear first, then hind legs. Gills can be seen shrinking. Tail lengthens. Does not always completely develop into adult form.	Hind legs appear first, then front legs. Tail gets shorter and is absorbed entirely. Always develops into adult form in all respects.

Key to the Families of the Orders Caudata and Salientia in the United States[*]

Order CAUDATA—Amphibians with tails. Salamanders.

1. **Family Amphiumidae—The Amphiumas, or Congo Eels**
   a. Eel-like body
   b. Two *tiny* front legs. Two *tiny* hind legs
   c. Adults neotenous, but no external gills

2. **Family Sirenidae—The Sirens**
   a. Eel-like body
   b. Two small front legs. No hind legs
   c. Adults neotenous with external gills

3. **Family Proteidae—The Mudpuppies**
   a. Four toes on all four feet
   b. Adults neotenous with bushy red external gills

4. **Family Cryptobranchidae—The Hellbenders**
   a. Very broad flat body with deep wrinkles on each side
   b. Adults neotenous, but no external gills

5. **Family Salamandridae—The Newts**
   a. Adults usually completely transformed
   b. Costal grooves absent

6. **Family Ambystomidae—The Mole Salamanders**
   a. Adults usually completely transformed
   b. Costal grooves present and distinct in most species

[*] Adapted with permission of Cornell University Press from *Handbook of Salamanders* by Sherman Bishop, and *Handbook of Frogs and Toads of the United States and Canada* by A. H. Wright and A. A. Wright.

7. **Family Plethodontidae—The Lungless Salamanders**

    a. Adults usually fully transformed. A few species are neotenic.

    b. No lungs. Nasolabial grooves from nostril to lip are present.

Order SALIENTIA—Amphibians without tails. Frogs and toads.

1. **Family Ranidae—The Frogs**

    a. Skin on belly smooth

    b. Narrow waist. Relatively narrow body. Long legs

    c. Toes with considerable web

2. **Family Bufonidae—The Toads**

    a. Broad thick body. Broad head. Wide waist. Short hind legs

    b. Parotoid glands are present and distinct

    c. Skin is warty above, granular below

3. **Family Scaphiopodidae—The Spadefoot Toads**

    a. Broad thick body. Broad head. Wide waist. Short hind legs

    b. Large eyes with vertical pupils

    c. Skin fairly smooth

4. **Family Brevicipitidae—The Narrow-mouth Toads**

    a. Broad body. Wide waist. Narrow head with pointed snout

    b. No tympanum. No parotoids. Skin fold across the head

    c. No webs on fingers or toes except in *Hypopachus cuneus*

5. **Family Hylidae—The Treefrogs**

    a. Narrow waist. Relatively narrow body

    b. Round disks on all digits

    c. Skin on belly granular

6. **Family Leptodactylidae—The Robber Frogs**

    a. Narrow waist. Relatively narrow body. Skin on belly usually smooth

    b. Disks on digits, if present, are oblong, not round. No webs on toes

7. **Family Ascaphidae—The Tailed Frogs**

    a. Short ribs are present

    b. No tympanum. Eyes with vertical pupils

    c. "Tail" is present on male. Short anal tube is present on female

Scientific Classification and Common Names

The scientific classification of plants was first set forth by the Swedish botanist Carl von Linné, or Linnaeus, as he is usually called. In 1735 he published a book entitled *Systema Naturae,* in which every known plant was given two Latin names. These names described salient characteristics of the plant designated. Zoologists soon did the same thing for the animal kingdom. The tenth edition of *Systema Naturae,* published in 1758, is considered the starting point of modern zoological nomenclature. The scientific classification of plants and animals was further improved and better organized through the influence of the writings of the Frenchman Cuvier, in 1817.

All living things are placed in either one of two kingdoms, the Plant or the Animal. Under the Animal Kingdom there are several phyla (singular: phylum). Under each phylum there are various classes. Under each class are orders. Under each order are families. Under each family are genera (singular: genus). Under each genus are species. Under each species there may or may not be subspecies. There the matter usually rests, but it occasionally happens that there may be mutants under a subspecies. In addition to these main groupings, there may be superorders and suborders, superfamilies and subfamilies, and so on. These extras are, of course, for the benefit of further clarifying the relationship of the animal being studied.

Every animal is given two or three names. These names are always Latinized, and frequently have Greek or Latin roots as well. This is so that scientists the world over, no matter what their native tongue, will know what animal is designated. The rules for forming names for new species is laid down by the International Commission of Zoological Nomenclature. The animal's generic name comes first; this generic name is

271

always begun with a capital letter. The animal's specific name comes next in lower-case letters, followed by the subspecific name (if it exists), also in lower-case letters. If the subspecific name is the same as the specific name, the latter is often abbreviated by its first letter; we may write *Desmognathus fuscus fuscus* as *Desmognathus f. fuscus* for short. The entire scientific name is italicized in printed matter. In technical literature the name of the scientist who first named the species is written after the generic, specific, and subspecific names in nonitalicized type. Thus the American Toad would be written *Bufo americanus americanus* Holbrook. When we find the authority's name enclosed in parentheses, it means that this species was originally assigned to a genus different to the one in which it is now placed. For instance, the Southern Rough-skinned Newt, *Taricha granulosa twittyi* (Bishop) used to be called *Triturus granulosus twittyi* Bishop. (Notice the different generic name.)

To make the system clear, we shall classify an amphibian with which most of us are familiar. The Northern Leopard Frog, *Rana pipiens pipiens,* obviously belongs to the Animal Kingdom. (There are some examples where this is not so evident.) This animal has a notochord that is an internal stiffening rod, a nerve chord dorsal to the notochord and pharyngeal gill slits, making him a member of the Phylum Chordata, together with Amphioxus, fish, reptiles, birds, and mammals. He is placed in the subphylum Vertebrata. The members of this subphylum have the notochord replaced in part or wholly by a chain of cartilage or bone in the mature animal. Gill slits are present only in the embryos of certain of these vertebrates. A well-developed chambered heart and never more than two pairs of paired limbs or fins are other characteristics of this subphylum. The Northern Leopard Frog is an animal with a naked skin, three-chambered heart, with the young different from the adults in form, which places him in the class Amphibia together with salamanders and caecilians. The Northern Leopard Frog belongs to the order Salientia, a group of tailless vertebrates with a compact body and four-segmented hind legs. Thus far, the characteristics of this frog are more or less self-evident. However, when we wish to classify the Leopard Frog beyond this point, we encounter trouble, for internal skeletal and muscular differences are not visible to us. At present, osteological differences are the principal criteria used to distinguish one amphibian family or genus from another. However, the Wrights (*Handbook of Frogs and Toads*) feel that these alone are inadequate, and believe that much more study is needed before the classification of amphibians is on as firm a basis as that of birds or mammals.

In our classification of the Leopard Frog, we shall point out just a few of the characteristics involved. The Northern Leopard Frog belongs to the suborder Diplasiocoela, a name that describes the type of vertebral column it possesses. It belongs to the family Ranidae, which is separated from other families by osteological and cartilaginous differences. It belongs to the subfamily Raninae, the genus *Rana*, species *pipiens*, subspecies *pipiens*. A complete classification of the Northern Leopard Frog would appear thus:

Kingdom—Animal
Phylum— Chordata
Subphylum—Vertebrata
Class—Amphibia
Order—Salientia
Suborder—Diplasiocoela
Family—Ranidae
Subfamily—Raninae
Genus—*Rana*
Species—*pipiens*
Subspecies—*pipiens*
Authority—Shreber

Frequently, throughout this book, we have mentioned that scientists were not in accord over the number of subspecies into which a given species should be divided. When is a subspecies a subspecies? When is it a mutant, a hybrid, or a variation? These are questions that require comparison with other forms, and detailed anatomical and genetic study of the animal involved. Thus we begin to understand why we, as laymen, cannot enter into these fascinating taxonomic disputes with herpetologists.

The scientific names used in this book are, with a few exceptions, those listed in the check list of *Common Names for North American Amphibians and Reptiles* published in *Copeia* (see Bibliography). Where these scientific names differ from those used in Dr. Conant's book, we have used his names; his book is the more recent work, and he tells us that it is completely up to date as of December, 1959. For the foreign species discussed, the scientific names used are those used by either Noble, Rose, Cochran, or Liu, depending on the species.

While scientific classification (and therefore scientific names also) are constantly changing, popular or common names, when properly chosen, tend to remain stable. Although the common names of birds have been fairly well standardized for some years, the common names of amphibians varied from one region to the next, and frequently one species might have several common names or, even more confusing, several species might have the same common name.

Within the last decade, herpetologists have made an attempt to standardize the common names of amphibians. In this book the common names are those recommended by the Committee on Herpetological Common Names (see Bibliography). The Committee believes that writers of technical literature should henceforth use common names as well as scientific designations in their works. Dr. Karl Schmidt in his 1953 check list paved the way for other herpetologists by including popular names in this work. Nontechnical writers will of course continue to use common names; since these are now more standardized, a greater accuracy in their work will be ensured. All this will make it easier for the lay reader to understand just what species is being discussed, a fact not always apparent in the past.

Bibliography

BOOKS

BARBOUR, THOMAS. *Reptiles and Amphibians: Their Habits and Adaptations*. Houghton Mifflin Co. Boston, Mass. 1929. 129 pp.
Interesting account of various habits of herptiles, with the emphasis on foreign species. Illustrated with photographs (many of them of preserved, not living, material). Good bibliography. Nontechnical.

Bibliography of Amphibians and Reptiles. Prepared by the Department of Amphibians and Reptiles. The American Museum of Natural History. Central Park West at 79th Street. New York 24, New York. Free upon request.
This is not a complete bibliography, but it is annotated, and contains many of the books on our native amphibians. Only one book on foreign amphibians is listed; names of others may be obtained on request.

BISHOP, SHERMAN C. *Handbook of Salamanders: The Salamanders of the United States, of Canada, and of Lower California*. Cornell University Press. Ithaca, New York. 1941. xiv and 555 pp. Price: $6.00.
Detailed accounts and photographs of all salamanders found in the area. Good key for identification of adults. Descriptions of all known eggs and larvae. Much general information in the introduction. The definitive work on our salamanders. Complete bibliography. Semitechnical.

COCHRAN, DORIS M. *Frogs of Southeastern Brazil*. United States National Museum Bulletin 206. Smithsonian Institute. Washington, D.C. 1954. 423 pp. Price: $2.00.
Almost completely taxonomic, with only a few details on habits. Many

species illustrated by drawings and photographs of mostly preserved animals. Complete bibliography. Technical.

Common Names for North American Amphibians and Reptiles. Prepared by the Committee on Herpetological Common Names of the American Society of Ichthyologists and Herpetologists. Reprinted from *Copeia*, 1956, No. 3. 26 pp. Price: $1.00. (See information listed under *Copeia* below to obtain.)

A list of all common and scientific names of herptiles in the area.

CONANT, ROGER. *A Field Guide to Reptiles and Amphibians of Eastern North America.* Houghton Mifflin Co. Boston, Mass. 1958. 366 pp. Price: $3.95.

Identification of all *adult* herptiles in the area is made very clear and simple through identification marks and illustrations, most of which are in color. Maps delineating range. Good bibliography. Nontechnical.

CROXTON, FREDERICK E. *Elementary Statistics with Applications in Medicine and the Biological Sciences.* Dover Publications, Inc. New York. 1959. Paperback. 376 pp. Price: $1.95.

Very clear presentation of some of the elementary statistical methods and their concrete applications. The material is so well presented that even an individual with no mathematical aptitude or training can understand it. A combination of treatise and textbook.

DICKERSON, MARY C. *The Frog Book. North American Toads and Frogs with a Study of the Habits and Life Histories of Those of the Northeastern States.* New Nature Library. Doubleday Page and Co. Garden City, New York. 1914. Vol. 6 Part 2. 253 pp. (Out of print.)

A wonderful book, though scientific names are, in some cases, out of date. Keys for identification of adults. Many very good large photographs, some hand-colored. Detailed accounts of many species. Nontechnical.

GOIN, OLIVE B. *World Outside My Door.* The Macmillan Co. New York. 1955. 184 pp. Price: $3.50.

The wife of the eminent herpetologist Coleman J. Goin shows how she and her husband observe the activities of herptiles, birds, mammals, and invertebrates found in their half-acre Florida yard. Good not only for Florida residents but for nature lovers everywhere. Nontechnical.

GRAY, JAMES. *How Animals Move.* Cambridge University Press. London and New York. 1959. Paperback. Pp. 75, 77, 90–104, Photograph #6.

A brief treatment of the biophysics of movement with excellent pictures and diagrams of frogs jumping and a newt walking. The section on the relative jumping abilities of a man, a frog, a kangaroo, a grasshopper, and a flea is especially interesting. Nontechnical.

HOLMES, SAMUEL J. *The Biology of the Frog.* The Macmillan Co. New York. 1927. 386 pp.
A good textbook on the frog written for college undergraduates.

LEUTSCHER, ALFRED. *Vivarium Life: A Manual on Amphibians, Reptiles and Cold-Water Fish.* Cleaver-Hume Press, Ltd. London. 1952. 230 pp.
Summaries of various animals suitable for keeping in aquariums and vivariums, with notes on distribution, identification, habits (including food), and breeding. Certain insects and crustaceans, as well as other miscellaneous groups, are covered, with instructions for their culture as food or for study. Drawings of all animals described. Nontechnical.

LIU, C. C. *Amphibians of Western China.* (*Fieldiana: Zoology Memoirs,* Vol. 2.) Chicago Natural History Museum. 1950. 400 pp. Price: $7.50.
Detailed accounts of adults, tadpoles, and eggs of all species known to be in the area. Completely illustrated by line drawings and some magnificent colored drawings. Complete bibliography. Technical but very readable.

MORGAN, ANN H. *Field Book of Ponds and Streams: An Introduction to the Life of Fresh Water.* G. P. Putnam's Sons. New York. 1930. Price: $5.00.
All fresh-water life covered. Some of the commoner frogs and salamanders (pp. 347–388) are briefly covered. Sections on aquatic insects are especially good. Good bibliography. Exact but nontechnical.

NOBLE, G. KINGSLEY. *Biology of the Amphibia.* McGraw-Hill Book Co. New York. 1931. Reprinted in 1954 by Dover Publications. New York. 577 pp. Price: $4.95. Paperback edition $2.95.
Contains material on the origin, habits, biology, and classification of foreign and native amphibians. Illustrated. Complete bibliography. Semitechnical but easy and absorbing reading, and should be among the first additions to the serious amateur herpetologist's library.

OLIVER, JAMES. *The Natural History of North American Amphibians and Reptiles.* D. Van Nostrand Co. Princeton, New Jersey. 1955. ix and 359 pp. Price: $6.95.
Much interesting up-to-date material of herptile ways and habits. Illustrated by drawings and a few very good photographs of living animals in action. Brief bibliography. A good book. Nontechnical.

ROMER, ALFRED S. *Man and the Vertebrates.* Penguin Books Inc. Baltimore, Maryland. 1957. Vol. 1, pp. 43–79.
Account of the origin of the class Amphibia together with an excellent summary of the anatomy and physiology of the present-day frog. Well illustrated by drawings and photographs. Nontechnical.

————. *Vertebrate Paleontology.* Second Edition. University of Chicago Press. Chicago, Illinois. 1945. Pp. 127–162.
The evolution of the amphibians is well covered with the classification of both extinct and present-day amphibians outlined. Intended for use as a college textbook. Good bibliography.

ROSE, WALTER. *The Reptiles and Amphibians of Southern Africa.* Maskew Miller Ltd. Capetown. 1950. Pp. 1–119. Price: $6.00.
Detailed accounts of habits of all species in the area. No keys or lengthy descriptions. All species photographed alive. The author's observations are accurate, interesting, and humorous. Nontechnical.

WARDEN, C. J., N. T. JENKINS, and L. H. WARNER. *Comparative Psychology: Vetebrates.* The Ronald Press Co. New York. 1936. Pp. 97–137.
Summary of information on behavior, sense organs, intelligence, and instinct. Interesting, but this material is well covered in Noble, *op. cit.*

WILSON, E. BRIGHT, JR. *An Introduction to Scientific Research.* McGraw-Hill Book Company. New York. 1952. 375 pp. Price: $2.95.
Good introduction to research and how to go about it. A few chapters require a knowledge of statistics for fullest comprehension. Others are more general. Unfortunately, because the author is a chemist, most of the illustrations to prove his points are from chemistry and physics rather than from biology; nonetheless the book is helpful. For the individual who has no mathematical training, parts of it should be read in conjunction with the Croxton book, listed above. Technical.

WRIGHT, A. H., and A. A. WRIGHT. *Handbook of Frogs and Toads: The Frogs and Toads of the United States and Canada.* Third Edition, 1949. Cornell University Press. Ithaca, New York. xii and 640 pp. Price: $6.50.
Detailed descriptions, accounts, maps, and photographs of all species in the area. Keys for identification of adults, eggs, and tadpoles. A wealth of information on breeding sizes, transformation sizes, secondary sex characteristics, and so on. The definitive work for our native salientians. Complete bibliography. Semitechnical.

PERIODICALS

Copeia. The publication of the American Society of Ichthyologists and Herpetologists. 4 issues a year. Membership, including a subscription, is $8 a year. $6 a year for foreign and student members. Address inquiries to Dr. James A. Peters, San Fernando Valley State College, Northbridge, California. Technical.

Herpetologica. The Journal of the Herpetologist's League. 4 issues a year. Subscription and membership $4 a year. Address inquiries to Dr. Wilmer M. Tanner, Department of Zoology and Entomology, Brigham Young University, Provo, Utah. Technical.

For other periodicals, see Scientific Supply Houses listed below.

RECORDINGS

BOGERT, CHARLES M. "Sounds of North American Frogs: The Biological Significance of Voice in Frogs." Folkways Records. Album FX6166 plus 20 pp. booklet. 12" 33⅓ r.p.m. Price: $5.95.
We have not heard this recording, but it should be excellent. More than 50 voices of Salientia are recorded. Booklet illustrates all species and contains explanatory material.

"Voices of the Night: The Calls of Thirty-four Frogs and Toads of the United States and Canada." Cornell University Records, a division of the Cornell University Press. Ithaca, New York. 12" 33⅓ r.p.m. Price: $6.75.
The calls of 34 Salientia, principally those found in the eastern half of the United States. A very fine record.

SOME SUPPLY HOUSES FOR PRESERVED OR LIVE AMPHIBIANS

General Biological Supply House, 8200 S. Hoyne Avenue, Chicago, Illinois
Publishes *Turtox News*, which is distributed free only to biology teachers or to other biological workers. Not available even on a subscription basis to others.
General catalogue free, on request, to all, contains but a small fraction of the stock. Orders for specific items not listed may be filled on request.

Quivira Specialties Company, 4204 West 21st Street, Topeka, Kansas
Specializes in herptiles both alive and preserved. General catalogue lists most offerings, and is free. This company also sells technical and popular books and magazines on natural history and science. Many are listed in the general catalogue but the company offers to get any magazine or book, technical or popular, which is in print, for you, and will furnish price quotations upon request.

Glossary

AESTIVATION Prolonged sleep induced by heat and drought.

ALGA (plural: algae) A simple flowerless green plant. Seaweeds and pond scum are both algae.

ALLOPHORE Red pigment cell.

AMPLEXUS Sexual embrace in frogs.

ANALOGOUS Similar in function but of different origin and structure.

ANATOMY The study of the organs or parts of an animal through dissection.

ANUS The cloacal opening found on the underside of the amphibian between the hind legs.

APEX The top or tip of a triangle.

AQUATIC Living in the water.

BALANCERS Armlike appendages, just in front of the gills on either side of the head, found on certain species of newly hatched salamander larvae.

BRANCHIAL RESPIRATION Respiration by means of gills.

BUCCOPHARYNGEAL RESPIRATION Respiration through the lining of the mouth and throat.

CAUDATA Tailed amphibians. The salamanders.

CIRRUS (plural: cirri) A slender appendage found below the nostrils on the edge of the upper lip of some Lungless Salamanders over which the nasolabial groove extends.

CLASPERS *See* BALANCERS.

CLOACA The chamber into which enter the products of the urinary, intestinal, and reproductive systems.

CHROMATOPHORE Pigment cells.

CORNIFIED Hardened skin.

280

COSTAL GROOVE   Vertical grooves found on the sides of many salamanders.

CRANIAL CRESTS   Bony ridges on the heads of many toads.

CREPUSCULAR   Active during the dusk or twilight hours.

CUTANEOUS RESPIRATION   Respiration through the skin.

DEPRESSED   Flattened.

DIFFUSION   The spreading out of fluids or gases from the area of greatest concentration to an area where a lesser concentration occurs.

DIMORPHISM   Differences in color, form, or structure between members of the same species.

DIPTERA   An order of two-winged insects, such as flies, mosquitoes, gnats, and so on.

DIURNAL   Active during the day.

DORSAL, DORSUM   Pertaining to the entire upper surface of the amphibian. The back.

DORSAL FOLD   In frogs, a skin fold dividing the back from the sides, and extending from in back of the eye to a point midway between the snout and the hind legs.

DORSOLATERAL FOLD   *See also* DORSAL FOLD. The dorsolateral fold extends from behind the eye to the insertion of the hind legs.

EUSTACHIAN TUBE   A tube connecting the tympanum with the mouth.

ECOLOGY   The science that deals with the interrelation of animals, plants, and their environment.

ENTOMOSTRACAN   Tiny crustaceans, often visible only with a microscope. Fairy Shrimp, Water Fleas, and so on.

EXCRESCENCES   Horny protuberances found on the forearms, fingers, and sometimes the chest of certain amphibians during the breeding season.

FEMUR   The first segment of the hind leg.

FOSSORIAL   Equipped for digging.

FROG   An ambiguous term. Properly, a member of the family Ranidae. Also synonomous with Salientia.

GILL   A filamentary organ for respiration.

GRANULAR GLANDS   Skin glands, found on the amphibian back, that secrete a thick milky acrid fluid. This fluid helps to protect the animal. The glands usually function only under pressure.

GRAVID   Filled with eggs.

GROIN   That region of the sides which is concealed by the hind legs of a frog when it is in sitting position.

GUANOPHORE   White pigment cell.

GULAR FOLD   A fold of skin found at the base of the throat of some salamanders.

HEDONIC GLANDS   Glands found on some salamanders, especially on the chin, cheeks, or tail, whose secretions attract the females during the breeding season.

HERPETOLOGIST   A scientist who specializes in the study of amphibians and reptiles.

HERPTILES   Reptiles and amphibians.

HIBERNATION   Prolonged sleep induced by cold.

IMPLANTATION   The union of the sperm with the egg.

INGUINAL   Pertaining to the groin.

INSTINCT   Inborn inheritable patterns of action.

INTERORBITAL CRESTS   The two bony ridges found between the eyes of certain toads.

IRIS   The diaphragm regulating the size of the pupil opening that is in the center of it.

LABIAL TEETH   Not true teeth, but toothlike ridges found on the upper and lower labia, or lips, of tadpoles.

LARVA   The immature form of an amphibian, especially an immature salamander.

LATERAL LINE ORGANS   Sense organs found in rows on the sides of all larval amphibians and a few aquatic adult salamanders.

LIEBESSPIEL   The courtship dance of salamanders.

LIPOPHORE   Yellow pigment cells.

MANDIBLE   The horny beak of tadpoles.

MELANOPHORE   Black pigment cells.

METAMORPHOSIS   The change from an immature form to the adult form, which is generally quite different.

MORULA STAGE   In embryology, the stage in which the egg has reached a division into 16 cells. So called because the eggs resemble mulberries at this point.

MUCOUS GLANDS   Skin glands, found all over the body of amphibians, which secrete a clear fluid to keep the skin moist. The fluid may also be of a protective nature.

NASOLABIAL GROOVE   A groove running down from the nostril to the edge of the upper lip. Present on all Lungless Salamanders, and on them only.

NEOTENY   The retention of certain juvenile characteristics in a sexually mature salamander.

NICTITATING MEMBRANE   The third eyelid, which is transparent and is raised up from behind the lower lid.

NOCTURNAL   Active during the night.

OPERCULAR FOLD   The fold of skin that covers the gills of tadpoles.

OVIDUCT   A tube connecting the ovary to the cloaca, through which the eggs descend.

OVOVIVIPAROUS Producing live-born young hatched from eggs retained in the mother's body, but not attached to it. Do not confuse with the following terms: VIVIPAROUS—producing live-born young from eggs that are attached internally to the mother's body; and OVIPAROUS—producing eggs that hatch outside the mother's body.

PALEONTOLOGY The study of fossils.

PAPILLAE Small nipplelike projections.

PAROTOID GLANDS Elevated granular glands located behind the eyes and above the tympanum in many toads.

PECTORAL Pertaining to the chest.

PHOTOSYNTHESIS The process by which green plants make carbohydrates by uniting carbon dioxide and water when exposed to light. Oxygen is given off as a waste product of this process.

PHYSIOLOGY The study of the functions of organs and parts of the body of the living animal.

PITUITARY GLAND A gland of internal secretion governing, among other things, growth and metamorphosis, and stimulating the production of eggs and sperm.

PREMAXILLARY TEETH Teeth found on the premaxillary bone in the center of the upper mouth.

PREPAROTOID LONGITUDINAL CREST A bony ridge attached at a right angle to the postorbital crest, and extending down toward the parotoid gland.

POSTORBITAL CREST A bony ridge found behind the eyes of certain toads.

PULMONARY RESPIRATION Respiration by means of lungs.

PUPIL The opening in the center of the iris. When contracted in darkness, it may be either catlike, when it is termed erect or vertical, or it may be horizontal.

REFLEX An instinctive movement or action.

RESPIRATION The process of taking in oxygen and giving off moisture and carbon dioxide. Breathing.

SALIENTIA Amphibians that are tailless when adult. Frogs and Toads.

SNOUT The front part of the head.

SOLE TUBERCLE A small wartlike protuberance found on the bottom of the hind foot of certain toads. If it is near the body when the animal is in sitting position, it is an inner-sole tubercle. If it is near the outside edge of the foot, it is termed the outer-sole tubercle.

SPERM Used in this book as a synonym for spermatozoa.

SPERMATHECA The chamber found in female salamanders that receives the spermatophore.

SPERMATOPHORE Stump-shaped objects of jelly containing the sperm of salamanders.

SPERMATOZOA Mature male sex cells.

SPIRACLE   The opening through which the water passes after it has gone over the gills. Found either on the left side or the underside of tadpoles.

STAGHORN GILLS   Flat leaflike gills characteristic of certain terrestrial salamander larvae.

STAPES   The bone that carries the sound vibrations from the tympanum to the inner ear. Often called the columella.

SUPRAORBITAL CREST   *See* INTERORBITAL CREST

TADPOLE   The immature form of a salientian.

TAIL CRESTS   The filamentary part of the tail on the upper side and underside of the muscular part of the tail.

TAXONOMY   The scientific classification of plants or animals.

TERRESTRIAL   Living on land.

THIGH   The femur.

THYROID GLAND   The ductless gland, found in the region of the throat, that governs metamorphosis in the amphibian.

TIBIA   The second segment of the hind leg.

TOAD   An ambiguous term. Properly, a member of the family Bufonidae.

TRANSFORMATION   *See* METAMORPHOSIS.

TROPISM   An involuntary or instinctive turning movement toward a stimulus (positive tropism) or away from a stimulus (negative tropism).

TUBERCLE   Any small protuberance. *See also* SOLE TUBERCLE.

TYMPANUM   The membranous eardrum found below and behind the eye in some frogs.

UNPIGMENTED   Light in color—white, yellow, or some other very pale shade.

VASCULARIZED   Well supplied with blood vessels.

VENT   The anus.

VENTER, VENTRAL   The belly. Pertaining to the entire underside.

VENTRAL DISK   A round fold of skin in the middle of the venter of some Robber Frogs.

VITELLUS   The egg exclusive of any jelly envelopes.

WAIST   The distance between the hind legs of a salientian. Measured across the venter.

Index

Page numbers in **boldface** type refer to illustrations.
Page numbers in *italics* refer to principal discussions.